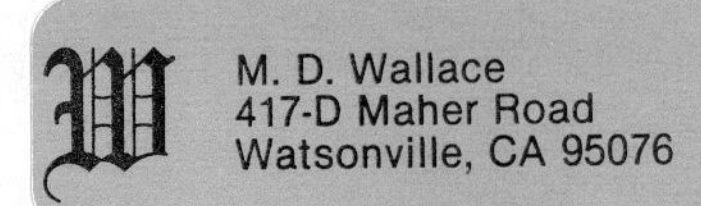
M. D. Wallace
417-D Maher Road
Watsonville, CA 95076

D0210362

OLD INDIAN TRAILS

SUNSET FROM LOOKOUT BUTTE (*page* 197)

OLD INDIAN TRAILS

BY WALTER McCLINTOCK, M.A.

With illustrations
from photographs by the author

HOUGHTON MIFFLIN COMPANY
Boston New York London

Photos by the author courtesy of the
Yale Collection of Western Americana,
Beinecke Rare Book and Manuscript Library

CIP data is available.

ISBN 0-395-61155-5

Printed in the U.S.A.

AGM 10 9 8 7 6 5 4 3 2 1

TO MY MOTHER

CLARA CHILDS McCLINTOCK

CONTENTS

ILLUSTRATIONS

FOREWORD

If there really are such things as American longings — desires we possess as a people — surely one of them must be the wish to put aside our modernity with all its emptinesses and complex disturbances and to go live as the Indians did before the Europeans descended here. Perhaps even better, to join a tribe with old ways and discover whether life with people only slightly beyond a stone-age culture is sweeter than ours, to learn whether tribal Americans truly built their lives around a harmony and balance between humankind and the rest of nature.

Although some Indians still live as removed from contemporary existence as one can on the eve of the twenty-first century, I suspect no one does so without conscious rejection of our times. A stone-age life lived intentionally today is different from the unchosen one of preceding generations. We may dream of escaping our own era and emulating what Walter McClintock did in 1896, but we cannot. I believe he was impelled to search out the last days of an American aboriginal people as much by his romantic longings as by his awareness that such a journey would soon be impossible. In this way, he is a time traveler, and the route he found into another age began on the shore of Swan Lake on the western slope of the Flathead Range of the Rocky Mountains in northwestern Montana, and the time machinery that transported the twenty-six-year-old was his feet, his horse, and the desire of a visionary Blackfoot leader to defend the cultural resources of his clans from assaults by white bureaucracies and economics and to see them preserved for his descendants and honored through understanding by others.

Some Indians today — especially mixed bloods — grow wroth over any outside inquiry into aboriginal practices, and I can imagine a Blackfoot today resentful of McClintock's recording of the life a century ago. But that Blackfoot should remember McClintock's work was possible only because Siyeh (Mad Wolf), a chief of the Southern Piegans (one of three divisions of the Blackfeet, the other two in Alberta, Canada) wanted a full record made. The penetration of McClintock's writings and photographs, if nothing else, attests to the wide acceptance of his presence by the Blackfeet. To them, he was not an inconsiderate voyeur opening tribal secrets but a respected preserver of ways that then teetered on the fringes of extinction. Without his work (and that of other ethnographers he informed and inspired, such as John Neihardt's interviews with the Lakota holy man Black Elk), awareness of ancient North American cultures would today be considerably poorer, especially among the Blackfeet themselves. Indian and non-Indian, we all are in his and Mad Wolf's debt.

Walter McClintock, born in Pittsburgh in 1870, graduated from Yale (where most of his papers and photographs now are) in 1891. He joined the family carpet business for two years, then worked for a steel manufacturer for a couple of more until he contracted typhoid fever. Like many Americans in the later nineteenth century, he went west to regain his health, which he accomplished by a long horseback tour through North Dakota, Wyoming, and Idaho. He returned to Pittsburgh, but soon went west again, this time as the photographer for a federal commission looking into management of national forest reserves in Montana. It is at that point his book begins. He stayed with the Piegan (ignore the spelling and pronounce it pay-GAHN) three years, then went home to Pittsburgh, where he took a job in a tile company that allowed him to revisit the tribe and its Canadian relations in the springs or summers over the next decade.

From his first journey into Blackfoot territory until his last, he carried a notebook as well as glass plate sheet-film cameras. Although he came to feel a part of the tribe, he was first of all a reporter and — at his best — a capable ethnographer. I understand we no longer have his field notes or any manuscripts of his two books written from those notes, so we can only surmise how squarely his reporting follows his actual experiences. I especially wonder whether he spoke the difficult Algonquian language well enough to be able to report conversations as precisely as he does. We do have, however, something else, something unusual: McClintock published his first book, *The Old North Trail or, the Life, Legends, and Religions of the Blackfeet Indians*, in England in 1910 soon after his last visits to the Blackfeet. Because of some distribution problem in the United States, to make the book widely available here while avoiding copyright infringement, he completely rewrote and considerably reorganized it. Houghton Mifflin, that venerable Boston publishing house, brought out *Old Indian Trails* in 1923 (seven decades afterward, dealers offer mint copies for nearly two hundred dollars; the first book, by the way, is available from the University of Nebraska Press).

The Old North Trail contains many more photographs, more ethnographic details, and is more plainly written with less colored prose than *Old Indian Trails*, but this later book reveals much material not in the first version. Together, despite some rephrased repetition, the two books give a rich account with a splendid immediacy that McClintock's eyes and ears bring; I find these works superior in all ways to his more famous predecessor among the Blackfeet, James Willard Schultz, whose *My Life As An Indian* must be considered fiction despite its frequent factuality. Coming closer to pure ethnography than either man's work is George Bird Grinnell's classic *Blackfoot Lodge Tales*, even though it is not so abundant in particulars as McClintock's trail books. (For more recent studies of the tribe, today numbering about seven thousand people in the United States, see John C. Ewers's *The Blackfeet: Raiders on the Northwestern Plains* and William Farr's *The Reservation Blackfeet, 1882–1945: A Photographic History of Cultural Survival*).

Soon after his first return to Montana, McClintock began giving hand-colored lantern-slide lectures on his experiences with his adoptive tribe. In fact, after he became financially independent, he devoted the rest of his life to presenting his views of the Piegans in hopes of educating Americans away from the view that native peoples were foul brutes bound in a debased, unenlightened, and sinister culture. He even produced an opera about the Blackfeet, titled *Poia* (Scarface).

As a writer who has tried his own hand at making photographs to accompany my reporting, I am continually struck by the excellence of McClintock's pictures (I've found working in the two disciplines at the same time, as he did, most difficult). Unlike nineteenth-century photographer Edward Curtis and others, McClintock avoided manipulating and adding props to his subjects or their activities. In 1949, not long before his death, he wrote: "The pictures were not posed, nor were the scenes constructed for the occasion. They are of real life." No one has made a full study of his contributions as an ethnophotographer — especially his sequential pictures, like the two dozen virtual time-lapse images of the construction of a Sundance lodge, yet they are a rare resource for students of aboriginal America.

At times I do wish McClintock's verbal and visual documentation included depictions of the new reservation itself. Of his more than two thousand photographs, he made many only yards away from Browning, Montana, but it doesn't appear. From his work, we might conclude that reservation life was yet to come to the Blackfeet, although, in truth, when McClintock lived with them they were beginning their first years under conditions set out by the sometimes baneful Bureau of Indian Affairs. As an artist — if not as an ethnographer — it was his prerogative to examine the last days of the bison culture and to exclude the doled-out-canned-meat era, a decision brought about, I think, because of his occasional tendency to idealize and romanticize the Indian. Still, he could argue for his emphasis because he saw disappear the generation which witnessed the earliest incursion of the whites. (Meriwether Lewis, on the great expedition of 1804–06 became the first American on record to shoot down a Blackfoot, one of only two Indians killed by the expedition;

Reuben Fields, in the same fray, stabbed to death the other, also a Blackfoot. The tribe, whose name may derive from the color they dyed their moccasins, were fierce defenders of their territory both from whites and other Indians.)

Some months ago, I recommended to Alan Andres, an editor at Houghton Mifflin, that he consider republishing this book, but, for the life of me, I could recall correctly neither the title nor the author's name. On the remote chance I might find the volume, I went down into the dim Houghton basement archives, among the long and wonderful — if haphazardly organized and uncatalogued — shelves of its publications. At random, I picked a center aisle, took a few steps down it, glanced up just above my head, and there — among the thousands of books — was *Old Indian Trails*. I carried it up to Alan's desk and left it. You may interpret the coincidence as you like, but I take it as a sign of good medicine seeking outlet, and I am happy you can now share what McClintock, at Mad Wolf's invitation, so painstakingly and cherishingly left for us, all of us: a people's life, their vision of encompassing harmony.

WILLIAM LEAST HEAT-MOON
Columbia, Missouri
2 April 1992

PREFACE

In the spring of 1896 I went into northwestern Montana as a member of a Government expedition which was appointed by President Cleveland to recommend a national policy for the United States Forest Reserves and to advise the Secretary of the Interior as to the reserving of certain other forests.

Our expedition, which went in advance of the main Commission, was composed of Gifford Pinchot, Chief of the Forest Service (now Governor of Pennsylvania), and Henry S. Graves, later Chief Forester and Dean of the Yale School of Forestry; I went as photographer and to help in the forest surveys. We had two guides, William Jackson, an Indian scout of the Blackfoot tribe, and Jack Munroe, a white man who was married into that tribe.

We examined the forests in northwestern Montana, both on the eastern and western slopes of the Rocky Mountains. We came into contact with the natives of the region, both white men and Indians. We made surveys in the country where the Flathead Forest Reserve was later established, and in the region now known as Glacier National Park. Then it was a paradise for hunting and fishing, a wild and unfrequented country, visited only by Indians, trappers, and a few hunters of big game.

We made our last survey in the heavy forest on the western side of the Rocky Mountains. Then Graves set out for Kalispell and civilization; Pinchot, with Jack Munroe and our bear dogs, started south for Fort Missoula; I was left alone with the Indian scout.

We crossed the mountains together and joined the tribal camp of the Blackfoot Indians on the plains. There I met many of their leading men; among them Chief Mad Wolf, who adopted me as his son, in ceremonies lasting through two days, and made me a member of his tribe.

I maintained intimate associations with my Indian father and his tribe through many years, keeping records of everything that I saw and heard — their customs and legends and religious beliefs, our hunting trips, and the flora and wild life of their country.

But into the region where we wandered civilization came with its automobile highways and great modern hotels. The old generation of Indians have died and their children are civilized. The Blackfoot are no longer nomads and hunters, following the great herds of buffalo and other game; they till the soil and live in houses like white men. Their ancient customs and tribal life have passed away forever.

My purpose, therefore, in writing this book, is to record the results of fifteen years' close association with the old Blackfoot chiefs, medicine men, and common people. I have retained the narrative form of my original notes, in order to give as faithful a record as possible of their character, environment, and family life.

W. McC.

OLD INDIAN TRAILS

OLD INDIAN TRAILS

∴

CHAPTER I

MY INDIAN GUIDE

It was an evening in early summer. The stars shone bright and our Indian tepee glowed with light from its inside fire. My guide, a famous scout of the Blackfoot tribe, smoked in silence; while I lay on my comfortable bed of robes and blankets, listening to the sounds from the forest — chirping of crickets, last songs of the thrushes and vibrating chant of an ovenbird.

That night by our lodge-fire I said to the scout: "Tell me about your home." And he replied:

"On the prairie beyond the Rockies, I have a ranch with many horses and cattle. The mountains are near, the hunting good; our streams and rivers are full of fish. Come with me to my country, to my tribe, the Blackfoot Indians. In our valley the head men of the tribe live; you will meet there our leading chiefs."

For a moment I was silent. The plan of the scout accorded with my own desire. All my life I wanted to live away from the city, among the mountains and wilds. I was weary of the turmoil of the city, the dreary grind and slavery of business, from early morn until night in an office-prison; away from the sunlight and from birds and flowers in the spring-time. I wanted to shake off the shackles of social convention, to leave the worry and stress of the modern city, where business and the making of money are the chief end of man.

I thought to myself: "If I go with my guide, I can live out-of-doors all day and all night. I shall become strong in body and mind and be happy. And, instead of striving for money, I will go on a quest. I will stay with the scout and visit his tribe, to find whether they are more happy and contented in their primitive life, than civilized people in great modern cities."

Now Indians have a way of masking their feelings; they never show enthusiasm. So I said quietly to the scout: "I want to go to your home and your Indian tribe." This ended our talk for that night; but I had a keen desire to go.

My guide was near middle age. He had the swarthy complexion, black hair and high cheek bones of an Indian; but he did not look like a full-blood. He was tall and slender, with an impressive manner; fluent of speech and polite and suave. His father was a white man named Jackson, an early pioneer, a Rocky Mountain hunter and trapper, his mother an Indian woman. The son was called Billy Jackson by white men and Siksikaí-koan (Blackfoot Man) by the Indians.

But Siksikaí-koan was an unusual half-breed. He raised himself above the popular prejudice against half-breeds. He was liked and respected by both white men and Indians. Honest and industrious, generous and kind, he was always ready to help any who came to his ranch. He stood high in the councils of the Blackfoot tribe; and served honorably as scout for Generals Custer, Miles, and Reno in the Indian wars.

The scout was a good guide in the wilderness; on him I could depend. He knew the trails of the plains and mountains and handled with skill the wild Indian horses. Self-reliant in time of danger, he had the quiet manliness and courage that knew no fear; a keen sense of humor and a wonderful knowledge of nature — information not gained from books.

A SMALL LAKE ON THE WESTERN SLOPE OF THE ROCKIES

OUR INDIAN TEPEE

He knew woodcraft; that moss generally grows on the north side of trees, more on evergreens than on those which shed their leaves in winter; that pines are more frequently struck by lightning than birch or cottonwood; that the toughest side of a tree is to the north, because the winter winds and cold come from that direction.

He knew Indian legends and traditions and stories of war and adventure. He told me about a family of lost children who went to the sky and became the constellation of the Pleiades, and the woman who left home and children to live with the Man-in-the-Moon. He spoke English fluently, also the Blackfoot, Cree, and Sioux tongues; and was familiar with the ancient customs and traditions of his Indian tribe.

Our camp was on a small lake on the western slope of the Rocky Mountains, in the region now known as the Flathead Forest Reserve. We had a good "pack outfit," a herd of fifteen horses, a comfortable Indian tepee and plenty of food. Our government work was finished and we were free to wander.

Next morning the mists were heavy over the lake, which lay like a mirror beneath the surrounding mountains and forests. The sun came up red and flashed bright shafts of light through the big trees; the shadows from their branches made odd patterns on their smooth trunks. Grass and undergrowth were wet with heavy dew and hanging cobwebs shone like diamonds in the sunlight. By the time we broke camp and had our horses packed, the sun's rays were hot on our backs.

The scout led the way through the forest, while I followed and drove the pack horses. How different they were from the horses of civilization! They had learned to think for themselves and to rustle their own food. On the trail they were always scheming; I had to watch them and be on the alert. Their leader was a crafty mare with a bell fastened to her neck. All the herd were devotedly attached to her. She was a good baggage carrier and careful of her pack. She never let it scrape or bump trees. But she knew how to make things easy for herself. No matter how poor the feed, she was always fat and in good condition. She took the lead and kept the other horses in order. If one of them tried to pass, she met him with bite or kick and put him back in his place.

All of our pack were gregarious by nature. My saddle horse was uneasy whenever I dropped behind. He pawed the ground, whinnied and danced until I started; then ran with delight to join the others. This feeling held all of our horses together on the trail, and kept them from wandering at night.

It was the beginning of summer — just the time for birds and wild flowers. I saw fields of Indian basket grass with tall stalks and dense caps of cream white flowers; along the trail were beds of yellow adder's-tongues, pink twin flowers, white lilies and flowering dogwood. I heard the wild cry of a loon from a lonely lake and olive-backed thrushes along the shores. In the deep forest were winter wrens, golden-crown kinglets and myrtle warblers. Then, for the first time, I heard the flight song of a Macgillivray warbler; and found his nest in some blackberry bushes close to a lake.

Finally we entered the valley of the Flathead and camped in a grove of larch and yellow pine. In that broad and fertile valley with plenty of free sunshine, the yellow pine is a noble tree with symmetrical spire, straight round trunk and slender shaft. The needles are long and yellow green, the bark smooth with deep fissures and arranged in massive plates.

There was plenty of good grass, a godsend to our horses after their long stay in the forest. We removed packs and saddles, attended to sore backs and picketed the bell-mare. It was our custom to keep her near camp at night, that it might be easy to catch the rest of the herd in the morning.

I slept outside under the stars, making my bed close to a thicket of fragrant pines and masses of wild roses. It was one of those days that come only with early summer. A crescent moon hung over the forest; from a bank of clouds the first star shone. In the east, beyond an outer range of forest-covered mountains, I saw a line of white, glittering peaks, remote and ethereal, glowing in the soft tints of the sunset, like the realm of another world.

Then the lure of the wild stirred my blood strangely. Again I told the scout I wanted to stay with him. I had a new sense of freedom, as though a load had been rolled from my back. I felt like a boy just freed from school and longed to explore that mountain world, to discover what lay beyond.

That night we sat by our camp-fire through the long northern twilight. The scout smoked in silence, while I dreamed of mountain trails and Indian camps and bright days ahead.

CHAPTER II

CROSSING THE ROCKY MOUNTAINS

WE left the Flathead Valley and came to the South Fork of Flathead River, entering a gorge, narrow and precipitous, where the river roared and thundered against huge rocks. The current was swift, swollen by the melting of mountain snows under a hot sun. On both sides of the gorge were sheer cliffs, and, because of the rocks, it was hard and dangerous going. We followed the river, seeking a place to ford, until we came upon open flats, where the channel was wider; then with shouting and shooting of guns, we drove the frightened horses across.

We camped near a band of Kutenai Indians. Their smoke-colored tepees stood on rising ground. Near by was a grove of trees where a woman was chopping, and a stream with groups of children swimming and playing in the water. In a broad meadow many horses were grazing, men driving picket pins and looking after their horses for the night.

The Kutenai were famed for their good horses. In former days they brought them across the mountains to run buffalo on the plains and to race with the Blackfoot. Whenever the scout visited their country, he traded for horses and took them back across the Rockies to his ranch on the prairies.

That evening I went with the scout to the Kutenai camp and saw the men gathered in a gambling game. They sat in a circle, the players in the center, surrounded by a throng of women spectators. It was a guessing game, played with marked sticks of bone, with horses and blankets for stakes. The players sang gambling songs; they joked and taunted each other; they beat with sticks and drummed. The game came to an end, when one of the sides which was led by the chief of the Kutenai lost all their counting-sticks; and then the scout began to trade.

In the meantime, I was on the lookout for a good saddle horse. Near the circle of gamblers I saw a fine bay tethered. He was a stocky horse, built from the ground up, a four-year-old with a white star on his forehead. He had a sleek and glossy coat, slender legs, and a beautiful pair of brown eyes. He belonged to the chief of the Kutenai, the Indian who lost the gambling game. He saw me looking at his horse and came near. He wore a suit of deerskin decorated with colored beads, a beaded necklace of many strands, white shell earrings, and his hair in long braids over his shoulders.

We bargained in the sign language, and our trading was short. I asked him "how much," by holding out my closed right hand and opening the fingers, one after the other. He sold me his horse for nine dollars. And with the money he opened again the gambling game. This time he won all the counting-sticks and the game was his, while I was the owner of a fine saddle horse. I named him "Kutenai," after his Indian tribe.

Then we entered a broad timber belt, where the forest was dense and the trees large, for the most part giant cedar, hemlock, larch, white pine, great silver fir and canoe birch. The forest floor was covered with a thick carpet of moss and ground pine. Sun and wind did not penetrate. Along the trail the light was dim and the air still. But overhead, through the tops of the big trees, I heard the rushing of the wind.

We rode through glades rank with dense clumps of fragrant ferns and grasses growing shoulder high, forded streams and passed foaming cascades and chains of lovely lakes hidden in deep recesses of the forest. On the western slope of the Rockies the vegetation is luxuriant and the forests dense, because of the mild climate and abundant rainfall. Just across the Continental Divide, on the eastern slope, the climate is cold and dry, with extreme changes of temperature.

When the trail was blocked with fallen trees, the scout went ahead and chopped our way through, while I followed driving the pack horses. He had the marvelous instinct of an Indian for direction and keeping his course. On the trail he was cheerful; he never disputed, found fault, or cursed. He rarely said whether he liked or enjoyed anything. He was courteous and had the quiet manners of a gentleman. If I made mistakes, I found it was better to remain silent than to apologize, or try to make excuses.

We camped near the forks of two streams, where a huge white pine towered above the rest of the forest. I heard the ringing, rippling song of a water ouzel, almost fierce in its wildness, as if sung by a free and untamable spirit. So wild was he, and continually on the alert, he reminded me of a watchful Indian. Springing from rock to rock, he ran along the shore, filled with nervous energy, ever shaking himself and bobbing up and down.

That night by our camp-fire Siksikaí-koan told about his life. Most of his youth was spent north of the Line among the Cree Indians in Canada. In those early days on the plains, he was daring and reckless, and suffered permanent injuries. In 1874, he was scout for General Custer on his expedition to the Black Hills of Dakota, and went with him against the Sioux. He served under General Miles and General Terry, and the Government of the Northwest Territories in the Riel Rebellion. Some of his scouting companions in the Cheyenne Service were the warriors, White Bull, Beaver Claws, Shell, Two Moons, and Brave Wolf.

On the day when General Custer and his battalion of the Seventh Cavalry were cut to pieces by the Sioux, Siksikaí-koan was with Reno's command. With fifteen scouts he made a stand and tried to stop the Indians. In that charge, all but two of those brave scouts were killed. Bloody Knife and Siksikaí-koan alone were left. Then Bloody Knife shook hands and said: "This is the last day I shall ever fight." He rushed among the enemy, killed two and was slain himself. But Siksikaí-koan escaped; he hid in the underbrush, and lay in the river close to the bank. After two days and nights of terrible exposure and without food, he made his way with two white soldiers to Reno's command on the bluffs above the river. In the night, Siksikaí-koan led them past the Sioux sentinels, through his knowledge of the Sioux language.[1]

We left our camp at the big pine in the early morning, when the mists were lifting from the valley, and came that afternoon to a fine meadow surrounded by the forest, where we camped because of good pasture, grass in full seed and thistles, of which the horses were very fond. We hobbled and tethered them, caught a mess of trout, and a grouse which the scout killed by a skillful throw of a stone. The day was warm and bright, and the trout were rising in the river. The scout used bait in deep water and caught many fish. I stood on a high bank where the facilities for fly-fishing were of the best. In the clear swift water I saw many fish swimming over the gravelly bottom, but they scorned a fly. Finally the scout called: "Try the white entrail of another fish." So I baited my hood and cast toward a place where the current eddied in a deep pool. For a moment I let it lie. Suddenly there was a swirl and a big form broke the water. I struck and saw a golden flash as he sprang from the river. "Hold him fast!" shouted the scout. "Don't slacken your line." The fish rushed upstream and across; he struggled in vain. I reeled him in and pulled him to the shore, and the scout landed him on the clean stones. He was a five-

[1] This incident is referred to in the Report of General W. T. Sherman, Secretary of War, 1876, p. 33.

pound fish, the biggest I had caught. The scout called him a bull-trout, but he is also known by the name of "Dolly Varden" (*Salmo clarkii*). He had a large mouth filled with sharp teeth, and was dotted all over with small black spots. The upper half of his body was yellow, the lower half pink, and silvery white underneath. He was good eating; we had him with the grouse for our evening meal.

In the night I wakened to the sound of the ever-rushing river, and saw the forest lighted by moonlight; it made shadows on the trunks of the big trees and lay in patches on the ground. The air was fragrant with the smell of leaves, the freshness of the woods and the subtle perfume of the earth. At daybreak I heard the early chorus of the birds, and went after our horses in the meadow, wading through masses of wild flowers and tall grass growing in bunches. I felt in accord with the world, as though I belonged to the forest. My heart was light; I was as free as the air.

When I found Kutenai, my saddle horse, he gave a gentle whinny of recognition and rubbed his soft nose against my hand. He was a good and faithful companion, just the horse for the Indian country. He was young and spirited, yet gentle and friendly; I could trust him, and rode him without saddle or bridle.

Before the sun was high, we had our horses packed and were on our way toward the Blackfoot country. Our trail led through a broad valley and along the banks of a swift stream, where the current dashed against moss-covered boulders. The peaks of the Continental Divide sparkled in the sunlight, revealing snowfields and glaciers, which overhung tne mountain sides like ice cataracts. Early in the day the water of the stream was clear, but in the afternoon changed to a milky white, from glaciers melting under a hot sun.

I saw a water ouzel dive fearlessly into the foaming rapids

and flit about in the spray. The more boisterous the water, the better he seemed to enjoy himself. He sat on a rock in midstream and burst into a cheerful song with delicate trills. Then flew like a flash to his moss-covered nest on a ledge, so close to the rushing water it was continually bathed in spray.

We passed through a forest of fir and spruce, the trees tall and straight, and soon had high peaks and massive mountain ranges towering over us. We rode along the base of a great mountain, which rose precipitously several thousand feet. There were lateral valleys with cirques, formed by the erosion of glaciers. Through each of these valleys flowed a stream, which had its source in an overhanging glacier at the head, pine forests sweeping upwards in long and gentle curves.

Finally we entered a great basin, a vast amphitheater. In the center was a sparkling blue lake with wooded shores, surmounted by walls of rock several thousand feet in height. The lake was fed by many streams springing from glaciers and snowdrifts; they fell over high cliffs with an incessant roar, which reverberated like thunder from the surrounding walls of rock. We crossed high rock ledges, ravines and gullies, jumped fallen trees, and forced our way through windfalls and thickets of balsam and fir.

I marveled at the endurance and sure-footedness of our Indian horses. In the worst places they rarely stumbled; I did not see one of them fall. In emergencies they never lost their heads. They walked serenely along the edges of precipices where I shuddered to look down. Steep places did not bother them; they sat back on their haunches, bunched their feet together and slid.

But we had one rattle-brained pack horse. If he happened to get in the lead, he wavered and hesitated and held back the outfit; he wandered from the trail to try fool routes of his own, and tore his pack against rocks and trees.

Our last camp on the western slope of the Rockies was in

a grassy park surrounded by groups of tall firs, spruces and thickets of balsam, close to huge banks of snow and the precipitous cliffs of the Continental Divide. A stream of water, cold as ice, flowed through a meadow of rich grass, fine food for our horses, tired and hungry after their hard climb.

Hoary marmots greeted us with shrill whistles from the cliffs, and a red fox barked sharply and ran into his den. We saw a herd of Rocky Mountain goats feeding on a high shelf in an inaccessible part of the mountain. They lay in the sunlight near a cavern in the wall-rock, while their sentinel, an enormous billy with long white beard, stood like a statue close to the edge of a precipice.

Then from a high elevation above our camp, where everlasting snowdrifts lay under the shadow of huge rocks, we had a view of massive mountain ranges, with fields of snow and ice glistening in the sunlight; great valleys with sky-blue lakes and vast forests stretching toward the west to meet blue and distant plains. Through a massive rent in the rocky wall of the Divide, we looked eastward, toward the Blackfoot country and the end of our journey — a view of plains so vast and distant they looked like an ocean meeting the horizon.

North, lay Triple Divide Mountain, the Crown of the Continent, where the watershed divides between the Pacific Ocean, Hudson Bay, and the Gulf of Mexico. To the northwest was Mount Blackfoot and the Blackfoot Glacier, a vast expanse of snow and ice; Mount Cleveland (10,438 ft.), a lofty and massive dome; Mount Siyeh (10,004 ft.), named after the Blackfoot chief who was to be my Indian father; and Mount Jackson (10,023 ft.), named after my Indian guide Siksikaí-koan (William Jackson), because he was the first to climb its steep and rocky slopes.

CHAPTER III

OUR CAMP NEAR THE SUMMIT

THE scout said a big storm was coming. That day the sun went down with a rayless glow and a warm wind sprang up from the south. But the sky was clear and the night had a multitude of brilliant stars.

At dawn we broke camp and packed our horses. We hastened across the Divide to the east side of the range, where we camped in a sheltered place, between two small glacier lakes with banks of snow and ice along their shores.

As we crossed the summit, I saw black clouds coming up across the western horizon. They had an ominous look, extending into the north like a great wall; they ascended towards the zenith and were advancing over the entire sky. There was a strange stillness. The air was sultry with no wind; birds and insects were silent. Then came a vivid flash of lightning, a deafening peal of thunder, and after a stillness a second peal.

Suddenly a strange moan seemed to fill the air. Sinister-looking clouds swept down from the Divide. I heard a roar like ocean surf and the tempest burst with hurricane force, bearing masses of rock and shale and whirling the water of the lake into the air. A canvas pack cover was caught by the wind and carried towards the sky. It soared over camp like a monstrous bird, frightening our horses which stampeded through thickets and snowdrifts. In spite of the gale our tepee held fast. We anchored it securely by a lariat noosed round the apex of the poles and made fast to strongly driven stakes; and weighted down the pegs and sides of the lodge with stones. The bottom, too, was sheltered from the wind by thickets of gnarled and stunted spruces.

For three days and nights a heavy wind with rain and sleet blew out of the northwest. But our Indian tepee was a snug shelter. We lay by our lodge-fire, cosy and comfortable. In my warm blanket-bed, I liked to listen to the roar of the wind in the spruces, the creaking of the lodge-poles, and the beating of rain and sleet. We had sumptuous meals of trout, and tenderloin and heart of a Rocky Mountain ram, which the scout had killed near the summit. He passed the time telling me about his home and Indian tribe. He told about their ancient customs and strange religious beliefs, Indian legends and tribal tales about the very region where we were camped.

Now an Indian is generally slow to speak his innermost thoughts and to talk about his religious beliefs. But during that big storm, the scout was in the mood to talk. He said:

"The Sun is the Great Power. He is in the birds and wild animals, lakes and streams, prairies and mountains. He brings the leaves in the spring-time. He makes the grass and berries grow; and upon them the birds and animals depend for life.

"The Thunder is a great bird. It flies with the clouds, and brings the rain. From its eyes the lightnings flash.

"The blizzard is a person, who runs before the storm and shoots his arrows.

"Long ago an Indian, who camped in this valley, saw the Wind Maker rise from the waters of a lake. He was like a monster bull elk. When he flapped his ears, the wind blew hard; and when he sank again beneath the water, the wind went down.

"My people are afraid of spirits. We believe they are everywhere — underground, in the air, in the forest, in rocks and streams. We are afraid of ghosts which take the form of

AN OLD INDIAN TRAIL
Golden snow lilies in bloom on both sides

owls and come in the dark to harm people; ghosts of disembodied relatives and friends often come around. The Blackfoot are happy on the open plains. In the mountains they are afraid; the forests are dark and gloomy and they hear strange sounds.

"Last summer an Under-Water-Spirit took a child of Bear Paw. He is my friend and lives near me on Cutbank River. One day Bear Paw went into the mountains to cut lodgepoles. He camped at the edge of the forest, near a bend in the river, where a big rock stood and the water was deep. His wife went there for water and saw the rock move; and that night she had a strange dream. The Rock stood over her and said: 'Give me your child.' The woman was so frightened she went to the river and sacrificed some of her ornaments; she threw them into the water close to the Rock. Soon after that one of her children died. Now they believe it was taken from them by the Spirit of the Rock."

The scout related a story which Heavy Breast, another friend who lived in his valley on Cutbank River, told him.

Heavy Breast and the Grizzly Bear

"When one of my children died last autumn, I felt so badly I did not want to see any one. So I went alone to the forest on the mountain. It was dark and gloomy and I felt lonely. But the only animal to be feared was the grizzly bear and I knew he would do me no harm, because I am the guardian of the Bear Medicine. Through its wonderful power I have cured many people.

"One night I came to a cave near the forks of a stream. It was raining and I decided to stay there, because in the cave I would have shelter from the storm. I built a warm fire and lay down to sleep. When I awoke the sun had not risen, but, through the mouth of the cave, I saw that day was beginning to dawn. I heard a noise outside, like some animal sniffing the air. I thought one of the dogs had followed from camp and was nosing around, trying to get my scent. Then I heard heavy footsteps and knew it was a large animal. So I was careful. I made no sound; I scarcely even breathed.

"My back was towards the mouth of the cave, so I turned my head very slowly, very carefully, and saw close to the entrance a huge grizzly bear. Then I said to myself: 'If this bear is angry, he has me caught in a trap.' I have often laughed at animals in traps, but I did not feel like laughing this time. Again I said to myself: 'This grizzly can do me no harm; my Bear Medicine will protect me; it has often helped me to cure the sick; besides I have always had a friendly feeling for bears, as if they were my relatives; I must be bold and make a strong talk; I must make this bear understand that I am his friend.'

"Then I thought: 'Perhaps he intends to play with me before he kills me.' And this made me feel very queer.

"Now, all this time the bear did not move. He stood with his head down and gazed into the mouth of the cave. Oh! How big he looked! He stood high in front and had a broad head; and his great feet had long sharp claws. He did not make a sound, but I knew he was angry; his hair stood straight up on his back.

"Then I remembered an old medicine man saying, that a bear never harms a person who does not move and talks to him in a friendly voice. So I lay with arms stretched out and head on my hands, like a bear does. Thus I lay and looked straight into his eyes. And then I began talking in a friendly way, using the softest and kindest voice I knew. I flattered him the best I could. I said:

"'Brother Bear, you are very good-looking; you have nice eyes and white teeth; you are big and strong. I have never killed bears; I do not care to hunt them. Yes! I have always liked bears. I look upon them as my relatives.'

"While I talked, his hair began to flatten, so I talked again harder than ever. I kept on flattering him; I told him some of the secrets of my Bear Medicine. I saw that he liked my talk; he was in a good humor; and then I began to pray, saying:

"'Brother Bear, pity me! I am poor and in trouble.
Brother Bear, I am the keeper of the Bear Medicine.
Brother Bear, it is I who guard the Bear Secrets.
Brother Bear, I ask you to go away and to leave me in peace.'

"Now, the bear was no longer angry. The hair on his back all went down smooth. Soon he turned and walked slowly from the cave; and after that I saw him no more."

Thus my guide, an Indian belonging to a tribe of the stone age of thought, told me about their religious faith. They believed in the power of the Sun, and that birds and wild animals were endowed with his wisdom and supernatural power. They communed with the wild animals, looking upon them as brothers; they believed they had tribes like men, with head-chiefs, councils and dances; that they were friendly, and had power to help people in trouble. Nor did they exclude the animals from the spirit world, the place where they expected to go after death.

We were storm-bound in our summit camp for several days. But, on the morning of the fourth day, we awoke to find the heavens a vast expanse of blue. A foot of snow had fallen. The surrounding mountains were covered with a white blanket. After the great storm, the air was strangely clear and sparkled with myriads of shining particles. The clouds had rolled away towards the east, revealing the entire chain of Rocky Mountain peaks, their white summits glowing under the bright rays of the rising sun.

Then we made ready to break camp and leave the snow and ice of the high altitude for the milder climate of the valley; but the devil was in our horses that day. It took many weary hours to catch the herd. We made a series of corrals with lariats and pack ropes. By the time we had the horses packed and ready to start, the sun had long passed the meridian. The scout led the way down the mountain, while I followed on foot with camera and tripod, driving the horses and leading my saddle horse Kutenai, loaded with baggage, because one of our pack horses had escaped us down the mountain. Then the contrary bell-mare ran into the underbrush and bucked her pack loose, and the horse of the scout ran away and threw him off. I found him lying senseless on the ground, with blood flowing from nose and mouth. When he came to himself, he made light of his accident; he said that he had been weakened by his former life of exposure in the Indian wars.

We camped that night on the floor of the valley, in a park surrounded by a dark forest of lodge-pole pine and spruce; the air was mild; bunch-grass grew luxuriantly and many varieties of wild flowers — blue camas, orchids with pale green flowers, and yellow columbine with lovely pendant blossoms.

Our last day in the mountains, we followed a trail down the eastern slope, a well-known Indian route across the Rocky Mountains, famous in legend and war story. We passed through the long forest-covered valley of Cutbank River, between two massive snow-covered mountain ranges, and rode through the foothills with their lovely lakes and meadows, groves of aspen and thickets of willows, crossing high grass-covered ridges, closely following one another like great waves of the ocean.

Finally, from the crest of a ridge about twenty miles from the foot of the mountains, we looked down upon a scene I shall never forget. On a broad stretch of prairie and on the shore of a lake lay the tribal camp of the Blackfoot; many

TRIBAL CAMP OF BLACKFOOT ON THE PRAIRIE
Rocky Mountains in the distance

hundreds of smoke-colored tepees, pitched in the form of a great circle more than a mile in circumference. In an open space near the center of camp was a throng of Indians, taking part in the ceremony of the Sun Dance. The surrounding meadows were bright with blue lupines, shooting stars, camas, and yellow sunflowers. Smoke from the evening fires rose from the tepees. Many horses were feeding contentedly on the hills. As we stood looking down at the great camp, a light breeze carried distinctly the shouts of men and women, crying of children, barking of many dogs, neighing of horses, and the rhythmic beating of Indian drums in dances and ceremonial gatherings.

On that first night, we slept on the open prairie with only the sky for a roof. Late in the night, I was wakened by Indian horsemen riding through the camp, singing strange melodies, giving at intervals shrill war whoops, jingling bells keeping time with the slow and measured trot of their horses. Their songs had a lilt and wildness, and were sung with a vigor and enthusiasm that made me long to record them.

Excitement was in the air. Flaring inside fires lighted up the lodges, casting weird shadows of the inmates on the outside coverings. I heard the booming of drums, shrill cries and shouts of dancers, laughter and cheers of the crowds. From the center of camp came a solemn chanting of many voices, accompanied by heavy beating of rattles on the ground. At intervals the low monotone of men singing in unison, united with the shrill voices of women. Then the mysterious chanting died away and I fell asleep.

CHAPTER IV

HOME OF THE SCOUT

NEXT day the scout took me to the lodge of the head-chief White Calf and his wife Catches-Two-Horses. These were the givers of the Sun Dance ceremony. We talked with the venerable chief Running Crane, and saw his wife who was fasting, because of a vow to the Sun. We went to the tepees of the war chiefs, Little Plume and Little Dog, and smoked a friendly pipe, also with the judges, Shoots-in-the-Air, Curly Bear and Wolf Plume, and the medicine men, White Grass and Bull Child. In this way I met some of the head men of the tribe, and among them chief Mad Wolf, an orator of renown and the owner of the ancient Beaver Bundle, an important religious ceremony. This was the beginning of a friendship, unusual between an Indian and a white man. It lasted as long as Mad Wolf lived, and had a strange influence upon my life in the years to come.

When the Sun Dance came to an end and the big camp broke up, I went with the scout to his ranch on the prairie, in the valley of Cutbank River, near the homes of the chiefs, White Calf and Mad Wolf, and of the medicine men, White Grass and Ear-Rings.

The scout had a cabin built of pine logs from the mountains, with sod-covered roof and clay-chinked walls, also corrals and low-lying sheds, a garden, and herds of cattle and horses. His wife was an Indian woman named White Antelope, and they had a family of four children.

She was young and good looking, but had a high temper. She liked to take things easy, to dress in Indian finery and go visiting, leaving ranch and children to the care of the scout.

But he was patient with her; he was kind-hearted and always tried to keep things smooth. She cooked and waited on the table, when she felt in the mood; she and the children ate after the men. If she was moody, the scout prepared the meals.

Their family all slept in one room and I in another. My bunk of rough boards was built against the walls. But, in good weather, I slept outside the cabin and under the stars, on the grassy bank of the river, with a shady grove of cottonwoods near by, and a lovely landscape of meadows and distant snow-capped mountains.

Siksikaí-koan was a good friend, honest and trustworthy. He stood high in the councils of his tribe and was liked by all the people. He was always ready to help any who came to his ranch, to advise his people in their struggle towards civilization. Through him, I met Indians both old and young. I made friends with them, and tried to understand them and to see things their way.

Every morning before sunrise, the scout wakened me to go into the hayfields. He mowed while I drove the horserake; and then came days of pitching and stacking. Then every part of me seemed sound and sane; I was light-hearted and happy, untrammeled and free. On those broad prairies were no worries nor pessimists, no laws nor creeds, nothing but a wonderful peace and contentment; something I had longed for all my life.

The west wind blew fresh from pine forests on the mountains, from meadows with odors of wild flowers, sweet grass, and ripe strawberries. Bees hummed in the air, western meadow larks sang on the prairie, willow thrushes and white-crowned sparrows in the river valley.

But the scout could not stand heavy work in the hayfields. He suffered from the hardships of his former life on the plains, from an injury by a wild horse, and wounds received in the Indian wars.

Then Yellow Bird came to help in the haying. He was a relative of the scout, a young half-breed of my own age, strong, full of life, and a good worker when he felt like it. But he was wild and could not be depended upon. Like young men of the Blackfoot, he wanted to be gay and craved excitement. He liked to wander, to hunt, to rope cattle and ride wild horses, to see friends and visit new places, to be always on the move; he liked jolly companions and people who gave him a good time; but he loved to go with girls best of all.

He took me to Indian camps to dance and see the girls. On our way home at night, he liked to gallop past ranches where they kept packs of ferocious dogs. They rushed after us and he had the fun of riding at a mad gallop, yelling and shooting at them on the run. He was thrilled at the idea of being chased by their angry owners, and of hearing bullets whizzing harmlessly in the dark.

We attended a meeting held by a white missionary in our valley. I led the singing and sat in the front row with Bear Chief and Eagle Child, who were prominent Indians. They listened gravely and attentively but understood not a single word. They were broad-minded chiefs and came as an example to other Indians; to show they approved of the missionary and of his religious ceremony.

Thus with Yellow Bird I entered into the life of the people. I wanted to see them natural and without restraint. With them I talked not of my life in civilization, but of things of their everyday life, of horses and cattle, hunting and wild animals, dancing and ceremonies. In this way I became one of them, and they saw I was not critical of them nor of their ways.

After we stacked eighty tons of hay at the scout's ranch, Yellow Bird and I rode the range after stray horses and cattle. We skirted the base of the mountains, along the foothills and edge of the forest, until we came to a well-worn trail, which led to an open park far back in the mountains. Many cattle were there, seeking refuge from the swarms of flies and mosquitoes on the grass-covered prairies. Then we found a herd of mares and geldings. Their leader, a fiery young stallion, tried to drive us off. But we rounded them up with the cattle and drove them back to the ranch, feeding them salt, that they might not again stray away.

When we wanted to break a new team for the wagon, we drove that wild herd of range horses into the corral and lassoed a roan and a three-year-old sorrel. We tied them with ropes while we put on the harness, then hitched them to the wagon and took blankets and provisions; we knew not how far they might run.

At the start the broncos bucked and plunged; then ran and tried to tear themselves loose from the rattling wagon, bounding over rocks, swinging as though it would turn over. After running many miles, our broncos broke into a stampede so wild that Yellow Bird turned them up a butte and put the brakes on hard. They galloped up one side of that steep butte and down the other, our wagon plunging over ruts, stones, and badger holes, and into a swamp in the valley of a stream, where they sank deep into soft muck and the wagon went down over the hubs. But they soon freed themselves, and, with their sides covered with foamy sweat, they pulled us through to firm ground. Then they ran again and did not stop, until we were far out on the open plains. That night we tied up our wild team and slept peacefully under the wagon, twenty-five miles from the ranch.

Sometimes in the evening, after our work at the ranch, we saddled our horses and rode down the river to see two sisters who were home from school, Katoyísa and Nínake. Their father, Lone Wolf, was dead, and they lived alone with their mother, a quiet, pleasant-faced woman. Their log cabin of three rooms had low ceilings, and walls of hewn logs chinked and plastered, all whitewashed and clean. The floor was spotless and covered with skins of wolf, bear, and mountain goat; in the windows were grasses and ferns and wild flowers, and a dish of fragrant red apples on a table.

Nínake, the younger sister, was the favorite of Yellow Bird. She was lively, a great talker, and gave him a good time. But I liked Katoyísa better, a quiet bashful girl of nineteen, with shapely head and good features. Her black hair hung in two heavy braids almost to her knees. She wore homemade cotton gowns of thin material which showed her slender graceful form. From the look in her eyes and expression of her face, I knew she had courage and character. In her was the stuff of our bravest pioneers.

After we had finished with the hay of the scout, Yellow Bird and I went to their ranch to help with their crops. The girls cooked and gave us good food, fresh vegetables from their garden, beef, bread and butter and milk.

Many years have passed, but they have not dimmed the memory of those happy days without a care in the world, the primitive simplicity of that family, and the way they made me one of them. We both enjoyed our work, we were near the girls from morning till night, and that kept us in a good humor.

Then the scout wanted timber from the mountains, so we took two teams and made ready the wagons. We threw off their beds and placed the wheels far apart by means of a long reach, to hold the heavy logs. Yellow Bird drove one wagon and I the other. For me it was a new thing to drive a team of broncos. I sat on the reach, on a gunnysack stuffed with hay. I had to wield a whip with a long lash, and had a heavy chain for binding the logs together.

We left the ranch soon after sunrise and went to a burned stretch of timber on a slope of the Rockies. We felled only trees that were sound and well-seasoned, cutting them into logs and snaking them down the forest trails to be loaded on our wagons.

At first it was hard to chop hour after hour with an axe. I blistered my hands and was drenched with sweat; my arms and back ached; I felt weak in the knees and had a consuming thirst. Then I became accustomed to the work and had a feeling of exhilaration. I liked the fresh odor of the wood, the ring of my axe and the feeling of a good stroke, to know my sharp blade was cutting deep.

There was always danger of being cut with an axe, from felling trees that had lodged, and from Yellow Bird; sometimes his trees fell perilously near. Once I was nearly struck by a pine that let go at the roots; I heard a sharp crackling, saw it coming towards me and jumped just in time.

But for me the hardest work was the loading of the wagons. The heavy logs were twenty-five feet long and from one to two feet in diameter. The roads were steep and rough and our brakes would not hold. But we always joked about hard work and danger, and had to look out for ourselves.

Soon Yellow Bird tired of ranch work and wanted a change. He proposed that we ride across the Montana line into Canada, to visit relatives in a camp of Blood Indians, a northern division of the tribe. So we rounded up the wild herd of range horses and drove them into the corral. We each chose a saddle horse, Yellow Bird a brown with silvery mane and tail, I a powerful sorrel. My gentle horse, Kutenai, I left to graze at the ranch.

In handling horses that ran wild on the range, we were always ready for trouble. To control them was a question of mastery; they took kind treatment as a sign of weakness. When I tried to saddle my sorrel, he rose on his hind legs and with forefeet high in the air tried to bring them down on my head. In mounting, I held his bit in one hand, the pommel with the other, and made a flying leap upon his back. Before I was in the saddle, he sprang forward like a race horse at a desperate gallop. He had an easy motion and I kept my seat; but to stop him baffled all of my endeavors.

We went north across the open plains, without fences or roads to bar the way. Our horses ran like the wind; we gave them free rein and held on. I rode Indian fashion, letting myself go freely with the motion of my horse and kept a firm grip with my knees.

The first night we stopped at the cabin of a squaw man, near a rocky peak which rose abruptly out of the prairie, standing apart from the main range of the Rocky Mountains. Our host was a white man with an Indian wife and four half-breed children, the oldest a girl of seventeen. She and Yellow Bird were sweethearts; and while they made love by the river, I went into the meadow to help the old man with his hay. He was one of those poineer settlers of early days, short and sinewy in stature, and with a heavy beard. His life had been filled with hardships, toil, and little pleasures. He was suspicious by nature, and liked to talk about free silver; but at heart he was a good fellow, resolute, brave, a hard worker and hospitable. His Indian wife was a laughing, broad-faced woman, good-natured and lazy. Their cabin was dirty and swarmed with flies. The second daughter was strangely pretty, with flashing black eyes, jet black hair, and marvelously clear olive skin. She had a pet colt which followed her like a dog. He came into the cabin for supper. When they put him out, he ran to the open window and poked me in the back with his nose; he whinnied and grunted and made such a fuss that his young mistress went to the window and gave him sugar.

Soon after sunrise on the following morning Yellow Bird

and I saddled our broncos and moved on. To the west rose the mighty frontier range of the Rockies. The rugged valleys and peaks still had a thin veil of morning mist. In the cool air our horses had wonderful speed. They chafed at the bit and were tireless, as though their sinews were of steel. But, after that first day, they were not so hard to hold.

We crossed buttes on the run, up hill and down, it was all the same; in steep places our horses put their feet together and slid. They jumped streams, rocks, and badger holes; galloped over ledges and sharp volcanic rocks, across hills and ravines; it was beautiful to see them go; they never stumbled, but lifted their feet cleanly up and over, and always planted them securely and firmly. We passed lakes and marshy ponds, starting noisy flocks of ducks and other water birds, crossed Boundary Creek, and were over the Montana line into the Province of Alberta.

We came to the ranch of a Frenchman named Big Steve, far out on the prairie. He and his wife were pitching hay in a meadow. She was buxom and smiling, with rosy cheeks and did the work of a man. Both were friendly and wanted to talk, but we could not tarry; our horses were wild and hard to hold.

At midday we dashed into a Mormon settlement, and a number of men came to meet us. They all looked alike, over six feet in height, with smooth faces and prominent features. They were good-natured and hospitable and gave us all the food we could eat. But it was a dreary place on a barren plain, a group of board shanties, without trees or vegetation. I thought to myself: "How dull an existence compared to our life in the Indian country, with dances and games, feasts and ceremonies!"

Near the border line we entered a region of bandits and law-breakers. We saw a white man who tried to hold us up, but we spurred our broncos and they ran so fast he gave up the chase; then a band of Blood Indians closely muffled in their blankets; they were on their way south and kept their faces hidden. We passed another rider, who was followed by the North-West Mounted Police; they said he was leader of a gang of cattle thieves.

We came that afternoon to the end of our journey in a camp of the Blood Indians. Yellow Bird took me to the home of his relative, an elderly man named Strong. In his lodge we met some of the head men of the tribe — Thunder Chief, Spotted Calf, Running Coyote, and Grasshopper. They were all friendly and glad to see us. They greeted us with "How!" shook us by the hand and welcomed us to their feast.

For refreshments, they had a meat stew and hot tea. Their manner of eating was different from that of people in civilization. They ate with their fingers, gulped down the food, sucked their teeth, and drank with a hissing intake of the breath. But with them these were not breaches of good manners; they were not sensitive to any of these things. While eating they did not talk; and after the manner of Indians showed no enthusiasm. None of them said the food was good, or that they liked anything; nor, on the other hand, did any one grumble or say the food was bad.

After the feast they smoked a large pipe of polished redstone, which was handed stem first to each person. Then they talked, speaking rapidly, in guttural voices that were not harsh, and making graceful gestures with their hands. The Indian named Grasshopper had a reputation as a wit. He kept them laughing — all but Thunder Chief, who was head man and had his dignity to maintain.

Grasshopper wore a coyote-skin cap with the tail hanging down behind and an eagle feather on top; slung over his shoulder was a polished buffalo horn. He had beaded moccasins and leggings, and a blanket coat with bright stripes. After we had eaten, he turned to me and said with a laugh:

"You look like an eagle. You sit straight and with your head up. Now is the time to shake your tail feathers, like an eagle after it eats." This was Indian humor and made the others laugh.

Grasshopper was the life of the party. He said his parents died when he was small. He was raised by a chief named Red Crow, who had started many boys in life; he had become a successful man, because he followed the advice of his adopted father.

Grasshopper was pleased when he saw me recording his conversation in my notebook. He said: "Now I am going to tell you some stories." I sat waiting, but he did not begin; so I said: "Go ahead; I am ready."

To make the others laugh, he held out his hand saying: "How much do you pay?" I took his outstretched hand, shook it and said: "That is what I pay."

Then every one laughed, even the dignified head chief joined in. They liked the repartee and wanted more.

Grasshopper said: "Well, instead of paying he only shakes." He turned to the head-chief and said: "This white man is a great traveler. I like him and want him for my partner. We had better keep him here with us."

And then he said to me: "Why don't you join our tribe and stay with us? You could take an Indian wife; you could hunt and trap and make a good living."

That evening we sat outside the lodge and watched the sun go down fiery red, with its glow reflected in a near-by stream. Then the moon, nearly full, rose over the distant hills of the prairie, like a ghostly phantom in the twilight.

Then by the lodge-fire the Indians told stories of their hunting trips and war expeditions of former days. They talked far into the night, and next morning we saddled our horses early and rode back to Montana.

CHAPTER V

STORIES BY THE SCOUT'S MOTHER-IN-LAW

ONE day Two-Bear-Woman, mother of the scout's wife, came to our ranch. She pitched her lodge in the meadow, not far from my bed on the river bank. After dark I watched it, glowing with yellow light from an inside fire. And, when the dying fire made shadows dance on the lodge wall, there was an air of mystery about her tepee. At night I heard the old woman praying and chanting weird songs of old days, in a quavering voice and beating on a tom-tom. The sound was mournful and made me feel sad; I lay awake and listened until late in the night.

Two-Bear-Woman was the widow of a famous medicine man named Four Bears. She was said to have occult powers and was looked upon as a wise woman. She could see visions, dream dreams, doctor, and do mysterious things. She was something of a shrew, with sharp tongue and quick temper, but industrious and skilled in all the arts of Indian women — tanning, making clothes and lodges, and the knowledge of herbs and plants.

The scout never went near the lodge of his mother-in-law, nor could she visit her daughter while her son-in-law was at home, according to tribal custom. A mother-in-law had no dealings with her son-in-law, nor could they even speak to each other.

So I went with White Antelope to call upon the old woman. One evening by her lodge-fire she talked about her husband. She said he was a man of influence and stood high in the tribe. When danger threatened, the chiefs used to call upon him for help. As head medicine man it was his custom to officiate at tribal meetings and ceremonies. He was mediator between the Great Spirit and his people. He fasted and prayed and helped the tribe by means of his supernatural power. He was both prophet and priest. Besides being a man of mystery, he had a reputation as a doctor. His power to heal came from the buffalo through a vision, after long fasting and prayer. When he doctored, he wore an old buffalo robe decorated with a yellow buffalo head. He carried a medicine drum which was painted yellow, also his body, with a crescent on his forehead for the moon and marks over his temples for sun dogs. He wore a wonderful belt which had supernatural power, an otter-skin to keep him young and an eagle feather to ward off danger in battle. The old woman said that after the death of her husband his ghost had come every night to protect her from harm.

Then, as we sat and smoked and the fire burned low, Two-Bear-Woman told legends and stories. She liked blood-curdling tales and gloated over one of a warrior who went mad.

The Warrior who ate his Foot

"Long ago, two warriors named Arrow Top and Black Horse went to war against their enemies the Crow Indians. They left home in the early summer and did not start back until it was time for snow in the autumn. They had a hard time; the weather was bad and their food gave out. One evening at dark, they came to two old shelters made of willow branches, which stood close together. It was snowing and cold, and they were tired and hungry. They had no food, so each crawled into a shelter and lay down to sleep.

"In the night Arrow Top was wakened by a queer sound — his friend was hacking with his knife. Then he smacked his lips and drew in his breath, saying: 'Mmmmmm, this foot is fine, it is tender and juicy and has a good taste.'

"He shouted: 'Hai there! Arrow Top! Come and eat.

I have plenty of meat. This leg is tender and juicy; I have a good slice for you.'

"Then Arrow Top peeped into the other shelter and saw a terrible sight. His friend was covered with blood. He had cut off his own foot and was roasting a piece of the flesh over a fire. Then he hacked at his leg, and when there was nothing left but the bone, he began digging out the marrow with his knife.

"Again he called, and getting no answer he shouted: 'Arrow Top, I say, come and join in my feast; I have saved a fine piece of juicy meat for you.'

"By this time day was beginning to dawn and Arrow Top tried to run away. But Black Horse saw him and followed; it was a cold night and the blood of his wounded leg froze. He ran on his mangled stump, shouting for his friend to wait. He begged him not to go and leave him alone.

"Arrow Top was so frightened he climbed a tree and tried to hide in the branches. But Black Horse saw him. He was so mad he foamed at the mouth. He came to the tree and shouted:

"'You dog-face, I see you there. I asked you to come and eat with me, but you ran away and left me to die. You can't escape me. I am going to catch you now and kill you.'

"He struck at Arrow Top with his knife and tried to climb the tree. He fell down because of his mangled leg; he got so mad he ran at the tree. He kicked the trunk with the sharp bone of his leg, until it stuck fast in a crack. He wept and raved; he twisted and turned and tried to tear himself loose.

"Then Arrow Top jumped from the tree and struck out for home. He did not stop running until he came to the camp. He told his story to the head men and they took a band of warriors. They found Black Horse dead, with the sharp bone of his leg still fast in the crack of the tree."

CHAPTER VI

MY ADOPTION BY MAD WOLF

NEAR the end of summer, I met Mad Wolf on the prairie. He was alone and signed that he wanted to talk with me. He was mounted on a restless bronco, and held a rawhide quirt in his hand. From his neck hung a bone whistle, made from the wing of an eagle; and in his hair a single eagle feather stood erect. He dismounted from his horse and stood waiting; and when I came to him, he shook hands; then looked earnestly into my face, and said:

"From the time you first came to live in my country, I have been watching you, and my heart feels warm towards you. I have never taken a son from the white men; now I want to adopt you, because I believe that some day you will be a chief among your people. I am growing old, and it is probable that I shall go before you to dwell with the Great Spirit, for you are still a young man. After I am gone, you will then be left, to help and to advise my people."

I told Mad Wolf that I wanted to be his son. He pointed towards the north and said:

"My lodge is out yonder on the prairie. It is beyond that long range of hills and cannot be seen from here. Come tomorrow when the sun is high. I will hold a ceremony. I will paint you with the sacred paint; and in the presence of my relatives and friends, will adopt you as my son."

In after years, I saw more clearly Mad Wolf's purpose in taking a white son. His tribe were rulers of a vast domain of plains and forest-covered mountains. Great herds of buffalo and other game furnished them with an abundance of meat for food and skins for clothes and shelter. But the coming of the white man caused the disintegration of his tribe. The herds of wild animals quickly disappeared and with them the chief support of the Indians. An advancing tide of white settlers came like the invasion of an enemy; they introduced smallpox, measles, scarlet fever, and other contagious diseases. The white men were shrewd and unprincipled. They traded whiskey and debauched the Indians; they occupied their country; they always got the best of them in their deals. Indian children were sent to white men's schools; they did not learn their native tongue; old tribal customs, traditions, and religion were no longer handed down.

When a white man whom he trusted came to live among his people, Mad Wolf decided to adopt him as his son. He foresaw the doom of his tribe. He wanted a son among the white men upon whom he could depend; one able to help his tribe, who would go to the Great Father at Washington and intercede in their behalf. The old chief was wise; he saw that an Indian could not accomplish his purpose.

The following morning, I rode Kutenai across the prairie in search of Mad Wolf's summer camp. From the summit of a ridge, I saw the white tepees in a meadow amid grass-covered hills. The sky was overcast and a strong wind shook the lodges, which were anchored to the ground by long ropes around their tops. I heard the sound of chanting and beating of drums. For a moment I waited on the hill, listening to the weird singing and thinking of the days when the lodges of Mad Wolf's tribe were numbered by thousands and they were the rulers of their country.

After the song had ceased, I rode down from the hill. Dismounting before the large lodge of the chief, I lifted the door-flap and looked inside. Mad Wolf saw me and shouted, "Okye!" (Welcome.) I entered and saw Mad Wolf seated at the back, the position of honor, with the fire between

MAD WOLF

himself and the door. He shook hands and motioned me to a place at his left, among the other men, and said: "Bring a robe for him to sit upon." Morning Plume, who was nearest, greeted me with a smile and made ready my seat. Other Indians present were, Blessed Weasel, Heavy Breast, Double Runner, Middle Calf, Bear Child, and Many-White-Horses, so named because he owned many horses of that color. The men were all seated on Mad Wolf's left, the women and children on his right.

Between Mad Wolf and his wife Gives-to-the-Sun, who sat on his right, lay the sacred Beaver Bundle. It contained the skins of beaver and other wild animals, which were believed to contribute Sun Power to the Bundle.[1] It was opened in a religious ceremony, given in behalf of the sick, or on other important occasions. From the lodge-poles hung beaded clothing and sacred bundles with long leather fringes hanging from their sides and decorated with painted designs.

Mad Wolf was a noble specimen of Indian chief. His long gray hair fell loosely over his shoulders, and his face had a kindly and benign expression. He was large in stature and of majestic presence, with broad forehead and high cheek bones, keen eyes and firm mouth. From the waist up his body was bare. He had broad shoulders and chest and his arms were muscular and well formed, like those of a young man. He wore leggings of deerskin, moccasins decorated with colored porcupine quills and necklaces of deer bones and bear claws. A medicine whistle, with which he led his beaver ceremony, hung by a thong from his neck.

All sat in silence, waiting for the ceremony of adoption to begin. Then Gives-to-the-Sun, wife of the chief, whispered to a young woman; she straightway rose and stirred a large kettle of service-berries and tongue, which was cooking on the fire. Mad Wolf pointed to her and said to me: "She is

[1] For descriptions of Beaver Bundle, see Chapters VII and VIII.

your Indian sister, Strikes-on-Both-Sides. We gave her that name because, in battle, I once struck down enemies on both sides."

Gives-to-the-Sun brought forth a forked stick. She went to the fire, and, lifting out a live coal, placed it in front of Mad Wolf, who burned dried sweet grass upon it. Soon a fragrant perfume like incense filled the lodge; and they began to sing a low chant in a minor key, in which all the Indians joined.

Then Mad Wolf and his wife knelt by the burning sweet grass; they placed their hands in the rising smoke; they seemed to grasp the smoke; they rubbed it over their bodies and passed it over their heads, shoulders and arms; they breathed it in; thus purifying themselves without and within.

Suddenly the clouds broke and the sun shone into the lodge. Its bright rays came through the smoke hole and lighted up the ground in front of Mad Wolf. Again he held his hands in the smoke of the burning sweet grass. He passed them over his arms and breast for a blessing; and turning his face towards the sun, he chanted:

"See! Our Father, the Sun, shines into the lodge.
His power is very strong.
At night our Mother, the Moon, shines into the lodge.
Her power is very strong.
I pray Morning Star to shine into the lodge and bring long life."

Mad Wolf took a willow branch, which was painted red. He placed it in turn on his right and left shoulders, and prayed for long life. He handed the branch to me; and I laid it on both my shoulders, while he prayed to the Sun that I might live to be old. Then the branch was passed round the lodge for every one to pray with.

Mad Wolf and Gives-to-the-Sun knelt by a long bundle and sang four times. After the fourth song, they began to loosen the thongs of the bundle, but they still sang, chanting a slower and more monotonous song. After the thongs had been untied, Mad Wolf chanted and prayed and removed the cover, revealing a large redstone pipe. For a moment the old chief bent over it in silence; then raised it slowly and tenderly, addressing it in a soft caressing voice; he pressed it to his lips and prayed to it. He passed it over his arms for a blessing, then over his shoulders and both sides of his head. Again he chanted, moving the pipe in time with his song:

> "Pity us! O Sun! O Moon! O Stars!
> Mother Earth! Pity us! Pity Us!
> Give us food and drink.
> Bless our children, may their trails lie straight."

Mad Wolf passed the pipe to Blessed Weasel, who held it before his face; he prayed long and earnestly with bowed head. Then Blessed Weasel handed the pipe to me. I held it reverently for a moment and passed it to Morning Plume; and thus it went round the lodge, until it came to the women, who also prayed with it, and passed it over the bodies of their little children, believing it would help them, too. People who did not pray, went through the motions of touching the pipe to both sides of their heads and shoulders. Some prayed aloud and others only whispered. But every one who prayed made the sign for receiving a blessing, and, at the same time wished for something.

Finally the pipe came back to Mad Wolf. He arose and danced round the fire with it, while the others sang in unison. He moved the pipe in time with the song, blowing on his medicine whistle, and facing, first towards the east, then south, west and north, following the direction of the sun's course through the heavens. After he sat down, the pipe was passed around the lodge for every one to smoke.

Then Mad Wolf turned his face towards the Beaver Bundle, which contained the skins of many birds and animals. He prayed solemnly and earnestly:

"Hear! Above-Spirits and Underground-Spirits, birds and animals, our secret helpers. Pity us! Pity us! Give us long life! May we live to be old! Listen, Spirits! This young man with the light hair, let him live. Care for him and let no harm come to him from evil men or wild animals. May all his relatives live long and have plenty. Let our young people grow, and our men, women, and children have a full life and be happy."

At the end of the prayer, all in the lodge united in a long-drawn "Ah-h-h-h-h," meaning "Yes" or "Amen."

Then Mad Wolf brought forth a small pouch of red clay, the sacred paint. There was an impressive silence while he prepared it in his hands, and said: "Now is the time for my white son to come." He motioned to me. I went before him and knelt, while he painted my forehead, chin, and both cheeks, describing a circle and representing the sun's daily course through the heavens. He took a beaver-skin from his sacred bundle, and passed it down both sides of my head, shoulders, and arms; then ended with an upward sweep, by which he imparted his blessing, and prayed:

" Before you, my Father, Great Sun Chief,
I now adopt this white man as my son.
Let the red paint be like the sunlight,
To protect and bring him health and strength.
May all my people be kind and help him,
That he may be happy, as long as he remains among his
Indian brothers and sisters.
My Father, the Sun, keep him from harm,
When he goes again to his home towards the rising sun.
Give him light by day,
That his path may be free from danger.
If he should go into the wrong trail,
Lead him safely back,
That his path may be firm and downhill to old age."

After the prayer, Mad Wolf and Blessed Weasel opened a bundle of buffalo and elk hides, which were spread before the men. Rattles of rawhide, containing small pebbles, were

MAD WOLF PRAYING

MAD WOLF'S SACRED BEAVER BUNDLE

also distributed among them for beating on the hides. Mad Wolf handed two of the rattles to me and said: "You are now my son and should take part in the ceremony." Then kneeling with the Indians, I joined in the chants and in beating time with my rattles on a buffalo hide.

One song we sang represented a porcupine on a hill, watching a beaver at work. The porcupine said: "I will take my bow and arrows and kill you." But the beaver escaped by swimming under the water. We also sang the song of the war eagle, soaring high over the mountains and at times swooping down for its prey.

At sunset Mad Wolf brought the ceremony to a close with the prayer:

> "Father, the Sun! Continue to give us light,
> That the leaves and grass may grow.
> May our cattle increase, and our children live to be old.
>
> Mother, the Moon! Give us sleep,
> That we may rise again like our Father, the Sun.
> May our lives be strong.
> May our hearts feel good towards our white brothers,
> We are all your children."

After the feast of soup made of service berries and tongue, Mad Wolf made a sign that the ceremony was over; and all rose and filed out of the lodge.

CHAPTER VII

MAD WOLF TELLS THE LEGEND OF THE BEAVER BUNDLE

AFTER the ceremony Mad Wolf reclined upon his couch and smoked with half-closed eyes. I sat near him, gazing at the sacred Beaver Bundle, thinking of its mysterious power over the Indian, and its strange superstitions handed down through many generations. There was a long silence; the fire burned low and twilight settled over prairie and camp. Finally Mad Wolf knocked the ashes from his pipe. He signed for me to help him remove the robe which covered the Beaver Bundle. For a moment he allowed me to gaze upon it, when the robe was reverently replaced. Then Mad Wolf said earnestly, as though he were thinking back into the distant past:

"Before the white men came into our country, we lived content, and were happy in our religion. We worshiped the Sun. In those days we had many powerful chiefs and wise men. There were no white men, and we wandered wherever we pleased. We had plenty of food. We killed buffalo in great numbers by driving them over cliffs, and the young men who were good in the buffalo drives were famous.

"The information I have came from wise men of the older generation, and what they told me was true. Never before have I talked in this way to a white man; I have always been afraid to trust them. But I tell you these things, because I believe in you. I feel towards you as a father to a son. I want to hand down my secrets through you.

"I come from a long-lived family. My father's name was Big Bonnet and that of my mother, Bear Woman. My father taught me many things; but he died when I was ten years old. In my youth I was wild, like many others, and I was still a young man when I had a narrow escape from death. When the danger had passed, I felt glad to be alive. I looked up to the Sun and made my first vow. After that I became thoughtful and wanted to do something to help my tribe. The following summer at the Sun Dance, when many people were assembled, I stood before them and made known my vow. Then for the first time I took part in the ceremonies in the sun lodge; and I have continued to do so ever since.

"When my wife was ill, and I thought she was going to die, I made a vow to the Sun, that if she recovered, I would take the Beaver Bundle. White Calf, the head-chief, was then its guardian. It came into his care from an Indian of the Blood tribe. Now if a man makes a vow to take the bundle, the owner cannot keep it. So, when my wife was restored to health, I made known my vow. I had to make payment to White Calf in many things—horses, robes, and blankets. But my friends and relatives helped. These people now own shares in the bundle. Some of them have become beaver men and now take part with me in the ceremony. When I took over the bundle, I had to learn the songs, prayers, dances, and movements, which make up the ceremony. I had to pay for everything, and I found that a man must have a good memory to remember it all. My woman helps me with the bundle, and it is necessary for her to take part in the ceremony. She leads the other women in their songs and dances, and directs them in whatever they do. The bundle is kept at the back of the lodge and should be taken outside only when we move camp."

Mad Wolf gave me an old medicine sack woven in different colors, containing the two rattles which I had used in the ceremony of adoption, with the instructions to always carry them with me, that I might be ready to take part, whenever he gave a ceremony. He also gave me a buckskin bag with seeds of the tobacco, and said:

"Tobacco was first given to us at the same time with the Beaver Bundle by the Chief of the Beavers. These seeds are sacred, because they came from the 'Dwarf People,' who look after our crops of tobacco. We try to keep these little people in good humor, by giving them presents of clothes and moccasins and sacks of food, which we leave outside the tepee with the prayer:

"'Dwarf People! Here are clothes and food. We ask you to look after our tobacco crop.'

"No one should ever try to watch the Dwarf People at work. Any one who sees them is sure to die.

"We always give a beaver ceremony in the spring, when the tobacco seeds are planted; also because spring is the time when beavers are accustomed to leave their winter dens. For the crop we select a lonely place near a stream or a river, where the land is fertile. And before planting, we cover the ground with the dung of deer, antelope, and mountain sheep. This makes the tobacco grow fast, because these animals are swift runners. We never use the dung of elk or moose; they walk slowly and might retard its growth. We first hold the beaver ceremony, and then dig up the ground with sharp-pointed sticks. While planting we sing songs and burn sweet grass as incense. And when we have finished every one must go away. No one stays to see the Dwarf People at work, nor returns to look at the crop, until it is time for the tobacco to be gathered. If the season is dry and the tobacco needs rain, I take the otter-skin from the Beaver Bundle and tie it to a pole. It floats in the wind and is sure to bring rain. When the crop is ready I call the people together. We put up a large tepee for a dance and have a feast which lasts four days and four nights. Then the Beaver men pull up the plants.

We mix the leaves with those of the bearberry (kinnekinnick), and distribute it among the people.

"The owner of a Beaver Bundle has power to forecast the weather; he must keep track of the moons and be able to read signs in the sky. In winter, if the buffalo disappear, and the snow is deep and people starve, the owner brings out the Beaver Bundle and charms the buffalo back to the camp. Any one who is ill or in trouble can make a vow, and the beaver ceremony will be given in their behalf. They must pay the owner of the bundle a horse, robe, or blanket, whatever they are able to give.

"There is much trouble and expense in keeping a Beaver Bundle. But I am happy in giving the ceremony; and it brings good fortune to a family. It makes a man a greater chief, and gives his family a prominent position in the tribe. There are many rules in its care, which bring misfortune if not carefully observed. The sides of the tepee, where the bundle is kept, must never be raised, nor should any of the cooking be done outside the lodge. Food must be given to every one who comes as guest; and, when the owner of the bundle goes into another lodge, he must not change from the place where he first takes his seat. No one should ever pass in front of the beaver man when he is smoking. If he goes for a swim, he must sing a certain song before entering the water. He has power over the water, and must never show fear of water. If he comes to a deep stream, he must cross quickly, and not hesitate or turn away. He must not eat a beaver or strike a dog or kill any of the birds or animals that are represented in the Beaver Bundle. He must not beat his wife without singing first the appropriate song. But if she sings the 'Defense Song,' it makes her safe. Otherwise, she cannot escape from the beating, because it would be in vain to run away."

Legend of the Beaver Bundle

"The Beaver Bundle is very old. It came to us in the days when our ancestors used dogs instead of horses for beasts of burden. They had tools and weapons of stone and wore clothes made of animal skins. In those days of long ago lived a poor young man. He wore an old robe badly tanned. The corners were cut off. It had a queer shape, and the people called him Round-Cut-Robe. In the same camp was a chief named Red Horn who had three wives. The youngest was badly treated by her husband and the other two wives. Round-Cut-Robe was her secret lover. He was so poor he did not have a tepee of his own. He lived through the camp, wherever he could find shelter. One day he said to his sweetheart:

"'I shall go to an unknown place, because I am ashamed. I want to have a dream. Perhaps some of the birds or animals may pity me and give me their Sun Power. If I never come back, you will know that I am dead.'

"Round-Cut-Robe went alone over the prairies; no one knew where he went. He had no food and became thin and weak. He prayed to the animals for power; he wanted a dream to guide him. Finally he came to a place in the mountains where the beavers had a lodge, a big pool in a river where they swam and worked. Round-Cut-Robe made a shelter near their den. He stayed there night and day, crying and acting like an unhappy person; he wanted the beavers to pity him. For four days and nights he lay by their lodge, but none of the beavers appeared. Then he cried again and called upon the Under-Water-Spirits. He prayed:

"'O Sun! I put away all that is bad. Moon and Stars, pity me and give me power!'

"Then a small beaver came from the lodge and said: 'My father invites you.' He followed the little beaver into their lodge, and saw a beaver with his family gathered around. This beaver was white from the snows of many winters, and so large that Round-Cut-Robe knew he was the chief of all the beavers.

"The beaver chief asked why he traveled alone, and the young man said:

"'There is a woman who loves me. I am poor and am trying to get power.'

"Then the old beaver felt sorry for him and invited him to stay in their lodge, saying:

"'If you remain here with us through the winter, we will teach you many wonderful things; and in the spring you can go home again.'

"Round-Cut-Robe was glad to stay in their lodge. When the beavers went out to work, he went along and watched them cut down many trees and bushes for their winter food — birch, poplar, cottonwood, red willow and willow brush. They told him to take back four things into the lodge; and, in the night, when the moon was high, the beaver chief changed them into food for his winter supply — pemmican and ripe berries.

"The beavers closed their lodge when the river began to freeze; but left a hole for air at the top. On the coldest days they kept Round-Cut-Robe warm, by laying their tails across his body. He made friends with them all, but he liked Little Beaver the best. He was the cleverest, and the favorite child of the beaver chief. During the winter the beavers taught Round-Cut-Robe many wonderful things. They gave him the paint, and showed him how to use it to ward off sickness and death. They taught him how to count the moons and gave him the first seeds of the tobacco, showing him how they should be planted with songs and prayers; and they told him about the different herbs and plants, which the Indians have used ever since for eating and healing.

"One day Little Beaver said to his friend: 'Spring will soon come. When the ice breaks up in the river and the trees begin to bud, it will be time for you to go home. But, before you leave our lodge, my father will offer you something to take back with you. Choose only the beaver-gnawed-stick which hangs at the head of his couch. He will not want to part with it. He will try to persuade you to take other things. But if you get that stick, you will become a great chief, because his power goes with it.'

"When the snow had gone and the ice was breaking up in the river, Round-Cut-Robe said it was time for him to go home. The Beaver Chief offered him anything he saw in their lodge to take with him. Then Round-Cut-Robe remembered the advice of his friend Little Beaver and asked for the beaver-gnawed-stick. The Beaver Chief tried to make him choose something else. But at last he gave him the stick and said:

"'With it goes my power with water. If you should ever be in trouble and call upon Little Beaver, he will be your helper.'

"Before Round-Cut-Robe left, the Beaver Chief gave him the Beaver Bundle. He taught him the songs, prayers, and dances that go with the ceremony; and said that, if any one were ill or dying, and a relative made a vow to the bundle, the sick person would be restored to health. The ceremony should be given every new moon, keeping track of the moons with counting-sticks. When seven moons were counted, the winter would be over, and it would be time for the beavers to open their lodge for the summer.

"It was the beginning of spring when Round-Cut-Robe came home. But he did not enter camp at once. He sat on a hill in plain sight until the people saw him and a messenger came out. Then many people came to meet him on the hill, and he told them how he had lived seven moons in the lodge of the beavers.

"After Round-Cut-Robe came back, he gathered together the sacred bundle as the Beaver Chief had instructed. He called upon many birds and animals of the prairies and mountains to add their power. And, when the Beaver Bundle was finished, he invited many people to the ceremony. He showed them the way the beavers danced and they heard for the first time the songs and prayers that went with the ceremony."

Round-Cut-Robe goes to War

"Now in those days the Indians used to have a woman's dance. The women who danced stood in a circle, and the people who watched were on the outside. If a woman loved a man, she dressed like him and took part in the dance; in that way every one would know. The people had a lively interest in this dance. They liked to stand around, to joke at the women and to guess the names of their secret lovers. If a man saw his wife in the dance, he recognized the costume she wore. The men encouraged their wives in this dance and then the women were not afraid. When it became known that women were free to dress like their sweethearts, they had a good time. They imitated each other and took pride in having side-husbands.

"Soon after Round-Cut-Robe came back, after living with the beavers, the woman's dance was being held. The people were crowding round and shouting at the dancers. Red Horn, the chief with the three wives, came near. He saw two of his wives in the dance, but the youngest wife was not there. She alone stayed away. Then he found her in his tepee. He taunted her and said:

"'How does it come you don't dance like the others? Maybe you wait because your lover is a bashful man.' He said this to make fun of her. And the girl replied:

"'I shall go to the dance. I shall get his clothes.' So she

went to Round-Cut-Robe. She dressed herself in his clothes and painted her face as he was accustomed to do. But before she left him to enter the dance, her lover said:

"'All those other women dancers are going to talk before the crowd. When it comes your turn, don't be afraid. What I tell you to say will come true.' And then he told her what she must say.

"Then the girl went to the dance and found all the other women in line; she was the last to come. They had finished the first song. Every one stared at her; and they laughed because she was poorly dressed. She had red earth on her cheeks, and wore an old robe that was badly tanned. It had the corners cut off and had a queer shape. Some one in the crowd shouted:

"'Those are the clothes of Round-Cut-Robe. She must be his sweetheart.'

"Then all the people laughed and her friends and relatives were ashamed, because she had a lover who was poor. The head-chief shouted for them to go on with the dance. So the women sang their second song; and after that they made their talks. The crowd called for the poor girl, and she stood up before them. In her hand she held a beaver-gnawed-stick. She said:

"'Listen, men and women! I know my relatives are ashamed of me, but what I tell you now will come true. When the rivers are warm (midsummer) I shall go to war. A river will be high, but deep water cannot stop me. I shall swim across and kill an enemy.'

"Then the crowd laughed. They said: 'We know that her lover cannot do this. He is poor and has never been to war.'

"After that a war expedition made ready to go south against their enemies, the Snake Indians. Round-Cut-Robe said to his sweetheart:

"'I shall go to war with them, and all that you promised will come true.'

"He took no weapons, only his beaver-gnawed-stick. He followed behind the other warriors; he did not go with the rest. They were on the road many nights, and came at last to the Yellowstone River. The Snake Indians were camped on the other side. But the water was high, and they could not cross to fight. Then Round-Cut-Robe went to Little Dog, their war chief, and said:

"'Over there is the head-chief of the Snakes. I shall go across and kill him.'

"But Little Dog laughed at him. He said that the current was swift and he would be drowned. Then Round-Cut-Robe made ready. He tied up his long hair and thrust into it a stone knife. He sang his beaver song and prayed to Little Beaver for help. Holding the beaver-gnawed-stick in his mouth, he struck the water like a beaver and dove. Halfway across, he came up and sang his beaver song. Again he dove and swam under water, until he came to the other shore; and then he stood up, holding the beaver stick in his mouth. The head-chief of the Snakes saw him coming. He sang his war song and ran into the water. He threw his long spear at Round-Cut-Robe. But it struck the beaver stick, and did him no harm.

"Then Round-Cut-Robe seized the spear and killed that Snake chief; and all the Blackfoot warriors set up a great shout. He swam across the river, pulling after him the body of the dead chief by the hair. He dragged it ashore and took the scalp. He stood with his foot on the head of the Snake and sang his war song. After that Round-Cut-Robe and the Blackfoot warriors started for home. They came to the summit of a hill overlooking the camp. There they waited until a messenger came out. And when the people heard the news of their victory, they ran to tell the sweetheart of Round-Cut-Robe. She was out on the hills gathering berries. They said to her:

"'Your lover is now a great chief. It was he who killed the head-chief of the Snakes.'

"And, when the girl heard this, she was so excited she spilled her berries.

"The returning warriors stood together on the hill and sang a song of victory. Then they marched down, with Round-Cut-Robe in the lead, holding up the scalp and spear of the Snake chief. All the people came out from the camp; and the girl, Spilt-Her-Berries, was before all the others. It was she who met the new chief first and gave him a kiss. She sang the song of victory:

"'My lover has killed the Snake chief and all his people mourn for him.'

"Round-Cut-Robe gave the scalp and spear to his sweetheart, saying:

"'Give these to Red Horn, your husband, and say to him: "My lover sends you these, even though he is a poor man. Your other wives have rich lovers, but they have never done anything for you like this."'

"Then they paraded round the camp, with Spilt-Her-Berries carrying aloft the scalp and spear of the Snake chief. She took them to the lodge of Red Horn and gave them to him. Then every one was proud to know the girl, and they gave her many presents of fine clothes.

"Red Horn invited the head men of the tribe to his lodge. He gave a big feast and told Spilt-Her-Berries to bring her lover; and after the feast he said:

"'Round-Cut-Robe is now a great chief. He is above all of us. There was a time when I was ashamed to know him. But now I am proud to have him at my feast. He gave me this spear and scalp. In return I give him his sweetheart and my tepee. As for myself, I will move into some other place.

May this new husband of Spilt-Her-Berries have a long life and good luck!'

"Round-Cut-Robe became head-chief of the tribe and lived to be very old. He kept the Beaver Bundle in his lodge as long as he lived. It was he who taught the Indians how to give the beaver dance.

"That is the origin of the Beaver Bundle."

When I was leaving Mad Wolf's lodge to return to my own camp, he said:

"You are now my son and have met my relatives and friends; I want you to come for another ceremony. It is now the moon when the leaves are turning yellow. Come again to my lodge at the next full moon — the time the leaves are falling. I will have White Calf, the head-chief here, and other prominent men, who will help me open the Beaver Bundle. We will select an Indian name for you, and will make you a member of the Blackfoot tribe."

CHAPTER VIII

I AM GIVEN AN INDIAN NAME AND MADE A MEMBER OF THE BLACKFOOT TRIBE

On the day of full moon, when the leaves were falling, time appointed by Mad Wolf for the second ceremony and opening of his Beaver Bundle, I rode across the prairie towards his summer camp. It was fine autumn weather, without a cloud in the sky. Eastward over the plains, through a bluish haze, rose the Sweet Grass Hills, like distant islands in an ocean. West stood the main range of the Rocky Mountains, extending into the north and disappearing into the far south, the majestic snow-capped peaks of Rising Wolf and Going-to-the-Sun looming sharp and clear against the deep blue sky.

From the summit of a grassy ridge, I at last looked down upon the camp of Mad Wolf. Smoke was rising from the lodges and bore the fragrant odor of burning cottonwood. Many horses dotted the hills, Indian boys riding to and fro and racing their mounts across the broad meadows. Among the rows of white tepees were groups of Indians in bright-colored clothes. They were seated about their outside fires, playing games and engaged in various occupations of camp life.

I rode to the large decorated tepee of Mad Wolf, and was greeted by my Indian sister, Strikes-on-both-Sides. She wore a dress of fine deerskin with beaded stripes. Her leggings and moccasins were decorated with colored porcupine quills. She had white shell ear-rings, and necklaces of elk teeth and deer bones. She shouted, "The Light-Haired-One has come back"; then saying to me, "I am glad that you are still smiling," she took my hand and led me inside the lodge to Mad-Wolf and her mother, Gives-to-the-Sun.

On the day appointed for the Beaver Ceremony, the chief's family rose before sunrise to cook food for the feast and prepare for many visitors. They made ready a kettle of service-berry soup and tongues; also dried meat mixed with wild cherries, and dried bear-berry leaves for smoking. I helped in the feast with a supply of raisins and fresh meat, dried berries, and a roll of strong Hudson Bay tobacco, which they liked to smoke mixed with bear-berry leaves. I also gave a blanket with colored stripes. It was looked upon as my offering to the Beaver Bundle; so during the ceremony it lay under the Bundle.

When the sun was high over the eastern horizon, the guests began to arrive. The head men of the tribe came with their families: White Calf, the head-chief; White Grass, a judge and medicine man; Heavy Breast, Middle Calf, Medicine Wolf, Elk Chief, Bear Child; Ear-Rings, a doctor and medicine man; and Double Runner. The tepee was filled to the door with eleven men, seventeen women and ten children. Mad Wolf as director of the ceremony, sat at the back and in the center. The men were on his left, the women and children on his right. The beaver men had seats in the front row. Beside Mad Wolf was White Calf, the head-chief, then White Grass, the medicine man, who helped him in conducting the ceremony. I was next to Maka, an Indian of unusual appearance. He was short and stout with a large head which was crowned with a heavy mass of hair.

While they were waiting for the ceremony to begin, Mad Wolf said to White Calf, so that all in the lodge could hear:

"Because you are my friend, I ask you to make the choice of a name for my white son." After that, the venerable chief sat in silence for a while, his head bowed and eyes closed, trying to think of a suitable name.

In the meantime, Middle Calf mixed the tobacco and filled the pipes; he had charge of the smoking outfit, while Bear Child looked after the incense of sweet grass.

The ceremony began by Bear Child taking a forked stick and selecting a live coal from the fire. He laid it on the ground in front of Mad Wolf, who placed upon it dried sweet grass. And the rising smoke soon filled the tepee with incense. Mad Wolf held up his right hand to command attention; then swaying his body to and fro, he chanted:

> "I am the Morning Star, child of Sun and Moon,
> My power is very strong."

He held both hands in the smoke, and, placing them upon the sacred bundle, sang a chant to the Sun. Then he raised his hands from the bundle and laid them upon his breast — the sign that Sun Power was thus communicated.

The Beaver Bundle lay at the back of the tepee, between Mad Wolf and his wife. It had a wrapper of elkskin painted red; and the tie strings were also of elkskin. To the outside were attached sacred implements — a long pipe, digging stick, and a set of smudge sticks.

During the ceremony of opening the bundle, the outside articles were removed first. And for this the four principals, Mad Wolf, White Calf and their wives, Gives-to-the-Sun and Catches-Two-Horses, chanted in unison, while the two women untied the strings and loosened the smudge sticks. The four together placed their hands upon the sacred sticks and held them in the sweet smoke. Then, each held a stick in imitation of beavers carrying branches of trees. They extended their arms together, with hands raised and parallel — the Indian sign for beaver den — and prayed in unison to the spirit of the beaver:

> "Pity us! Give us your wisdom and cunning.
> May we live to be old.
> May we always have plenty of food."

Buffalo hides were next unrolled and spread upon the ground in front of the beaver men during the chant:

"The buffalo bull stays in the mountains.
He comes down to the plains.
The mountains are his medicine."

In this chant the four principals held their hands with two index fingers curved towards each other, the other fingers being closed, in imitation of buffalo horns — the Indian sign for buffalo.

The two women raised the Beaver Bundle, while the men sang the chant:

"The buffalo bull came down from the mountains.
He lies upon the ground."

They moved the sacred bundle slowly and reverently and placed it on a buffalo robe, beside the burning sweet grass. Mad Wolf took some rattles from a woven Nez Percé bag and distributed them among the beaver men. He handed two of them to me and said: "You are now my son and should join with me in this ceremony."

These rattles, which were made of buffalo hide and contained small pebbles, were used by the beaver men to beat time on the buffalo hides during the chants and dances, in imitation of beavers striking the water with their flat tails.

Then, with the beaver men, I joined in the Raven Song:

"We fly high in the air.
Our power is very strong.
The wind is our medicine."

We cawed four times in imitation of ravens, and held our rattles vertically on the hides. After another raven song, we beat with our rattles, shook them in the air, and ended with four caws. I watched closely Mad Wolf's movements, and imitated his motions with the rattles, giving forward sweeps to the beats, as he did. This did not escape his keen eyes, for he said to me so that all could hear: "I like the way you swing your rattles. I am proud of my white son."

For the Antelope Song, the beaver men chanted in unison, holding their hands closed, one above the other, changing their positions by quick, sharp movements, in imitation of the quick and dainty rise and fall of the antelope's feet in walking.

We joined with Mad Wolf in the Elk Song and beat time with our rattles. The two women, leaning towards the Beaver Bundle, simulated dancing on their knees, and at the same time imitated elk rubbing the velvet from their horns. Mad Wolf untied the strings of elkskin, releasing the pipe from the bundle, and sang:

> "Our Father, the Sun!
> It is time you were rising.
> I want to dance with you."

Then he arose and danced with the pipe; while the beaver men beat with their rattles and all the people joined in the song. Mad Wolf blew on his medicine whistle and circled the fire in the direction the sun moves through the heavens. He gave the cry of the beaver and imitated the actions of a swimming beaver.

White Grass, the medicine man, danced after Mad Wolf; and passed the pipe in turn to the head-chief, who danced and returned it to Mad Wolf. My Indian father held the pipe in the sweet-grass smoke, and, bowing his head, prayed to the Sun in behalf of those who were ill.

Thus the Beaver Bundle, with its ritual of songs, dances, and prayers, was a medium through which Sun Power was transmitted to man, especially in the healing of the sick. It contained not only the skins of the beaver, but also many sacred relics, principally of birds and wild animals, all of which contributed their Sun Power to the bundle.

The time had now come for opening the bundle and taking out its contents. Gives-to-the-Sun and Catches-Two-Horses were distinguished from the other women by clothes decorated with red paint. They had both been sacred women in the Sun Dance, and were held in high honor by the tribe. The beaver men beat with their rattles and sang to the buffalo bull with the words:

"The head-chief of the buffalo is looking for something to hook."

The two women knelt beside the bundle and imitated the Bull hooking with his horns. Mad Wolf chanted the "Hurry" Song; and the women removed the elkskin cover. The inner bundle was wrapped in a rare and beautiful buffalo skin with the color of a beaver. Then Mad Wolf began a solemn chant, while the women opened this sacred buffalo robe, and revealed the skins and relics of many birds and animals of prairies and mountains. He took a beaver skin from the bundle and sang:

"I go from my lodge.
I see an enemy.
I dive under the water and am safe."

He moved the skin in imitation of a beaver swimming; suddenly it dove under the water to escape an enemy. At the same time the two women knelt beside the bundle and pantomimed with their hands the movements of beavers swimming and working on their dams. They danced on their knees, gracefully swaying their bodies to the rhythm of the drumming, while the rest of us sang a Beaver Song and beat time on the buffalo hides.

Then each of the women took the beaver-skin in turn and with bowed head held it reverently to her breast and prayed to the spirit of the Beaver:

"I take you, my child, that my relatives and children may be free from sickness."

Two more women knelt in front of the bundle. Then these four women together imitated beavers, moving their bodies in time with the chanting and drumming. They covered their heads to represent beavers hidden in their den under the water. Then the imaginary beavers rose to the surface of the water and swam around while working on their dams. Mad Wolf brought forth a bag of beaver-gnawed-sticks and handed them to the women. They held these sticks in their mouths, like beavers holding branches. They made swimming motions with their hands, and imitated beavers diving under the water, then coming to the surface and swimming in the stream. They went out upon an imaginary bank; and sat upright as if to cut down trees, brushing their faces with their hands as beavers do with their paws; looking carefully around, always alert for danger.

The four women danced together round the tepee, with hands crossed on their breasts. They kept turning and swaying their bodies in time with the chanting and drumming of the beaver men. Mad Wolf handed a beaver-skin to his wife who was at the head of the line. The singing and drumming of the beaver men now became louder, while the women circled the fire and gave the call of the beaver. Gives-to-the-Sun in the lead held the beaver-skin under her robe and moved it as though it were swimming round her waist and then round her neck. After she had danced once round the tepee, she handed the skin to the woman next in line, with the prayer:

"I do not give you away, my child (beaver), because I am tired of you, but because the child of this woman is ill. May it be restored to health!"

Catches-Two-Horses who received the skin prayed: "I take you, my child (beaver), that my husband and children may be from sickness; may they live to be old!"

She danced once round the tepee, with the skin across her shoulders. Each of the other women took the skin in turn, and then it was returned to the bundle.

The women held up two winter-skins of weasels. The

weasel, that great hunter, was included in the bundle, because of its power as a provider of food to its family. Mad Wolf began the Weasel Song; the beaver men beat with their rattles and joined in the song. White Calf, the venerable head-chief, rose and took one of the skins. He held it to his breast with a prayer, and then danced round the tepee. He blew on his medicine whistle to represent the cry of the weasel, and imitated its actions hunting for food. Finally he stopped in front of me and held up the snow-white skin, so that all could see. There was silence as he looked straight at me, and said earnestly:

"This is the white weasel, one of the sacred animals of our Beaver Bundle. We name you 'Á-pe-ech-e-ken' (White-Weasel-Moccasin), because your color is light and your eyes are blue. We pray this name may bring you long life and good luck."

Mad Wolf approved of this name, and moved to one side, so that White Grass, the medicine man, might take the leader's seat. The face of White Grass was painted red. In the center of his forehead was a black mark to represent the thunder bolt, from which extended yellow zigzag lines for lightning. He prayed:

"Father, the Sun, bless us all, men, women, and children.
Sacred Beaver Bundle, help us to lead straight lives.
Sacred Pipe, bless us, the rivers, mountains, prairies, birds, and animals.
— Mother Earth, give us food until we die."

Then White Grass sang the Paint Song, after which he took some red earth from the bundle and prepared it with his hands, swaying his body to and fro in time with the chant. First he painted the faces of Mad Wolf and White Calf; and in like manner the beaver men, Heavy Breast, Middle Calf, and Ear-Rings. I was seated next to Ear-Rings; and when my turn came to be painted, Mad Wolf exclaimed: "Here comes my white son."

White Grass signed that he was ready. I went forward and knelt before him, while he placed the red earth on my forehead, chin, and hands, because these are the places the beaver rubs himself with his paws. Mad Wolf started the Beaver Song, and all joined in, accompanied by the beating of rattles on the ground.

After the song, White Grass said to me very earnestly: "This tepee is sacred. And this Beaver Ceremony, in which we have painted you and made you a member of our tribe, is also sacred. We pray that you may never be ill."

Then Bear Child took a hot coal from the fire and laid it in front of White Calf. The head-chief placed sweet grass upon it; and holding his hands in the rising smoke, prayed:

"Father, the Sun, who gives us light,
Be good to this young man.
We have taken him into our tribe.
Keep him day and night from harm.
May he live long.
To return many summers to his Indian brothers and sisters."

Then Mad Wolf again took the leader's seat beside the bundle to continue the ceremony. It required a fine memory to conduct the Beaver Ceremony, with its great number of songs, prayers, and dances. Nobody knew how many there were; it was bad luck to count them; but there must have been between three and four hundred songs.

Every detail of the ceremony had to be performed accurately. It was believed misfortune would result if mistakes were made. Yet a mistake happened that very day in the dance of the lynx.

Mad Wolf took from the bundle the tail of a lynx, while the beaver men chanted and beat with rattles. Gives-to-the-Sun held up a stick painted red to represent a tree. Catches-Two-Horses took the tail and imitated the actions of a lynx hunting squirrels.

First, it walked round and then sat down and looked into

the tree. Several times it ran towards the tree after a squirrel, but each time came back and sat down. Finally it made a quick dash for the tree. Catches-Two-Horses then made the mistake of making the lynx go quickly up one side and down the other. Mad Wolf stopped the ceremony. Every one waited in silence. The beaver men began again their rhythmic drumming, while Mad Wolf took the tail. He represented the lynx running to the tree, just as the woman had done. But Mad Wolf made it climb more slowly; and held it for a short time on top, where it danced in time with the drumming. He then brought it slowly down the other side, clambering little by little like a cat, stopping frequently to look around, until it finally reached the ground.

Mad Wolf brought forth a pair of badger skins. He took them out backwards, the way badgers come from their dens. He imitated the timid actions of badgers, moving the skins this way and that, like badgers trying to escape. He turned them as though they were going to attack, but became frightened and fled back into their den.

During the song of the white swan, Mad Wolf made a mistake and stopped the ceremony. With bowed head and closed eyes, he strove to recall the song, while the entire company waited silently. Suddenly Mad Wolf raised his head. He looked straight at me and said: "There is White Weasel, my son. He had better continue the ceremony in my place." The Indians laughed and enjoyed the joke. The tension was thus relieved and Mad Wolf continued the song.

Then Mad Wolf took from the Beaver Bundle the head of a mallard duck. Elk Chief stood up and, drawing his blanket round him, circled the fire, imitating the movements of a duck. Across the tepee Soft Woman rose. Both danced gracefully towards each other until they met and together they circled the fire, representing in their dance a pair of ducks. Soft Woman held up her right hand and swayed her body from side to side, while Elk Chief spread out both arms, with hands extended, in imitation of a flying duck.

A woman entered the tepee. One of her children was dead, and she was in mourning. Her disheveled hair hid her face, and she had her blanket drawn closely about her. She was pale and emaciated from fasting, and her arms were bleeding from self-inflicted wounds — a sad and forlorn-looking creature. She stood silently before the assembled people, until Mad Wolf took pity on her. With some sage he performed the rite of purification and prayed that she might have a new and happy life. Then she withdrew as silently as she came.

Mad Wolf brought forth a prairie chicken and some of its tail feathers. He handed them to the two women who knelt facing each other. Then they arose and danced, praying to the prairie chicken. Gives-to-the-Sun held the skin and Catches-Two-Horses the feathers. This was a woman's dance. Gives-to-the-Sun knelt before another woman and Catches-Two-Horses did likewise. They knelt thus in pairs with heads close to the ground, and imitated the habits of prairie chickens. They made a clucking sound. They stretched out their blankets with their arms and shook them in imitation of wings. Their song was lively and the crowd enjoyed it. The beaver men drummed with enthusiasm and energy, singing and shaking their rattles in the air to imitate the sound of prairie chickens flying.

Mad Wolf again arose. He moved around the fire in a bear dance. He held his arms in front with hands hanging down, as a bear does its paws. He placed his feet together and moved backwards and forwards, with short jumps, imitating the deliberate and heavy tread of a walking bear, moving his face this way and that, as if looking about. He puffed and grunted and acted like a bear, digging in the ground, and turning over stones for insects. The two women, Gives-to-the-Sun and Catches-Two-Horses, arose and joined Mad Wolf in this dance. They held their hands with forefingers crooked on their heads for ears, and then in front, with hands down, as bears do their paws when standing on their hind legs. In this manner the women followed Mad Wolf round the tepee, and then danced up to their "potential husbands." They seized them roughly and forced them to dance, amid laughter and shouts of the spectators.

The lively air and quick rhythm of the Dog Dance made it one of the most popular of all the beaver dances. The beaver men sang their loudest and drummed so vigorously that many people rose to dance. They entered into it with spirit and dash, laughing merrily and joking with each other; while the spectators urged them on by barks and howls in imitation of dogs. Middle Calf's wife sat with her small daughter by her side. The little girl was excited by the singing and beating of rattles. She too wanted to dance. She was pretty, with bright eyes, and had jet-black hair falling over her shoulders. She wore a miniature squaw dress of red, fringed with elk teeth and decorated with colored beads. When the dance was at its height, her mother suddenly pushed her into the circle. At first the little girl was frightened, but quickly forgot herself and began to dance. She swayed her lithe body to and fro, in imitation of the other women, and hit the ground with her small moccasined feet in perfect time with the rhythmic beating of the rattles. The beaver men gradually quickened their pace; the steps of the dancers grew faster and faster until, wearied, they gave a series of dog howls and returned to their seats.

I saw two white-haired old women outside the tepee having a dance of their own. They were in mourning and debarred from the ceremony; but they could not resist the spell of the Dog Dance. They were surrounded by a group of children and young people, who urged them on with barks and howls.

For the Buffalo Dance, Mad Wolf took a string of buffalo hoofs from the bundle and handed them to his wife. She and Catches-Two-Horses arose to dance, wearing headdresses with buffalo horns. The Indians took great interest in this dance, because it represented the mating of buffalo, by women who chose their men. The two women knelt beside the Beaver Bundle with heads lowered. They represented buffalo cows. First they made motions of hooking the ground and digging wallows; then they stood up and pawed the ground and bellowed. They simulated buffalo throwing dirt and catching it on their backs, shaking themselves and throwing dust into the air. Then they danced with the string of hoofs, imitating the capers of mating buffaloes. Gives-to-the-Sun went round the tepee until she came to White Calf, and threw the string of hoofs near him. He arose and joined her in the dance, following her round the fire, like a bull after a cow. Amid shouts of laughter, he threw the hoofs to Strikes-on-Both-Sides, daughter of Mad Wolf. She danced gracefully round the tepee and threw the string of hoofs to me. She danced in front of me with quick steps, swaying her body in time with the singing and the beating of rattles. I heard much shouting and laughter and cheering. Some of the Indians called my name. They said: "White Weasel, you are a chief now; you must join her in the dance."

So I took the hoofs and followed my Indian sister round the fire. I danced like the others, swaying my body, holding my feet together, twisting and turning and bending my knees. There were shrill cries from both men and women. They shouted: "Good boy! White Weasel, you are a chief now." We stopped at intervals to bellow and imitate buffalo movements, digging wallows, kicking, pawing the ground, and throwing dust into the air. When my Indian sister stopped dancing, I completed the circle and threw the hoofs to the wife of Bear Child.

By this time the sun had set and the Indians prepared to go home. Horses were brought in, and the dancers changed their decorated clothes and moccasins for those of every-day use. Before they left, all joined in a feast of service-berry stew. The men were served first, but few of them ate their full portion. They called out the names of women and gave the remainder to them. I sent mine to the wife of Morning Plume, who had many children to feed. My friend Rattler, a kind-hearted old doctor, gave his share to his wife, before he partook of any food himself. Then he drew her aside from the crowd, and laying both hands upon her, he gave her his power to heal, because she was going to doctor a sick child.

The Beaver Ceremony ended with the close of day; and the Indians separated to their lodges. Peace and quiet settled over the camp, broken only by the cries of distant prairie wolves, and the answering barks of Indian dogs.

CHAPTER IX

HOME OF MAD WOLF

Mad Wolf, my Indian father, lived in the valley of Cutbank River. But in good summer weather it was his custom to take his herds of cattle and horses and camp about on the prairie. I remember well the summer camp, where he opened his Beaver Bundle and made me a member of the tribe. Our tepees were in a broad meadow of wild timothy and long bunch grass, bounded by a broken line of rounded hills. On this fine range fed his herds of cattle and horses, the grassy undulating hillsides glorious under a bright October sun.

The wife of the chief and his daughter, Strikes-on-Both-Sides, pitched my traveling-tepee between their own two lodges. It was small and easy to handle; decorated with picture records of war and hunting, also the Moon and Morning Star, and the constellations of the Pleiades and Great Bear.

Little Creek, son-in-law of Mad Wolf, and his wife Strikes-on-Both-Sides, lived close by in a lodge without decorations. But the chief had the Snow Tepee; it was believed to have power over storms and cold weather. It had a yellow top, the color of the sky at sunrise. On the north side was a cluster of seven stars for the Great Bear — the direction winter blizzards come from; at the back a red disc for the Sun; under the top four claws for the Thunder Bird; and at the bottom a yellow band for the earth, with green discs to represent the ice color.

Mad Wolf's women arranged everything for me — an inside lining to keep out wind and rain and help the updraft of the fire; provisions and cooking utensils were to the left of the door, with saddles and harness opposite. At the head of my couch was a back-rest made of willow sticks tied together with sinew, and supported by a tripod decorated with carved work; in the center, just under the smoke-hole, was a circle of round stones for my fireplace, and to keep the flames from spreading in the dry prairie grass. They roped down my tepee to a stake driven into the ground on the west side, to prevent it being overturned in a heavy wind. They showed me how to close the smoke-hole in a storm, and to keep the lodge from smoking by shifting the "ears" at the top with the changing wind. They brought me a bucket of fresh water from the spring; and for starting my fire, a bundle of resinous pine sticks and a supply of dry cottonwood branches.

After my adoption, the women of Mad Wolf's family were hospitable and kind and treated me as a relative. Strikes-on-Both-Sides, my Indian sister, came with her mother to my lodge and examined all my belongings. They emptied the bags containing my most personal possessions; but everything was carefully replaced. The old woman did not like the looks of my deerskin moccasins and changed them to suit her idea of the tribal style. She told me to use red earth on my face, the way Indians did; it would help my looks and protect my skin from sun and wind.

The women were hard workers — always busy, cooking, tanning skins, making lodge coverings, their own clothing and most of the men's, providing firewood, gathering berries and wild vegetables and herbs and plants for both eating and healing. Near Mad Wolf's lodge, they had some cowhides pegged to the ground hair-side down. On them were painted designs for cases, berry bags, and toy parfleches for the children, in red, yellow and blue, with the ring-bone pattern, also mountains, hills, arrow-points and buffalo trails.

Women considered it a disgrace for men to do any of their

work — put up lodges, tan skins, cook food at home or look after the provisions; all this was woman's work in which they were trained from childhood and they resented any interference from the men.

The men gave most of their time to care of horses and cattle, hunting, dancing, and religious ceremonies. Mad Wolf himself was away from camp most of the time, busy with public meetings throughout the tribe and with the ceremonies of his Beaver Bundle and Medicine Pipe.

Little Creek, the son-in-law of Mad Wolf, was of middle age, easy-going and good-natured, skilled in the handling of horses and cattle. He and his father-in-law were on the best of terms; but, in accordance with tribal etiquette, he never had any dealings with his mother-in-law. He always avoided speaking to her and they were never together in the same place. He explained that it was a custom handed down from their ancestors — a woman felt ashamed and humiliated to meet her son-in-law; she had to visit her daughter when he was away from home.

Often friends of Mad Wolf and their wives came to his tepee to spend an evening by the lodge-fire: White Calf, the head-chief; Ear-Rings, the doctor; White Grass, the medicine man; Middle Calf, Double Runner, and Morning Plume. The men sat on the north side of the fire; and according to custom, the women across from them, with Mad Wolf in the center and at the back, as owner of the lodge. The men had a large redstone pipe which they passed to and fro; the women a smaller pipe which they too smoked in turn. Visitors entered without ceremony, the men taking places on the right of the door, the women opposite and on the south side of the tepee.

In Mad Wolf's Snow Lodge many rules had to be observed; he was also the guardian of the sacred Beaver Bundle and owner of a Medicine Pipe. But his visitors were always well

WOMAN UNDER A SUN-SHELTER

Showing bead and quill work and meat drying on poles

WOMAN REPAIRING A TEPEE-COVER

informed and careful not to offend. They knew the bundles that Mad Wolf owned and their observances.

The Beaver Bundle forbade any one passing in front of Mad Wolf; no one should hang up their moccasins, or raise the sides of the tepee; dogs were not allowed to enter and the fire must never die out. Even the children knew that the word "bear" must not be spoken in the presence of the Medicine Pipe. If some one had to speak about a bear, it was referred to indirectly as "that-big-hairy-one," or "the-one-who-prowls-at-night"; to say the word "bear" would be sure to bring sickness and misfortune. No one should talk loud and people should enter without speaking; the occupants of the Snow Tepee could not reply to any one on the outside.

It was always rude to ask a man his name before a company of people; this reflected on his good standing and made him feel ashamed. If any one wore an odd-looking object, it might attract attention, but no one ever asked about it; it might be a charm; and it was a breach of etiquette to ask a leading question about one's personal medicine or experiences; the owner might talk about it, but the initiative must come from him.

Around the lodge-fire at night, Mad Wolf's friends liked to gossip, tell stories, and have fun; they were light-hearted and happy. I did not hear any of them dispute, find fault, or curse. They never talked loud and when one was speaking the others listened. They liked to exaggerate and to boast. But they always listened in silence to a speaker and did not interrupt.

One evening I asked Mad Wolf to tell about the days of long ago — how the Indians lived when buffalo were plentiful — before the white men came to occupy their country. He said:

"Oh! What happy times we had before we ever saw white

men! Then were many buffalo and we wandered where we pleased. In those days, we wintered far away from the mountains; we stayed in the 'Lower Country' — far down the Marias River until late in the spring, waiting for our horses to shed their winter hair and to get fat on the new grass.

"When the weather got warm and it came time to move, our chiefs shouted through the camp:

"'Make ready to pull up your lodge-pins; we are going to move towards the mountains.'

"And in the early morning, before sun-up, they called again:

"'This is the day; pack up your things and take down your lodges; we shall start before the sun is high.'

"We stopped to hunt buffalo near the Sweet Grass Hills. Before sunrise our chiefs rode through the camp and shouted:

"'The buffalo are close; a big herd is coming towards camp; get ready your long-winded horses and the hard-runners; soon we shall hunt.'

"Then we chased the buffalo until their carcasses were scattered all over. We rubbed our knives and cut open their backs; we skinned them from the back down, throwing out their kidneys and the yellow back-fat, splitting the tongues into strips and drying them for future use. The women cooked the back-fat and suet and boiled marrow from the bones, cutting the meat into slices and hanging it on scaffolds to cure in sun and wind. We had many feasts and ate the choice pieces; the old people and children were invited; all were happy and had plenty to eat.

"The strong women quickly got the hair off their buffalo hides and made them into parfleches, sacks, and clothes; some of the hides they tanned for lodges, oiling the skins with brains and liver mixed; they used the hides of the bulls for Indian trunks and made strings from the sinews and ropes from the long hair.

"After we had stayed for a while near the Sweet Grass Hills, our chiefs again shouted through the camp:

"'Come on! It is time to move. We shall go to pick berries. A young man who traveled far found that berries are ripe — service berries and raspberries.'

"We went nearer the mountains and camped on Milk River. In the morning the women and children went out on the hills and came back with berry bags filled; the bushes were so heavy with ripe berries, the sides of our horses were all red.

"Then we moved to Cutbank River to gather chokecherries, which the women dried and mashed with seeds; they mixed them with pemmican and put them away in calf-sacks for winter use. Near Cutbank were many buffalo and fat antelope and prairie dogs with sweet livers.

"In the fall we moved up to the mountains and chased elk. We made our camp in a big circle near the forest at the head of Cutbank River. Our women cut new lodge-poles, for the trees there grew tall and straight. They also gathered many roots and plants for eating and healing — gray leaves for stomach trouble, black-root for coughs, sage for heartburn, sticky-weed for the liver, and blueberry for bleeding at the mouth.

"After the first big snowstorm, we hurried to move away from the mountains, back to the Lower Country. We camped along the Marias River and hunted for a good place to spend the winter — with buffalo near and plenty of firewood and grass for our horses.

"Oh! Those were happy days from the food we all had and the clothes and warm buffalo robes. At the beginning of winter we ate the big heifers four years old and the heifers two years old; we liked them the best. Then, a woman who had ready her winter robes for husband and children had nothing more to worry about. To lie in a buffalo robe was so warm, it was like sleeping beside a fire. And now the dogs are all scattered, having had their evening meal," — an Indian expression for — my story-telling is ended.

In our prairie camp, my lodge stood a short distance from Mad Wolf's, but so close to Little Creek and his wife I could hear what they said. They were fond of each other and did not bicker or quarrel. Like most Indian parents, they indulged their children and rarely punished them. Sometimes they warned them to be quiet; but, as a rule, the children ran wild and acted as they pleased. For games they had follow-the-leader, hide-and-seek, stilts, and jumping rope. Boys had shooting contests with bow and arrow, spinning tops, hunting small game and horse racing. They were trained to hunt and fight and the care of horses and cattle; to have self-control and be firm and brave. Girls had hobby-horses and play-tepees with dolls; and little camps with miniature robes and blankets and cooking utensils. They were trained by their mothers in the dressing of skins, making of clothes, care of the lodge, and preparation of food; to be helpful and kind and virtuous; and to believe that a woman who was false to her marriage vow was a disgrace to all her relatives.

Small Otter, a boy of six and a grandson of Mad Wolf, was the favorite of our camp. He had a sunny nature, round face, bright eyes, and hair hanging in little braids over his shoulders. He liked to play at warfare with bow and arrow, and hunted for wild birds, rabbits, and ground squirrels. But his favorite sport was to ride bareback his grandmother's old saddle horse. She and Small Otter were inseparable companions. I often saw them together on the prairie, he holding her tightly by the hand, skipping and jumping and pulling her about, until weary she sank to the ground and watched him proudly, her face in her palms, while he hunted squirrels with bow and arrow.

One night I helped Little Creek when he was suffering from pain. He wakened me by his groans. With my medicine case I went to his lodge and gave him a remedy. In the morning he had recovered; thus I gained a reputation as a doctor.

I cut a barbed fish-hook from the hand of their daughter Anatapsa, a girl of fourteen. She came to camp with the hook imbedded so deeply they could not get it out. The women wailed and moaned at the sight of my knife. I dressed the wound with an antiseptic. It healed quickly and she had no pain. She showed her gratitude by giving me a piece of sweet-scented wood and a necklace of blue shells with little animals carved from stone. Then her mother, Strikes-on-Both-Sides, brought a medicine bag with painted designs and long fringe hanging down. She called it the "Iniskim" (Buffalo Rock Bundle). It was sacred and contained pieces of flint which resembled miniature buffalo. She told me the following story of its origin:

"Many years ago, when a band of Indians were starving, a woman who went alone from camp heard a strange singing. It came from these stones. She took the stones back to camp and taught the song to the head men. Then they sang the song together and gave a ceremony. The buffalo came back and the people had plenty to eat. That was the beginning of the Buffalo Rock Bundle. With it the Indians were able to call the buffalo."

Then Strikes-on-Both-Sides sang the old song and gave me directions for the care of my new medicine bundle. By day it must hang from a tripod behind my lodge. At sunset I should bring it inside and burn sweet grass as incense.

One day a strange Indian came to our camp. As soon as he entered Little Creek's lodge, I heard angry words from my Indian sister. She upbraided the visitor. She said he had a forked tongue; what he had said was not true; he spread the report that Little Creek was so ill that some of his relatives came in haste; they thought he was dying. It is offensive to an Indian woman to have a report spread about that anything is the matter with her man. She feels ashamed and humiliated, as though she had neglected him.

Near the end of our stay on the prairie, a storm came from the northwest, a sullen cloud mass with forked lightning and a whirling wind that smote Mad Wolf's tepee and twisted it out of shape. My lodge shook as though it were going over. Then the wind suddenly leaped into the south and the storm quickly ended. The women carried Mad Wolf's Medicine Bundles to a place of safety in Little Creek's lodge; and as soon as they had repaired the damage, they carried the bundles back.

Then Mad Wolf moved our camp from the open plains to his winter home in the sheltered valley of Cutbank River. The old chief led the way, riding at the head of our line, tall, erect, and stately, across the broad table-land. Little Creek and I were behind, driving the horses and cattle, riding backwards and forwards, rounding up and heading off, until we drove them back to his ranch in the valley.

There Mad Wolf had a cabin built of logs for shelter from winter storms and blizzards, also corrals and low-lying sheds for cattle and horses. But in good weather he and his family preferred living in tepees.

On both sides of the valley were cutbanks, which led to grass-covered plateaus overlooked by high hills — fine range for both cattle and horses. West were the snowy summits of the Rocky Mountains; east and south the Great Plains; and north a massive ridge grass-covered and bare of trees — the Hudson Bay Divide which formed an unbroken line of high hills against the horizon.

Strikes-on-Both-Sides pitched my tepee in the valley across a meadow from Mad Wolf's camp, near a large rock in a bend in the river where the dark water slowly eddied round and round in a deep pool. She was the favorite child of the old chief; always cheerful and kind and skilled in the arts of Indian women. She was so watchful and alert that no bird or animal near camp ever escaped her keen eyes. She brought me a present of brook trout just caught from the river, also some pulp from the heart of a cottonwood tree, a delicacy with a flavor like maple sap. She and her mother made braids of sweet grass for perfume to put with my clothes, and little buckskin bags of fragrant balsam and meadow-rue berries.

My Indian sister made fun of the rough sticks I used for lodge-pins; she was ashamed to have visitors see them. She said they might spread a report that the Mad Wolf family did not look after their white son. So she made me a set of twenty lodge-pins of conventional style — chokecherry wood with the bark peeled off and painted red, leaving two narrow rings of bark at the top, also a set of small pins for fastening together the front of my tepee.

In the afternoon, friends often came to go with Mad Wolf into the sweat-lodge — White Calf, the head-chief; Horn, an old hunter and trapper; White Grass, and Heavy Breast. The structure they used for their sweat was on the bank of the river. It was made of willow branches twined into an oval frame and covered with robes and blankets. Inside was a hole in the ground for hot stones. Four men entered at a time. They spouted water on the stones and kept wetting their hair. Because of the steam rising from the stones, the bathers kept their heads close to the ground and chanted and prayed to the Sun, Moon and Morning Star. After an hour, with four intervals for fresh air, they came out, and with shouts plunged into the cold river for a reaction.

The sweat-bath was used mostly by older men — never by women. Men who were ill went in to pray for healing power. It was used in ceremonies of all kinds, also to secure dreams and for pleasure. It was taken by men moved to anger, or depressed by the death of a near friend or relative.

In our valley camp, my days began and ended with the sun. When its first rays shone through the open door of my tepee, I took a plunge in the cold river; then lighted my fire and cooked breakfast. I watched the sunsets from a high ridge overlooking the prairie to the foot of the mountains. Near by were the graves of two young lovers. Water Bird, daughter of a prominent chief, loved Night Rider, a youth of her own age. But her parents made her marry an older man. The young lover killed the husband and fled with his sweetheart to the mountains. When the Indian police were about to capture them, Night Rider killed his sweetheart and then himself.

Our first night on the river, I stood beside these lonely graves and saw the sun go down in a sky of flaming red, and the evening star over the mountains. I heard the rhythmical beating of Indian drums from a camp in the valley, with the voices of men and women chanting in unison; and a young brave singing a love song to his sweetheart.

Then I returned to the tepee and lay on my comfortable couch of robes and blankets beside a small wood fire, watching the flickering flames and shadows dance on my tepee walls; listening to the last calls of the birds, the chirping of crickets, the rushing of the river, eddying and swirling in deep pools. There was something very cheerful and soothing in the rippling and surging of that mountain river.

Then my mind went back to a great modern city with its unrest and stress, its crowds of busy and hurrying people, leading indoor, artificial lives. I thought how good it was to be in the camp of my Indian father on the prairie; I loved the freedom and wildness, the quiet and peace. In me

SCAFFOLD BURIAL

A GRAVE ON A HILLTOP

was the instinct to live in the open, where the wind blows free and there is plenty of clear sunshine. My spirit was at home with this simple and primitive people. I felt as though I were one of them, as if I had known them ages ago; their thoughts and customs seemed in no way strange.

CHAPTER X
MARRIAGE CUSTOMS

Big Plume, a Blood Indian from the north, who had been visiting with his family at Heart Butte, stopped at Mad Wolf's camp on his way back to Canada. The morning after they arrived, I met Bluebird, a daughter of the northern chief; she was a comely girl of sixteen, active and strong, filled with energy and animal life. I saw her climb nimbly into a cottonwood tree after a woodpecker's nest and bring down the young birds one by one to her waiting brothers and sisters. That same evening our camp was alive with excitement. Bluebird went with some women and children to gather berries on the hills and did not return. No one knew what had become of her.

After several days, with no news of the missing girl, a band of Indians came from Heart Butte forty miles away, with the news that a son of Mountain Chief had also disappeared. He and Bluebird were lovers. They ran away together to the mountains.

Then Big Plume, her father, a silent and unassuming man, came to my lodge for advice. He had known that young Mountain Chief was in love with his daughter; he did not want him for a son-in-law. But the lover was aggressive. At night he lay in wait for the girl; he met her on the trails when she went after firewood, or to the river for water. It was for this reason they left Heart Butte and came to Mad Wolf's camp; and now his daughter was lost. He wanted to take his family back to their home in Canada, but he could not leave the girl with young Mountain Chief. He was poor and could not support a wife. Big Plume had no faith in him.

He felt bitterly towards the man who had stolen his daughter; it was no marriage and his daughter was disgraced.

In tribal life it sometimes happened that a lover asked his sweetheart to marry him through the medium of a relative. But as a rule it was customary for parents to decide on a suitable husband for a girl. A chief who was prominent would pick out a strong warrior for his son-in-law, that his daughter, a child of plenty, might be well provided for.

After the betrothal, it was customary for a girl to carry food to the lodge of her intended and to make moccasins for the members of his immediate family. Her parents gave a feast to which only his relatives were invited; and in this way the match became known.

If the girl's family were well off, they gave many presents — a bunch of horses and a new tepee completely furnished, with robes and blankets, back-rests, parfleches, and cooking utensils. They also gave their daughter a buckskin dress decorated with elk teeth, and a suit trimmed with ermine tails for her husband. They did this as a parade of their wealth and that their social standing might be recognized by the tribe.

The man presented a number of horses to the girl's father; and later he would be expected to share with his father-in-law the results of his war and hunting expeditions. If he brought back from a hunt three horses loaded with skins and meat, he gave his father-in-law one of the loads with the choicest parts of the meat. And in return, the father-in-law was expected to give of his property.

There was no ceremony; and the marriage form was simple. The couple took their places in the new tepee and began their domestic life. The husband hunted and looked after the horses. The wife prepared food, tanned skins, and made clothing. The husband had no obligations to his wife in regard to other women; but he held her to strict account for her actions with other men. A husband could kill an unfaithful wife, or cut off her nose, or the members of his society might be called upon to inflict this punishment.

But there was a stronger reason for a woman's chastity. Only a pure woman could make a vow to the Sun for the recovery of any of her family who were ill and give the Sun Dance in their behalf. Death was believed to be the penalty of a woman who vowed falsely. If a mother was not chaste she could not make the vow to save the life of one of her children that was dying. Besides it was a great honor for a woman to give a Sun Dance; she stood for what was best in Indian life; she had the respect and veneration of the entire tribe; none stood higher than she. Parents pointed to her as an example to their children; like her, they should live straight and be honored by all the people.

A man might have any number of wives, but no woman was expected to have more than one husband. Economic conditions regulated the number of wives. A man who was poor could have only one. A chief might have two or more, because he was expected to be generous and open-handed, ready at all times to share his food supply. He had to be hospitable and entertain friends, relatives, and strangers; as there were no servants, he needed more than one wife.

It was considered desirable for a girl to marry a chief with a number of wives; if she married a poor man who could afford only one wife, her life would be filled with drudgery and hard work. Prominent men sometimes had as many as five wives. But the first was his real or head wife. He cared more for her, and she sat beside him in his lodge. She took the woman's part in his ceremonies and looked after his sacred bundles. When he traveled, he expected his first wife to go with him. Thus she had to be more strict and careful of her actions than the other wives, who sometimes had secret lovers among the young men.

A man might marry a number of sisters. They were accustomed to living together and less liable to have friction. Then, too, if parents were satisfied with a son-in-law, they preferred such an arrangement. In this way they avoided the risk and social complications of having a number of sons-in-law.

The head-chief, White Calf, had three sisters for wives. Catches-Two-Horses, his middle wife, went to live with him when seven years old. And they were happy in their long life together; he died at eighty years of age.

It was not customary for a man to marry within his own band. There was a feeling that all the people of a band were related, and they always hung together. A girl left the lodge of her parents and went to live among the people of her husband; she and her children thenceforth belonged to his band. The different bands lived apart in the winter, but they always liked to come together every summer in the sun-dance camp.

A man was generally on the best of terms with his father-in-law, but it was not proper for him to ever meet his mother-in-law. It was a breach of etiquette for him to go into the same tepee with her. A mother could not go to visit her daughter if her son-in-law was home; she must wait until he went away. And in order that he might not risk seeing his mother-in-law, he always sent his wife with a customary meat-gift to the lodge of his father-in-law after coming home from a hunt. If he offended her, he must make amends by giving her a good horse. A man never spoke to his mother-in-law, nor to her sisters. He had to be careful what he said before his brothers-in-law and his female relatives; but he could talk freely before the sisters of his wife. They were looked upon in the light of "distant wives."

There was a "love-medicine," which was used by both men and women. It was a powder made from plants and roots, and contained in small buckskin bags. Any one who used it had to pray continually and carry out its requirements with the greatest care. Indians used it mostly in love affairs — to win the affection of one who was indifferent. There was also an antidote for persons who did not want to fall in love. But people regarded it with fear, because bad luck might come to the user.

Yellow Owl told me his experience with love-medicine. He tried it when his young wife left him. He said:

"I felt so badly at losing my wife, I tried to find a charm to make her fall in love again. I heard of an old medicine man among the Cree Indians, who was famed for the power of his love-medicine, and made a long journey north to find him. And when I came to his lodge, the old man said:

"'Do you believe that my love-medicine has power to help you? I will not give it to you unless you believe.'

"He asked me that question four times; and each time I told him I believed in his power. Then he gave me his love-medicine for which I paid him a horse. He directed me to get a hair from my sweetheart's head without her knowledge; I must twine it with one of my own hairs, and put them together in a little bag with the love-medicine and carry it everywhere.

"After that I came home to my tepee and did as the old man advised. I got a woman relative to steal one of my sweetheart's hairs; I put it with one of mine in a little bag with the love-medicine; I wore it fastened about my neck; and because of its power my wife came back to me. She came one day to my lodge and said:

"'You have some strange power over me; I cannot stay away any longer.'

"Then I told her she could remain with her father if she wished. But she would not leave me. She said some power was holding her. Now I will not release her. I still wear the love-charm of the Cree medicine man; and she has been my only woman ever since."

CHAPTER XI

THE HEAD-CHIEF AND HIS WIFE

White Calf, head-chief of the tribe, and Mad Wolf lived near each other on Cutbank River. They had been friends for many years. Mad Wolf secured his sacred Beaver Bundle from White Calf; and the ceremonies brought the two chiefs and their wives into close relations. Their families, too, were on intimate terms and continually visited each other. Dives-under-Water, granddaughter of White Calf, and Anatapsa, granddaughter of Mad Wolf, were bosom companions; and the four stalwart sons of the head-chief, Wolf Tail, Cross Guns, Two Guns, and Night Gun came often to our camp.

White Calf was then over seventy. But, in spite of his years, he still stood erect; rode horseback and walked with brisk step. For nearly thirty years he had been head-chief and was a real father to his people. He was called upon to settle all manner of disputes; and to make peace with those who quarreled. He had a gentle and benevolent spirit, and his kindness of heart showed in his benign countenance. He gave freely to the poor and helped widows and orphans. He was brave in war, deliberate and sound of judgment. But his most prominent trait was his love for fellow tribesmen. All his life he strove for their welfare with an earnestness and devotion rarely equaled by rulers of civilized peoples. In the defense of his tribe, he had a sturdy earnestness and devotion which the bullying threats of United States Government officials could not sway.

I remember a band of Sioux Indians who came as visitors to our camp. They had been on the way for over a month

— a journey of more than six hundred miles over the arid plains. As soon as they arrived, our Indian agent ordered them home; he refused to allow them time to rest their tired horses.

Then White Calf went to the Sioux camp and told them to remain. He warned the Government agent that his tribe would go on the warpath if their visitors were not allowed to stay; and the venerable head-chief had his way.

For sixty years White Calf roamed the plains, happy in his freedom. His tribe were free to wander from the Saskatchewan River to the Yellowstone in the south. Their hunting-grounds extended over thousands of square miles, and their war expeditions roamed as far south as Mexico. The conquering white men came. The herds of buffalo suddenly disappeared; and the Indians were confined to a reservation by the white men. Then White Calf advised his people not to fight, but to adapt themselves to their new conditions of living.

White Calf had three wives who were sisters. When I first met him, two of his wives were living, Catches-Two-Horses and Black-Snake-Woman. His first wife, the oldest of the sisters, was dead. Her grave was on a high hill near his home.

One day I went with Little Creek to White Calf's lodge and found Catches-Two-Horses. She was a fine type of Indian woman, a good mother, industrious and conscientious. She had been sacred woman in the Sun Dance and was beloved by all for her generosity and kindness of heart.

When we entered the lodge, Little Creek said: "Our white brother wants you to tell about the past." And Catches-Two-Horses answered: "Tales of the past should only be told after dark. I might become blind if I tell them in the daytime."

Her son Two Guns and his wife, a daughter of Little Dog the war chief, were also at home. She was young and lively;

like her father, she was always smiling. There were also visitors present from the north — a Blood Indian and his wife whom they called Sarcee Face. She was a wit and kept them laughing. She told about a swarm of bees attacking her while in the middle of a river; her face was still swollen from their stings. So I advised her to go to the river bank and cover the wounds with soft mud. She came back astonished at the success of my strange remedy. Then she made the rest laugh by saying: "I have a brother who is always being stung by bees. I am going to roll him in the mud when I get home."

I asked Catches-Two-Horses to tell about the Sun Dance. The lively young wife of Two Guns laughed and said:

"He wants to find out about the Sun Dance, because he thinks of taking an Indian wife and will want to give the ceremony himself." Sarcee Face made them laugh again by saying to me:

"You would make a funny medicine man. They would take off your clothes and paint you black all over; your white skin would show through and you would be a pink-looking medicine man."

By this time Catches-Two-Horses was ready to talk. She made an end of the joking when she said:

"I was seven years old when I became the wife of White Calf. My older sister was already his wife. I remember my age, because I had lived one year with my husband before I lost my first teeth. I have never cared for any other man, nor did I have a secret lover. My father was Black-Snake-Man. He was head-chief of the tribe many years ago. I remember when he first told our people they were going to get food from the Government. At that time we were camped at the place where the Yellowstone River flows into the Missouri. Then many Indians weie starving, because the buffalo had disappeared.

"During my life I have given three sun-dance ceremonies. I was a young girl when I saw my first Sun Dance; and looked for the first time upon a medicine woman. I wanted to be like her, to live a good life and be honored by all the people.

"I gave my first Sun Dance because of a battle with the Assiniboines. I made a vow in order that the Sun might keep some of my relatives from being injured in the fight. I gave my second, to fulfill a vow by my son Cross Guns. He made it in battle when surrounded by enemies. He looked up to the Sun and prayed:

"'Great Spirit in the Sun, have pity and spare my life. If I escape from this danger, I promise that my mother will give a Sun Dance in your honor.'

"Cross Guns escaped and came home. When I saw him I ran out to meet him. He kissed me and said:

"'Mother, I have made a lot of trouble for you. In a fight with the Crows, I was surrounded and thought I was going to be killed; I made a vow to the Sun; I promised that if I came through alive, you would make a medicine lodge (Sun Dance). I know this means suffering for you — to starve yourself and become thin and weak.'

"But I was glad. Quickly I made my vow; I kept praying day and night:

> "'Sun Above! Pity me!
> May I be pure and lead a straight life.
> May I be kind-hearted and good to every one.
> May my children and relatives live to be old.'

"Another time I was ill; the doctors said I was going to die. A messenger carried this news to my son Cross Guns who was camped on Badger Creek. It was midnight when he was told. He looked up to the sky and prayed:

> "'Moon and Stars! Have pity on my mother.
> May she live!
> If she recovers from this night,
> I promise you she will give the Sun Dance.'

"Cross Guns generally prayed to the Sun. But that night he prayed to the Moon and Stars, because they were in the sky. Next day he came to my tepee and made known his vow.

"We began our preparations in the early spring, before the snow was gone. We gathered tongues for the food and purchased a sacred headdress. I fasted and prayed day and night. On our way to the circle camp I had three travois, for the sacred tongues and my clothes."

Then the old woman changed from the subject of the Sun Dance and began to tell about her first experience with a Medicine Pipe. She said:

"Many years ago our people had a big camp at the lower end of the Cypress Hills. It was midsummer. The four tribes, Bloods, Piegans, Sarcees and North Blackfoot, came together in the same camp. It was so large that our chiefs formed two great circles, instead of one as was our custom. My father, Black-Snake-Man, and Lone Chief were head men; Little Dog was war chief and Four Bears head medicine man. I was then a girl of fourteen; and in that camp I first learned about the Medicine Pipe.

"One day White Calf had visitors at our tepee. He ran short of tobacco and asked me to borrow from his friend Four Bears, the medicine man. A large crowd was about his lodge, and inside many men dressed in fine costumes. I wondered what was going on; but I never thought it was a medicine-pipe ceremony. I stood at the door and asked Four Bears for the tobacco. At first he said he had none. Then I started to go away and he called me back. He left his seat at the back of the tepee and took some tobacco from a bundle hanging over the door. I saw him burn some incense and hold the tobacco in the smoke. He also made a prayer and said:

"'Here is tobacco. With it I give you the sacred bundle

that hangs over the door. From it you can take tobacco whenever you want.'

"I felt proud of his having given such a fine present. I took the tobacco to White Calf and gave him the message. He looked at me strangely and said:

"'Go back to Four Bears and tell him: "White Calf made a vow in his youth, that if any one ever offered him a Medicine Pipe he would take it.'"

"I was frightened at these words and the way my husband looked. But I went back and told Four Bears before his guests. Then they all began to sing and to beat on their drums. They came forth and marched towards our tepee, singing and drumming and shaking their rattles. Four of them put a robe about White Calf and took him back to the lodge of Four Bears.

"Then came the ceremony of transferring the pipe. Four Bears pitched a large lodge near the center of the camp. His wife came and dressed me for the occasion. I wore a buckskin dress with beaded leggings and moccasins to match, and a robe of soft tanned elkskin. My husband had a buckskin suit fringed over the shoulders and arms with scalplocks taken in battle, and a fine buffalo robe decorated with a band of colored beads. Four Bears gave us a bay horse with the Medicine Pipe, a saddle, whip, and painted rawhide rope. When we were ready to start for the big dance lodge, Four Bears led this horse bearing the Medicine Pipe and White Calf, with the buffalo robe over his head and extending back over the horse's flanks. I followed with my sister, Black-Snake-Woman, carrying the sacred bundles. In the dance lodge we had a pile of presents which our friends and relatives gave to help us pay for the pipe. We had to give Four Bears many horses, besides robes and blankets. Then he taught us the chants, prayers, and dances that go to make up the ceremony, and the rules we must follow in the care of the pipe.

"Soon after this ceremony five Gros Ventres attacked our camp and took some horses. White Calf followed with a band of our warriors and killed all of them. He took their scalps and we had a Scalp Dance. After that Four Bears, the former owner of the Medicine Pipe, and his two wives, took us to the dance. Because White Calf had taken the scalps, it was now proper for his wives to take part in the Scalp Dance. And this is the end of my tale."

CHAPTER XII

LEGEND OF THE SMOKING STAR

WHITE GRASS, the medicine man, lived in Cutbank Valley, between the homes of Mad Wolf and White Calf. He went by the nickname of "Shorty." He was a well-built, active little Indian, neat in dress and appearance, small in stature and good-natured. He had a prominent upper lip, sharp features, and a dry and wrinkled face, which, with an air of keenness, gave him a sly, shrewd look, like an old fox.

He had good standing as a medicine man, because of his knowledge of ceremonies and his social position. He was skilled in the conducting of ceremonies and handling of sacred bundles. He helped Mad Wolf, my Indian father, with his beaver ceremony; and was called in when any of the family were ill. He had reputation as a doctor and could treat certain kinds of troubles. His power over disease was believed to have been given him through supernatural experiences in visions and dreams. He was somewhat of a mind reader and mesmerist. He knew how to inspire confidence in his patients, which helped in their recovery. He also knew signs and omens both good and bad, and could tell people how to avoid bad luck. He was a great talker and liked to tell stories of the old days, when his tribe were free to wander and had many chiefs and medicine men. He spoke deliberately and in a low voice, using his hands freely in graceful gestures. He said:

"There is an ancient legend about a Smoking Star (Comet), that has been handed down through many generations. He came down from the sky to help old women and maidens who were in trouble.

WHITE GRASS, THE MEDICINE MAN

Showing interior arrangement of his tepee — couches and back-rests, society costume and regalia hanging from lodge-poles

"A camp of two lodges once stood far out on the prairie. In one of them lived an old man with his wife; and in the other their son-in-law who was married to their three daughters. The young man was a hunter. He provided food for both lodges. One evening a herd of buffalo came near. Early next morning the son-in-law shouted: 'Get up, old man, we will go together to drive the buffalo.' So the old father-in-law went with him to help in the hunt.

"Now this son-in-law was mean and heartless. He took it easy and made the old man do the work. He sat still and killed the fat ones, while his old father-in-law drove them past. But, when the hunt was over and it was time to cut up the animals, the son-in-law said: 'Go back to camp, old man, and tell the women to come out here. Your daughters can take back any share of the meat there is coming to you; you are too old to be of any use.' But he lied, for he did not want the old people to have anything to eat. That son-in-law kept on doing this every day. He made the old man go with him and drive the buffalo; but he would not allow the daughters to share any of the meat with their aged father and mother. He wanted to starve them.

"Now the youngest of the three daughters was the only one with a kind heart. She looked after the old people. Every day after the hunt, she hid a piece of meat under her robe. She carried it to them secretly and tried to keep them from starving.

"One day the son-in-law called as usual in the early morning: 'Hurry up, old man, let us go and run the buffalo.' They went together and hunted. As was his custom, the young man sent his father-in-law to drive the buffalo and do all the hard work, while he himself sat still. Now it happened that the old man walked alone in a buffalo trail. He saw a clot of blood which a wounded animal had coughed up. He said to himself: 'Here is something we can make into soup.' But he was afraid of his son-in-law; so he pretended to stumble and spilled the arrows from his quiver. Then he picked them up and put in quickly that clot of blood, placing his arrows on top. But the son-in-law was suspicious and said:

"'Old man, what were you doing so long in that buffalo trail? What did you pick up there?'

"'I fell and spilled my arrows,' said he. 'I was only putting them back into my quiver.'

"'Go home and tell the women to come out,' answered the son-in-law sharply.

"Then the old man went back to the camp and told his daughters their husband needed help with the meat. And the son-in-law kept all the food for himself. He gave nothing to the old people.

"When the old man got back to his own tepee, he said: 'Old woman, make the fire ready and the stone pot. To-day we have something to eat.' And he took the clot of blood from his quiver. 'Make haste,' said he, 'that we may eat before our son-in-law comes back.'

"Then his old woman hurried to put the clot of blood into the pot; and, when the water began to boil, they heard a child crying. It seemed to come from their pot. They looked in quickly and saw a baby. The old woman took the pot from the fire and lifted the child up. She said to her husband: 'It is a boy baby.' And he said: 'Old woman, take him out. By means of him we shall live.' So she wrapped up the baby and cared for him.

"When the son-in-law came home with the meat, he heard a child crying. He said to his youngest wife: 'The old woman must have a baby. Go over to their tepee and see. If it is a boy, I shall kill him; if a girl, I shall let her live.

"Now the youngest wife was the only one of the three daughters who cared for their parents. She went to their tepee and asked: 'What is the child? My husband wants to know.'

"And the old man said to her: 'It is a boy, but you must tell him it is a girl.'

"So the young wife went back to her husband and said: 'You will have another wife; it is a girl baby.' He was pleased and said:

"'Take some of these buffalo bones to your mother, that she may make soup with them and be able to raise the child.'

"But the young wife, on the sly, put some good meat with the bones.

"Now this all happened in the morning; and, when night came, the child (Smoking Star), kept looking at the lodge-poles and then at the old man. The old man was wise. He knew now that this child was supernatural and would help them. He took up the baby and held him first towards the lodge-pole on the south side of the door. The baby smiled; and they knew that this was what he wanted. So they held him towards each lodge-pole in turn, and after each pole the child grew larger. When he was halfway round the tepee, he was too heavy for the old man to hold; he stood him on the ground and kept turning him, until he faced the last lodge-pole on the south side of the door. By this time the child had grown to be a man.

"He said: 'I am hungry. Give me to eat.'

"The old woman replied: 'My son, your brother-in-law over there is trying to starve us.'

"Then she cooked him the last piece of meat which her youngest daughter had brought them. The young man said:

"'I am Smoking Star. I came down from my home in the sky to help you. And when I have done this, I shall return again to the sky.'

"He went out and made a bow for himself from the rib of a buffalo and used a tendon for the string. He also made arrows and flints for arrow-tips. When everything was ready, he asked the old man where they went to hunt, and said:

"'We shall start at break of day, before your son-in-law is awake.'

"In the early morning the old man and Smoking Star set out. Before they had gone far, they killed a fat buffalo cow. Smoking Star hid himself behind it and told the old man to stand by the carcass and wait.

"That morning the son-in-law came as usual and called for the old man to come forth to hunt. He said angrily to the old woman: 'He is late. It is time we were started.' When she told him her husband had been gone a long time, he shouted:

"'I have a mind to kill you first!'

"Then the old man saw his terrible son-in-law coming. But Smoking Star said:

"'Don't be afraid. Be eating some of the buffalo meat. And when he comes up you must talk back to him. This will make him so mad he will try to kill you. But he can't harm you, for I am here to help you.'

"The son-in-law came near and saw the old man eating beside the carcass of the buffalo cow. He shouted: 'Aha! There is no one to keep me from killing you now!'

"Then the old man mocked him and said after him: 'Aha! There is no one to keep me from killing you now!'

"The son-in-law was ready to shoot an arrow and kill him, when Smoking Star rose suddenly from behind the buffalo. At this the son-in-law was so frightened, he said: 'I was only going to shoot in fun.'

"'Now is the time for me to have fun with you.' He put an arrow in his bow and killed the wicked son-in-law.

"Then Smoking Star said to the old man: 'Take only the best meat from this carcass, for you are now the owner of your son-in-law's tepee and all his possessions. You will have plenty of good meat and robes to keep you warm.'

"He asked the old man which of his daughters had been kind to him. He said: 'The youngest was the only one who gave us food.' Smoking Star went to the lodge and told the youngest wife that she must look after her father and mother. He killed the other two women. He took their bodies and that of their husband and burned them together in a fire. He turned over both of the lodges to the old man and the old woman; and after that they had plenty to eat.

"Smoking Star had finished his work there, so he said: 'Father, I must now go on my way.' He left them and came to another Indian camp, to the lodge of some old women. They asked him how it happened that he came to the poor lodge of an old woman, when he could go to lodges where there were men. Smoking Star said: 'I am an old woman's child. I am not looking for men's lodges.'

"Then they gave him meat, but it was poor and lean. And Smoking Star said: 'Why don't you give me some fat meat?' 'Hush!' said the old women. 'Don't speak so loud. If the bears hear you, they will kill you. They always take the choice pieces of meat for themselves. They take all the good fat and give us only the lean. They live in the big Bear Tepee in the center of the camp.'

"Smoking Star said, 'In the morning I shall hunt buffalo.' He went through the camp and called to the people:

"'Go early to the corral, for I shall drive the buffalo over the cliff. There will be plenty of meat for all. Let every one come.'

"In the morning all the people came forth and saw the corral full of buffalo. Smoking Star killed the fattest cow and cut it up. He took the best parts for the old women. Some of it he lay in front of their tepee, in plain sight, where the bears could see. Soon they came forth to plunder. A young cub was first. He quickly smelled the meat and ran to the old women's tepee and seized the fattest piece. Then Smoking Star shouted:

"'Hey there! Young fellow! Go back where you belong.

I did not kill that buffalo for you. The meat belongs to those old women.'

"He cut the young bear across the face with his knife. It ran crying to its mother and said:

"'I was only taking a piece of meat when a man yelled at me and cut me across the face.'

"Then the old she-bear flew into a terrible rage; and the big father bear said: 'My son, take us over there. Perhaps that man will try to cut *me* across the face.'

"Smoking Star saw the bears coming. He drew his white-rock knife and ordered them to be off. But they ran at him. The old she-bear came first and her husband next. Smoking Star stabbed her and then the he-bear. He killed them both. Then he went to the bear lodge and killed all the other bears. There were none of them left; and he gave their big tepee and all of the meat to the poor old women. After that he left them.

"Then he came to a camp where he saw no young women. Again he went to an old women's tepee and asked how it happened. They pointed to a big Snake Tepee in the middle of the camp. They said:

"'The snakes have all of our young women. They take them by force and keep them in their lodge.'

"Smoking Star said: 'Now you will own everything in that tepee.' He walked into the lodge of the snakes and took a seat at the back. Soon the chief snake began to rattle, to rouse all the other snakes. Smoking Star took out his white-rock knife and waited. When the chief snake raised its head in the air, and was ready to strike, Smoking Star cut off its head. He killed all the other snakes and set the young women free; he walked through the camp and told the men to go after their wives.

"Then Smoking Star started again on his travels. He came to a lake where a terrible water monster lived. He stuck it with his knife and made it crawl. He jumped on its back and rode it into the water. He made it swim to the middle of the lake, where the water was deep. He called upon the Thunder and a big storm came up. The lightning struck the monster and killed it. The water of the lake was scattered and was never seen there again. Nor did any one ever find the body of Smoking Star. He went back to the sky, and became a star. Sometimes we see him in the southern sky in the evening. It was the Smoking Star who drove the big snakes and bears from the prairie. Those he let live fled to the mountains. And now the dogs have separated, after having had their meal." (The Indian way of saying — my story-telling is finished.)

CHAPTER XIII

MY NIGHT EXPERIENCE WITH A GRIZZLY BEAR

WHEN the leaves of the aspen and cottonwoods were turning yellow, the scout and I drove the herd into the corral and caught horses for a hunting trip to the mountains. That day a spirit of stubbornness possessed our horses. From the start we had trouble. Hard as I worked I could not hold them in line. Instead of following the scout, they hung back and wandered from the trail. They reminded me of people. Watching over them on the trail, they ceased to be mere beasts of burden, and became friends with individuality and characteristics of their own.

Brownie, the most ambitious, was happier in the lead. Strong and energetic, he was fitted for the place. Our blue horse was a nonentity; conscientious, honest and slow, but by nature a subordinate. Old Pinto, with a coat of red and white, had great endurance. He gave the impression of wisdom and experience. We had a large bay horse with a roman nose. He was headstrong and fiery, afraid of rattling things and of ropes dangling about his heels; he carried our bedding. A sorrel named Dandy was nervous and shy, too timid to assert himself; he was imposed upon by the others.

Baldy, my own pack horse, was small and wiry, surefooted as a mountain goat, but lazy and with diabolical cunning. He was too careful of his own safety to fall or wear himself out; sometimes he pretended to be nervous. But in bad places he never stumbled or faltered.

That day, while we were throwing on his load, he kept his legs spread apart and braced them firmly. He flinched and trembled as though receiving a heavy load — more than he could bear; and on the trail he groaned. But I took no notice of his complaints. His pack was light and I understood his tricks. Finally he stopped and lay down in the trail; he closed his eyes as if in pain; he trembled and gave groans that were pitiful to hear. I jumped from my horse and ran at him with my whip. He saw me coming and stopped suddenly in the middle of a groan. He struggled to get up, sneezed to hide his chagrin and ran after the outfit.

We had a buckskin horse with hide of yellow tan. His black mane and tail, black rings around his legs, and a black streak down the center of his back suggested a zebra ancestry. He was strong and stocky; hardest drives did not tire him. Buck was so reliable, we felt as if we could always depend upon him. But that day he gave us a surprise.

After a long rest at the ranch, Buck was feeling fine. When his pack slipped, he pretended to be frightened. He made a series of high jumps, landing stiff-legged on all fours; and gave his pack such a jolt that it turned. Then he threw his tail into the air and away he went. To frighten the other horses he ran among them, with pots and kettles rattling and banging. They were glad to stampede. The scout followed the main outfit; he took it as a matter of course. I rode after Buck who kicked off everything, even his pack-saddle. Then I caught him and went back over his trail, to find the precious contents of his pack and gather together our cooking utensils and kitchen outfit.

But we finally came to the mountains and entered the valley of the Cutbank, where there was a green forest of spruce and lodge-pole pine. In that whole region, the only broad-leaf tree in abundance was the aspen. The ground was covered with a soft carpet of moss and pine needles; and thimbleberry bushes full of crimson fruit. Then we turned into a side valley and followed a stream, where the trail was tortuous. At every turn the scene became more wild, until we came finally to a mass of burned and fallen trees. There we stopped to rest and feast on red raspberries fully ripe; and found an opening thickly covered with huckleberry bushes, bearing the largest berries I have ever seen.

There is nothing more trying than to drive obstinate pack horses through fallen timber. The main thing is to give them plenty of time. Sometimes they turned from the trail and went down the mountain side, or dodged through standing timber; and then their packs were torn and loosened by the trees.

At dusk we emerged weary from the forest and came into a basin with a meadow of green grass. A more romantic spot for a camp I have never seen — a narrow valley surrounded by high mountains and sheltered by trees. Through the meadow flowed a stream of clear water. Waterfalls dashed over the cliffs and fell into the stream below. We pitched our lodge on a carpet of green moss, near an ancient fir tree and a grove of spruces which sheltered us from the cold winds that sweep down the valley from the snowfields.

Soon after we turned our horses loose, I heard a kind of grunting, or roaring whine, answered by the frightened snorts of horses as they galloped away; and the scout shouted: "Hi, there! A grizzly bear! A grizzly bear!"

Among the hoofprints of the horses I found the tracks of a huge bear. But he had gone and we got no sight of him. I saw the place where he had been turning over stones hunting for insects and ant eggs, and tearing up the ground after squirrels.

At dark a cold wind came down the valley, and we gathered many logs and threw them on our camp-fire, till the big fir tree looked like a specter in the red glow of the flames. Then we lighted our pipes and sat by the fire. The scout had the gift of companionship; and when he talked I always felt at ease. He refreshed me with his knowledge of nature and of the woods, and stimulated my interest in Indians. That night he talked about the bear and said:

"In this valley a big grizzly has his range. He has lived here so long, he must now be very old. The Indians know him well and are afraid to shoot at him. He comes boldly into their camps and takes food. He is so big we believe he has supernatural power and call him the 'Medicine Grizzly.'"

After that there was silence for a while. The fire burned low and we sat gazing into the embers. By this time the valley was in darkness; but I saw the rugged outlines of the mountains against the sky, their snowy summits lighted by myriads of brilliant stars. I heard the rippling of the stream, the sound of the waterfall and the tinkle of the horse-bell where our herd were feeding. Then a wailing cry, probably the voice of some lynx or wolverine, arose from the depths of the forest. It made me think of the big grizzly in whose range we were camped. Little did I realize I would soon meet him face to face.

For several days the scout and I hunted on the mountains. We climbed to timber-line with its dwarfed and distorted trees. Above were the rocky heights and below the dark forest. In the front line were trees only a few feet in height, many hundreds of years old. Some were pushed partly over by storms and had all their branches pointing one way. They were battered and twisted by a thousand storms and overweighted by heavy snows. But we found no game, not even tracks.

Then the scout said he would go among the high peaks at the head of the valley. He took a light pack and went alone, while I stayed in our camp to guard the provisions and to look after the horses. In order to help in the hunt, I loaned him my large Winchester rifle of 45–70 caliber. Little did I realize how much I would need it myself.

After the scout had gone, I climbed the mountains for

camera pictures, caught trout in the stream and looked after our horses. Most of the provisions I stored inside the lodge, to be safe from wild animals and sudden storms. But I had an out-of-door kitchen at the edge of the woods, where I cooked in good weather and kept a supply of food.

One afternoon heavy clouds gathered over the mountains and a storm swept through the valley. Our horses left the meadow and came to the lodge, to pay me a little visit and to get a bite of salt all around; and then they strolled back again.

I passed that evening reading and writing by the lodge-fire. Finally I lay in my blankets and watched the fire burn low, until there was only a bed of glowing embers; and I fell asleep. In the dead of night, our horses wakened me by coming close to the lodge. I wondered at their leaving their feeding grounds again, and went out to drive them back. The storm was over. The clouds had broken and the moon was shining.

After the horses had gone, there was quiet. The wind had fallen and there was a strange stillness. I stood for a moment and looked reverently at the mystic mountains in the moon-light. I felt that uplift of spirit that I always have in the presence of giant peaks. I heard the solemn hooting of an owl, the distant cries of coyotes, and the rippling of the river rapids.

The night air was so cold I soon went back to my warm blankets. But I could not sleep; I had a feeling that something was near. Finally I raised myself and listened. Suddenly a rattling of pans came from my outside kitchen. Thinking one of the horses had come back, I jumped from my blankets. I seized a stick and ran out to investigate. A huge shadowy form stood against the black line of the forest. It looked like a horse and I was about to hurl my club; but this animal was no horse. It stood high in front and was low behind. It gazed steadily at me with lowered head, which moved slowly from side to side. Then came a sudden snort, a sort of snarling whine; and I realized that I was in close quarters with a huge grizzly bear. The thought of beating him with a stick made a chill run down my backbone; I felt weak in the knees; and I had the sensation of "my hair standing on end."

I remembered hearing that it was sure death to run from a grizzly bear, so I put on a bold front and backed slowly into the lodge. I started to build a fire; I thought the light might drive him off. But I was so excited it seemed ages before I could find either matches or knife. Had I my rifle I might have tried to shoot him; but we were in such close quarters and in the dark, he might have killed me.

No sooner had I a fire burning, than I heard his heavy footsteps; he was coming towards the lodge, but stopped near the door to examine my saddle. For a moment he stood sniffing and grunting; then came close to the side of the tepee, where we had the provisions stored. He raised himself on his hind legs, with front paws against the poles. I was directly underneath him; I saw the canvas press in and heard his heavy breathing. It seemed like a nightmare; again my hair stood on end. I shouted; and the sound of my own voice in that dimly lighted tepee sounded strange and far away. Then the bear got down on all fours and went back to his feast at my outside kitchen.

Believing the crisis was now past and that the old grizzly would do me no harm, I began to take a friendly interest and watched him through an opening in the door. He knocked a cover from a mess of trout; finished a bowl of delicious peaches and tore open bags of flour and sugar. At last he came to our "dutch oven," a heavy iron kettle for baking bread. In it I had stored, for safe-keeping, my greatest delicacy — a small piece of butter. For a moment his efforts were vain; the heavy iron lid held fast. Then he became angry; with his powerful forepaw he struck the kettle such a blow that the cover flew off; and I heard his rough tongue lick up the last of my provisions.

At the first sign of dawn, my dangerous visitor departed suddenly into the forest and I saw him no more. When the scout returned from his hunt, I showed him the tracks of the grizzly's huge feet and the marks of his long claws in the soft earth. They measured thirteen inches in length, seven inches across the toe and six at the heel. The scout said a grizzly of that size would weigh as much as a large horse. By the lodge-fire that night, he told me about the origin of the "Medicine Grizzly."

Story of the Medicine Grizzly

"The things I now tell you happened many years ago, when Mad Wolf, your Indian father, was a young man. He was the war chief of an expedition that went across the Rocky Mountains against the Flathead Indians. Two of his brothers were with him; but they both turned back before they reached the Flathead country. Mad Wolf and his warriors returned later by Cutbank Pass.

"Mad Wolf was riding in the lead, with the others following on both sides of the trail, as was the custom of war parties in those days. For fear of meeting enemies, they rode silently through the forest. Suddenly Mad Wolf heard footsteps and signed for the others to hide. It was a war party of Kutenai Indians. They ran into the ambush. In the fight, Mad Wolf singled out the Kutenai chief and killed him after a hard fight. On his body he found the scalps of his own two brothers, who had turned back. Mad Wolf sang his war song and ran back to help the rest of his party, who were by this time retreating. He roused them to fight harder; and together they killed all of the Kutenai, except one old woman. They spared her life and gave her to the Sun. They took the scalps from the dead Kutenai warriors and had a scalp dance. Then they painted the face of the old woman black. They spared her life and set her free, as a sacrifice to the Sun. They gave her food and presents — a warm blanket and dried meat. They put her on the right trail and started her towards home, with a prayer that the Sun would pity them, as they had their helpless enemy.

"After that Mad Wolf and his party crossed the summit and came down through Cutbank Valley. There they found the camp of some of our people, Running Wolf, Black Bear, and Middle Calf, who came into the mountains to cut lodgepoles. They were camped here, by this old fir tree.

"That evening they were all gathered at the lodge of Middle Calf to hear about Mad Wolf's trip. It was a warm moonlight night and some of the women were outside. Middle Calf told his wife to bring a pail of water from the stream. She came back frightened. She said: 'I met a stranger at the crossing. He jumped across the stream and ran into the forest.'

"Then another woman said: 'I just saw a man near the big fir tree. He looked into the lodge and ran away. He was an enemy. I could see his war bonnet.'

"Mad Wolf and the rest seized their weapons and ran out. They met a band of Gros Ventres who were ready to attack their camp. They killed all of the Gros Ventres except their leader. He escaped into the underbrush and stood them off. When his arrows were all gone, he fought savagely with his knife. All the time he made a noise like a grizzly bear. He dared the Blackfoot to come into the thicket. He kept shouting: 'Come on! I am not afraid. My power is very great.'

"After the Blackfoot had killed him, they found that he was a medicine man; his power came from the grizzly bear.

He wore the skin of a grizzly and had a necklace of big claws about his neck. They scalped the dead Gros Ventres warriors and had a scalp dance around a fire. But they burned the body of their leader; they were afraid some of his supernatural power might escape and do them harm.

"The summer after that, a party of Indians came into Cutbank Valley, to this same meadow. They pitched their lodges near this old fir tree where we are now camped — the place where you saw the big bear. That night this same grizzly came into their camp and took all the food he wanted. The dogs attacked him; but he killed some and put the rest to flight. He was so big they were afraid to shoot. We call him the Medicine Grizzly. We believe he is the medicine man of the Gros Ventres. When he was killed near this old fir tree, he changed himself into a grizzly bear."

CHAPTER XIV

INDIAN SUMMER

OCTOBER was fine that year, with days of warm sunshine and frosty nights — ideal for living in the open. Late in the month a party of Indians, both men and women, stopped at our ranch on their way to the mountains. Little Creek and my Indian sister were going; Yellow Bird, Onesta, and his wife Nitana; the sisters Katoyísa and Nínake; and they asked me to go along.

We put two old mares in the heavy wagon, to carry blankets and camp equipment; they were the only horses to be found near the ranch. Yellow Bird drove the team with Katoyísa and I rode Kutenai, my saddle horse.

Soon, one of the team became lame; and Yellow Bird went back for another horse. So I put Kutenai in the harness and mounted the driver's seat beside the Indian girl.

At first the going was good. The prairie was level and we had no trouble; but we were left far behind. Our wagon was heavy, the team slow and badly matched. Without a whip, I had to shout and swing my lariat to make the horses move along. Throughout the day we saw no big game, only jack rabbits and badgers and ground squirrels, chirping and standing straight up, like miniature prairie dogs.

Near the mountains we came to rough traveling, up hill and down. In bad places, with no road to follow, there was danger of breaking the tongue, a wheel or an axle. We had to cross gullies and washouts and streams with high banks; to find our way round ravines, and through thickets of alder and quaking aspen.

We did not talk much, but our silence was natural. Katoyísa only spoke when she felt like it. She was a quiet, self-contained girl, fearless and conscientious. She wanted to help her tribe in their struggle for survival; that they might learn to adapt themselves to the ways of the conquering white race.

That day I felt as though I were in a dream — like a pioneer of early days, on my way to a new land with this Indian girl. But, alas! I was brought suddenly back to earth. We crossed the summit of a high ridge and overlooked a terrible hill — a steep descent to a lower level of the plain, stretching to the foot of the mountains. The air was marvelously clear, and fragrant with the scent of pine and cedar.

We started down the hill; and I thought to myself: "If this heavy wagon ever gets started, the horses cannot hold it and we shall both be killed." The ground was smooth and hard, with a grass-covered gravel. When the tail of the wagon began to swing, Katoyísa was calm and unafraid. And, when the brakes did not hold, she was quick to act; she jumped from the wagon and held the heads of the frightened horses, while I blocked the wheels with stones. Then we rough-locked the wheels with ropes; and cut down a green tree and lashed it to the body of the wagon, so that it dragged on the ground in front of the hind wheels. Thus we made our way slowly down the steep hill, zigzagging back and forth until we came to a dangerous slant, where the wagon went on two wheels and began to topple. We thought we were turning over. But neither of us tried to jump. I put my arm about Katoyísa and we were ready. Then the wagon suddenly righted itself; I turned the horses into a low growth of aspens; and thus we came safely to the bottom.

We trailed the rest of our party across level prairie and along a river, passing through the broad entrance of a valley through lovely meadows of tall bunch grass, thickets of willows and groves of poplars, until we came to our camping place in the mountains — a high bench over the river and close to a green forest of pine and spruce.

In the northern Rockies the autumn nights come early. The sun was down by the time we had our camp ready, and the horses watered and picketed. Then we built a big campfire, for the night air was cold. We roasted meat on sticks over the hot coals, and stalks of wild parsnip to bring out the juice. My companions used neither knives nor forks; and like them I held the meat in my hands and tore it with my teeth; but it had a relish and flavor I never tasted in civilization.

In that autumn camp, the Indians were at their best. They were light-hearted and happy, as if they had not a care in the world. They were nomads by nature and loved to wander, to be free and live in the open. They sang Indian songs and told stories and tales of adventure. They talked about a mad Indian who roamed the plains and mountains; he traveled so fast every one was afraid; he killed people on sight, both Indian and white; he was on the warpath and wanted to kill as many as he could before he died; he came silently at night and shot people as they stood in the firelight.

Thus we sat and talked by the fire until late. We slept on the grass, under the stars. The women were together in one place, sharing their robes and blankets; the men in another, with our horses picketed near. As soon as the Indians lay down, there was quiet. But I lay awake, drinking in the clear fresh air and the fragrance of the forest, and watching the moon rise over the broad entrance of the valley. Then, suddenly it was morning. I saw the golden color of sunrise in the sky and the women cooking breakfast.

That day I went with Yellow Bird on a hunt for Rocky Mountain sheep. Our camp needed meat; and, in the fall, mountain mutton was the most delicious of all the game animals. We rode along an old Indian trail, westward through the valley, where the golden brown of ripened grasses covered the meadows; and came to a dark forest where the ground was fragrant with pine needles. We followed the shores of a chain of lakes, to a place where high mountains came close together on both sides of the valley. Yellow Bird was leading with rifle across his saddle. Finally he turned and signed with his hands, "Sheep on that mountain." High up, above timber-line, I saw a band of brownish gray animals with white rump patches. They were feeding on a grassy slope which extended to slide rock, near the summit of the mountain. I counted sixteen sheep — ewes and small rams. Suddenly, and for no apparent reason, they took alarm and ran swiftly along the mountain side. Then a big grizzly appeared against the sky-line, coming across the shoulder of the mountain. He, too, was stalking the sheep. He ran with head up, and I could see his long silvery hair rolling in waves.

Yellow Bird was excited and eager for a shot. So we tied our horses and made ready to climb, leaving our coats and everything we could spare. After a drink of cold water at a stream, we started with our rifles and cartridge belts, taking our course along the mountain side, so that the grizzly might not get our scent. We struggled through tangled thickets of evergreens, and windfalls where dead trees lay piled across each other in all directions. The forest seemed vast and lonely; everywhere silence, not a breath of air stirred. We climbed the southern slope in the glare of the midday sun. I was drenched with sweat and my breath came fast.

Near the edge of the woods at timber-line, we were careful not to snap a twig or make a branch rustle, expecting any moment to meet the grizzly. At every sound or movement in the trees, I felt a sudden thrill and peered through the forest with senses alert. But we did not meet the bear, to Yellow Bird's chagrin. He was a reckless fellow, always eager for a fight and confident of his skill with a rifle.

SUNRISE AT OUR HUNTING CAMP IN THE ROCKIES

We crossed the shale to the sky-meadow, where we saw the sheep; and to stalk them went towards the summit of the mountain, that we might approach from above.

Big Horn are the most difficult to approach of all biggame. They are wary and quick-sighted; the slightest sound startles them; and they are off like a flash. No animal is their superior in climbing; even in the most difficult places they never slip, nor make a misstep.

We hunted up-wind, keeping out of sight, using crags and boulders for shelter. When we came to a precipitous part of the mountain, we went slowly and carefully, to keep from making a false step and breaking our necks. We scrambled along the narrow ledges and rock-shelves, clinging to cold buttresses and to scant projections of the cliffs, careful not to start a loose stone or any crumbling shale.

At last we came to an overhanging crest. We crawled to the edge and peeped over the cliff. Below, on a narrow ledge, stood a ewe sheep. She was at the top of a precipice, with a view of the entire mountain side. By this time the sun was low in the sky. Now was our only chance for meat; we had to get down the cliffs, while there was still light to see the way. Yellow Bird fired and struck the sheep behind the shoulder. She jumped to a lower shelf, where my bullet finished her. The carcass fell over the precipice and down the barefaced cliffs; the hollow reverberations of its fall echoed from the mountain walls. It struck slide-rock and rolled over and over, going at terrible speed, until it landed against a big boulder far down the mountain — our fate if we should slip or make a false step.

Then we made our way back along the treacherous ledges and rock-shelves, where nerve and sure-footedness were necessary for every step. When we came to loose shale, we traveled fearlessly with long slides, down to the carcass of the sheep, near timber-line.

By the time we stripped off the hide and had the meat ready, night was beginning to settle over the surrounding mountains. Then, in the dark forest Yellow Bird was afraid. He sang chants to keep off ghosts and evil things, until we came to our horses on the floor of the valley. After the moon rose, the dark places were filled with its magic light, and the open parks and lakes were like fairyland.

At camp the Indians gathered around the fire to roast sheep meat, and to hear about our hunt. It was the night of full moon, without a cloud in the sky. Our fire was in a meadow, near the edge of the forest, where its red glow lighted up the big trees.

Like true children of nature, my companions acted as they felt. Sometimes they talked; and sometimes there was silence for a while. In the distance an owl hooted. It came nearer and nearer, until its call sounded from the top of a tree near by.

"Listen!" said Nitana. "He calls his own name — ears-far-apart, ears-far-apart, ears-far-apart (ka-ka-not-stoki, horned owl). One can tell the different members of an owl family by their voices — the deep call of the father, the higher one of the mother and the thin ones of the children."

After another silence the owl hooted again. My Indian sister shuddered: "Perhaps it is a ghost," said she. "Some owls are the unhappy spirits of people long dead."

"A medicine man told me," said Little Creek, "that people who have died and are unhappy in the spirit world, take the form of owls and come back to their old haunts. They travel only at night and dread the sunlight, because their deeds in this world were evil."

Again the owl hooted, this time from another tree. "Kyai!" exclaimed Strikes-on-Both-Sides, "there it is again. Just before my sister died, she saw an owl looking at the door of her tepee. She was so frightened, she told a medicine man;

he said to use black paint on her face; if the owl came back, the paint would ward off the evil. But it was no use; my sister died in a few days."

This ghostly talk by the fire, under the nocturnal spell of the forest, made the women afraid. To allay their fears, Little Creek said: "An owl never harms any one in a crowd, if he has a relative there." So he left the circle of firelight, and going to the edge of the woods shouted to the owl, "You are my relative."

Then the owl flew away, and I asked Little Creek: "What is the spirit world like?" He said:

"We call it the Sand Hills, a white alkali country — far east on the plains. It is surrounded by quicksands that the living may not enter. The ghost people chase ghost buffalo and antelope. They have wild berries and other things such as we like to eat. Old Person once died for a day and a night, but his spirit returned to his body. He told the watchers he had been to the Sand Hills, but was not allowed to enter; his time to die had not yet come. His body was wet with sweat when his spirit camc back; they drove him from the Sand Hills."

Nitana said: "Ghosts like to stay near forests and rivers. People who sleep alone in a thick forest are sometimes bothered by ghosts pulling off their blankets in the night and hitting them with sticks. But a person may never see the ghost. If it bothers him too much, he can offer his pipe with tobacco and pray: 'Ghost, pity me! I am poor and alone. Take this pipe and smoke. I pray go away and leave me in peace.' If the ghost will not leave, but keeps on bothering the person, it sometimes bestows upon him the power to doctor people."

"Ghosts of dead medicine men are the worst. They are known as 'the haunting spirits.' It is they who use the ghost shots, and kill people who go outside the tepee at night.

This fate often happens to sick people; they are shot at by ghosts; and when they go back to bed, they die in their sleep. Sometimes a person who goes outside at night, comes back breathing heavily, as if he were smothering. He tells his people that he saw something; and then they know that he was shot at by a ghost. But he can be cured by a medicine man who has power over ghost shots. This medicine man finds out the spot where he cannot breathe; and then he doctors him; he draws out the shot — he may suck it out with his mouth.

"Sometimes sick people see ghosts. Ghosts keep bothering them, coming again and again; the ghosts wait for them until they die, and then take them away. There are ghosts which scare horses at night, so that their riders fall off. Then they make a whistling sound and laugh."

After a silence Katoyísa said: "Tell a story about a ghost."

"Take care, the owl may hear you," answered Nitana. And then she continued: "There was a camp of two tepees in a lonely place, far off on the prairie. In one of them lived a couple without children, and in the other a man with his wife and daughter. No other people were near. One day the father sent his girl to the other tepee. On the way she saw a person seated on the ground. She supposed it was their neighbor and went towards him. He kept his blanket wrapped closely about him and she could not see his face. When he did not move, she threw a stone to attract his attention. Still he did not move or look up, so she went her way to the other lodge. There she found their neighbor and his wife. She told them about the stranger and they went forth to look. But the mysterious person had disappeared. There was no place to hide; the prairie was level with no trees. The girl was so frightened she ran back and told her parents. Throughout the rest of that day they watched, but nobody appeared.

"That same night, when both families were seated around

the lodge-fire, an owl lighted on one of the poles over their heads and began to cry: 'Oo-oo-oo-oo.' Then they knew the ghost had come back to trouble them. They begged it to go away and leave them in peace. But it stayed on the lodge-pole and kept crying: 'Oo-oo-oo-oo.' The girl said: 'I know he is angry, because I threw a stone at him.' So they filled a pipe with tobacco and offered it to the ghost. If he smoked he would do them no harm. But the ghost paid no attention to them. He was still angry, and kept on with his solemn crying. Then the father gave the pipe to his daughter. She held the pipe up and prayed: 'Ghost, smoke. I pray you go away and leave us in peace.' It paid no attention, but kept on crying. So they held the girl up into the smoke-hole of the tepee, where she was near the ghost. Again she offered the pipe. The ghost gave a loud cry and the girl fell over dead."

Then Little Creek told this ghost story about another owl:

"There was a man named Cross Bull who lived over north among the Blood Indians. He went alone to war. He had bad luck and started home empty-handed. One evening, after many days of hard traveling, he came to a river valley and went into camp in a grove of cottonwood trees. He had no food; he was tired and hungry. So he built a fire close to a log and lay down to sleep. In the night he was wakened by something coming through the underbrush. He had his back towards it. He dared not turn his head to look. He thought it might be a ghost. He heard it go into a tree, so he lay very still; he did not even move. Finally he raised his head and looked. In the forks of a big tree sat a ghost. A long white robe covered its bones. Whenever it swung its legs, the bones rattled. Cross Bull began to pray. He begged it to go away, saying: 'I am tired and want to rest.'

"But the ghost paid no attention. It stared at him from hollow eyes; it whistled and rattled its bones. Cross Bull prayed again:

"'O ghost, be kind.
Go away and leave me alone.
I am poor and have bad luck.
I am tired and want to rest.'

"Four times Cross Bull made this prayer. But the ghost paid no attention; it kept on whistling and swinging its legs. Then Cross Bull got angry. He took his bow and arrow and shot at the ghost. He saw an owl fly from the tree, and heard it cry in a quavering voice: 'You hurt me so badly, you hurt me so badly.' (Screech owl.)

"Cross Bull was so frightened he ran away in the dark. The ghost kept following; for whenever he stopped he heard it crying the same thing, over and over in a quavering voice: 'You hurt me so badly, you hurt me so badly.'

"Cross Bull left the valley. He did not stop running until he was far out on the plains. Then it was daylight and the ghost left him. But he kept on running until he reached the Blood camp. Next night Cross Bull died. And that is the end of my story-telling."

By this time it was late in the night and my Indian friends went to bed. I sat alone by the camp-fire. The moon was now in the west; and the handle of the Great Dipper, that wonderful clock of the north sky, pointed downward to the horizon.

Then I climbed the mountain side in the bright moonlight, to look out over the forests and the great plains stretching eastward. On the other side of the valley were mountains, with shining glaciers and snowfields. The aurora formed an arch of light across the north sky; streamers mounting to the zenith in yellow and yellowish red, and sometimes greenish white. They swayed backward and forward, now strong, now faint, until they faded and a luminous veil covered the sky, through which a bright star shone. There was no wind; and everywhere an impressive stillness, broken only by the river in the valley, and the solemn notes of the owl, "a haunting spirit."

CHAPTER XV

A FRONTIER DANCE

Two cowboys came to the ranch of the scout with a herd of cattle; one a half-breed, the other a white man, sinewy, tall and straight. He was a typical cowboy who had lived a life of adventure and hardship, rugged and bronzed by the sun. He wore a broad-brimmed hat, leather chaps, and high-heeled boots; a knotted scarlet handkerchief round his neck, and a cartridge belt with a six-shooter hanging from his hips. His fearless gray eyes looked straight out at me, and he moved and spoke with an easy, careless air of confidence. He had a smiling face and talked in a high squeaky voice that sometimes broke.

Yellow Bird told me, with mingled awe and admiration, that he was a famous bandit named "Slim." The United States Government had a reward on him dead or alive. Single-handed he held up a Montana stage, and an express train on the Northern Pacific Railway. Now he was trying to get a herd of stolen cattle across the border-line into Canada; they were "mavericks," or unbranded cattle, taken out of many herds.

Because of his adventurous life, Slim carried several bullets in his body. His right arm was so crippled that he could not lift his hand to his mouth. But, in spite of his wounds, he could still rope cattle and break wild horses; and was a dead shot with both hands.

I saw him break a vicious bronco to the saddle. He went into our high round horse corral, with smooth and easy gait, jangling spurs, and dragging his lariat which he coiled as he went. He lost no time and his movements were quiet and catlike. He did not seem to lift his arm or move; suddenly his noose shot out its full length and settled gracefully over the neck of the bronco. It bawled with rage and fear; threw down its head and sprang high into the air. It walked about on its hind legs, striking with forefeet and threw itself over backwards. But Slim finally mastered and tied it to the snubbing post. When he had finished his job, he could ride it without bucking, and led it about with a rope.

From the first I took a liking to this brave and hardy bandit, with smiling face and winning way and nerves of steel. He had a pleasant and easy-going disposition, with a broad and genial tolerance. He did not look down upon people with a different code, or hold it against me because my actions were within the law. To him there was nothing out of the way in robbing stages and trains and driving stolen cattle. He did not speak of these things, nor did he boast of them; to him they needed no apology. He was simple-hearted and generous — a type that would quietly face death without flinching, be faithful to friends and chivalrous towards women. But he would pursue an enemy with bitter and vindictive hatred.

Like all cowboys Slim loved excitement — especially a dance. That night there was going to be a party down the river at the Lone Wolf Ranch; and Slim asked me to go along.

Before dark we saddled our horses and rode together. I did not ask about his life; it was not customary in that country. But he told me of adventures in former days with wild animals and hostile Indians; and all the time he spoke his steel-gray eyes looked straight into mine. He talked simply and with a careless drawl, not seeming to feel there was anything unusual or exciting in his tales. But for me they had a strange charm — the way he told them, with a high squeaky voice, dry humor, picturesque cowboy language, and good-natured oaths.

With his partner he once roped a big grizzly, which charged from a thicket and chased them into the open. They were mounted on agile cow-horses that ran like the wind; but a fall would have meant death. Slim threw his lariat round the neck of the bear and his partner roped her hind feet. The grizzly bellowed with rage and foamed at the mouth. She tried to charge and floundered on the ropes; she reared and struck wildly with all fours; but in their grasp she was helpless. With ropes snubbed to their pommels and horses pulling in different directions they together stretched her out; and after a while turned her loose.

The dance at the Lone Wolf Ranch was given by the sisters Katoyísa and Nínake, and was free to all; every one in that region, both Indian and white, was welcome. People came long distances in wagons or on horseback — entire families — mothers with young babies. A log-shack close to the cabin was used by the women, and there they left their babies and young children to sleep on the floor.

The ranch cabin was lighted by lamps and candles; all three rooms, including the kitchen, were used for dancing. The front door opened upon the main room, a long apartment with low ceiling and walls of hewn logs, chinked and plastered, all beautifully whitewashed and clean. The windows and doors were decorated with green branches and pine boughs, with the Lone Wolf brand made out of juniper on the log walls, also the heads and horns of deer, elk, and mountain sheep. The guests were squaw men with Indian wives, cowboys, and half-breeds. But no men of the older generation of Indians came; it was not their kind of a dance.

The solitary musician was a half-breed who played on a wheezy accordion. He had only one tune, a sort of lively jig. But he played it over and over throughout the night, sometimes slow, sometimes fast.

Slim, Yellow Bird and I took partners and joined in a

square dance. At first there was little life or spirit; the dancers were stiff and self-conscious, until Slim took hold. He was a good mixer and a natural master of ceremonies. He was looked up to because of his brawn and genial disposition. He was the life of the party. He went from one room to another, shouting directions to the dancers; he was the caller-off and was witty and funny; he wakened up the half-breed musician and made every dancer "toe the mark."

Around the walls were bashful cowboys who had not the courage to ask a woman to dance, and breeds of all sorts and mixtures. It was hard to distinguish between Indians and whites. Among the spectators were elderly squaws in bright-colored Indian clothes, grandmothers looking after babies and children, while their daughters danced and had a good time.

At midnight I helped Katoyísa feed the hungry people. We had sweet cake — an unusual luxury — cold beef and bread. The people wanted nourishing food. They always had a craving for meat, especially beef; it took the place of buffalo meat and they felt abused if they did not get it.

We made tea in a great washboiler that nearly covered the stove. The people ate in relays; and we washed dishes in between. I helped Námo, a young Indian woman who had charge of the dishes; she was a great talker and good natured.

After supper even the bashful cowboys limbered up; although some slipped out of sight, because they had not the courage to dance. But never have I seen a crowd of dancers with more dash and enthusiasm.

After midnight only those who were experts in the square dance took the floor. Some had odd steps, like jigs, which they used at every chance. The dancers had no time to rest or sit down; and in their joy they stamped so hard the cabin was filled with dust.

In the early hours of the morning, old women and children lay asleep on the floors. And outside in the shack, they lay so close, there was no room to step, or turn over without waking the others.

At the height of the dance some women got excited and I heard exclamations of fear. They said they had seen a wild face look in at a window. They thought it was the Mad Indian — the murderer who came at night and killed people in the light. So they covered all the windows with blankets and shawls; and for a while no one was willing to open the door, or go out into the night. Perhaps somebody did look in. At the time I paid but little attention; Indian women are superstitious and have vivid imaginations. Besides, I thought the wild tales I heard of a "Mad Indian" might be a myth. But he was no myth. He turned out to be a real Indian, an outcast who had committed murder and was on the warpath — a menace to everybody in that country both Indian and white, seeking to kill as many people as he could before he himself had to die. Later I heard his story from one of the Indian Mounted Police who had captured him alive.

CHAPTER XVI

HUNTING ROCKY MOUNTAIN GOATS

WHEN the ducks and geese were flying south, Mad Wolf said the time had come to cut our winter firewood. So Little Creek, his son-in-law, and I went together to the mountains. We started soon after sunrise, with four powerful broncos harnessed to a timber wagon. Little Creek was a reckless and fearless driver. He stood on the axle between the front wheels and balanced himself skillfully, while I followed riding Kutenai, my saddle horse.

The wild broncos, frightened by the rattling wagon, galloped across the broad plateau. But it was an open table-land with an upgrade towards the Rockies, and Little Creek let them run freely. We passed through the foothills into a valley; and came finally to the edge of a forest of pine and spruce on the mountains. There we camped and pitched our lodge.

In the timber we selected only dead trees, standing and already seasoned for firewood. We cut them into logs and put them in piles, to haul later on the wagon. At midday we rested from our work, on a thick carpet of green moss by a small brook; we ate our midday meal and were refreshed by the fragrance of pine and balsam.

I watched a golden eagle soaring near the summit of a snowy peak; and a flock of white swans with long necks outstretched, winging their way across the deep blue of the autumn sky, the sunlight shining on their wings and breasts. Many flocks of ducks whirred close to the tree tops, in their level and rapid flight; and from far away came the honking of migrating geese.

"Geese are wise and can foretell the weather," said Little Creek. "Now they fly high; and it is a sign of a hard winter. Other birds and animals have also given warning. The curlew is not singing; many song birds gathered early into flocks; prairie larks have disappeared; the skins of otter, mink, and beaver are heavier than usual; and the jack rabbits are already turning white."

Next morning I stopped work in the forest to go on a hunt for mountain goats. I took my saddle horse and followed a stream through a canyon, into a basin with precipitous walls. There I left Kutenai and started to climb the mountain on foot. I came to an exquisite alpine meadow above timber-line, with a carpet of ferns and green grass. Little mountain chipmunks were gathering seeds from alpine plants, scampering and chattering in the warm sunlight. Then a hoary marmot gave a piercing whistle from his rock tower on a cliff, where he lay watching for enemies. Other marmots in their feeding grounds along the mountain side took up the cry and ran for shelter to near-by cliffs and boulders.

That day was strangely warm for the northern Rockies. Although late in the autumn, the sky was clear and the wind blew softly from the south. I ate my lunch of dried meat and bread beside a mountain torrent that had its source in an icy cavern and snowdrifts. It crossed the meadow and rushed tempestuously down a sheer and winding chasm to an unbroken cliff, where it leaped forth and fell into the valley a mass of spray, carrying chunks of ice which crashed upon the rocks far below.

Then I lay behind some gnarled and stunted firs to watch for game. The surrounding country with its crags and towering precipices was an ideal home for big horn and white goats. From my exposed place on the shoulder of the mountain, I had a far-stretching view — a wide panorama of unnamed peaks all towering into the blue, of valleys, emerald lakes, green forests, and white snowfields.

It was then so late I had given up hope of getting any game that day. Suddenly I caught sight of moving objects on a snowfield at the head of a valley. Through my glasses I saw a herd of five goats led by a large billy. They were the whitest things I have ever seen. It was only because of their jet-black horns that I could see them on the snow. Never shall I forget my feeling of exhilaration to see those wild animals in their native haunts, and my eagerness to get one for a hunter's trophy.

They were coming my way. They were traveling fast and were headed for a grassy knoll high above me. I waited until they were out of sight behind a shoulder of the mountain, then left my ambush and climbed with all my might. I crept along the side of a low ridge, hiding behind clumps of alpine fir and juniper. With my large 45–70 rifle, rope, and cartridge-belt, I had a heavy load for climbing. The ascent was steep and covered with broken rocks. Because of the high altitude, I was soon winded and felt weak in the knees. But my only chance for a shot was to reach the knoll first.

When I was close to the spot, I threw myself behind a patch of juniper — not a moment too soon. Before I could raise my rifle, the head of a billy appeared over the edge of the slope. First he took a look around; the others were behind and not in sight. Then he took a bite of grass and stepped into view. I raised my rifle very slowly, very carefully, and threw a cartridge into the barrel. The sound alarmed him, for he threw up his head. I fired and hit him behind the shoulder. He bounded into the air. I sent my second shot into another goat, wounding him. With my third shot, I killed the first goat; and in the meantime the second billy had disappeared. Then I saw him going up the mountain with discouraging agility. I followed and came upon a nanny with two young kids. I walked within a few feet, while they stood calm and unconcerned. The kids were beautiful little animals, like woolly toy goats. They stalked back and forth, wagging their ears and looking at me in a puzzled way. They were consumed with curiosity and hopped up on a big rock to get a better view. I wanted to stay and watch them, but went instead to find the wounded goat.

By blood marks I tracked him up the mountain towards some precipices. He ran to a series of ledges, made by the outcroppings of the rock strata. I saw him jump from one shelf to another, and hit him with a bullet. But, with vitality like that of a grizzly bear, he kept going. In the excitement of the chase, I never thought of danger and followed him along the shelves. He jumped to a lower series of ledges. If he went farther, I would lose him, so I leaned over the precipice and fired. The place where the goat stood was so narrow I thought he would roll over the precipice; but he fell dead in his tracks.

Then the difficulty was to get to the place where the carcass lay. With my rope in one hand and clinging to the rock wall with the other, I crawled along the tier of ledges. I could hear the rocky débris from my feet crashing on the boulders at the foot of the abyss. At last I reached the goat on the narrow ledge. But I had trouble in skinning. The carcass weighed two hundred pounds, and in such cramped quarters it was hard to turn over. With hide partly off, the goat smell was nauseating. But there was no escape. In front was a precipice which had a strange fascination, but I dared not look over. At my back was the rock wall which had such a slant I could not stand erect. Having unjointed the head and finished the skinning, I crawled from the carcass and sat down to rest.

Then, for the first time, I saw that a storm was gathering. Dark clouds were settling over the mountains. The air was sultry; and from the look of the sky a heavy snow was coming. I must hasten to a place of safety before the storm set in.

With lariat I lashed the head of the goat, with its long sharp horns, inside the pelt, threw one end of the rope to the shelf above, climbed up and pulled the bundle after me. The return trip was more difficult and dangerous; I had not the excitement of the chase to help. On hands and knees I crawled along the narrow ledges and climbed from tier to tier. I came to a buttress which blocked the way. I clung to the cold wall with my fingers and clutched the scant projections of the cliffs. It gave me a sickening sensation, when they crumbled and hurtled into the abyss.

On one of the shelves, I came to a steep pitch in the floor. I shoved the pack before me, but it began to slide. Quickly I freed myself from the rope. I lay flat and heard the dull thud of my pack as it struck far below. I thought all my labor was in vain; that the head had been ruined by the fall. But I found it at the foot of the precipice, saved from serious damage by the thick fur of the pelt. Then I skinned the other goat; the two heads and pelts in one pack made, with my rifle, a heavy load.

By the time I reached my horse on the floor of the basin, snow was beginning to fall. And when I got back to camp, the timbered mountain slopes were all white. That night we had the first heavy snow of the season. But in the morning the clouds lifted and unveiled the cliffs and canyons and high peaks.

Then I went forth for camera pictures, following the tracks of birds and animals in the snow. The valley was filled with winter scenes of wonderful beauty. As the sun rose over the mountains, icicles and ice draperies pendent from cliffs and trees glistened like diamonds in its bright rays. The branches of firs and pines drooped with heavy burdens of snow. The undergrowth was covered with delicate draperies; boulders and fallen trees had smoothly rounded caps. Brooks were covered with ice, crystal clear — with here and there snow arches and arcades and other marvelous ice structures.

Tracks of coyotes and timber wolves crossed and recrossed the trail. I saw footprints of a snowshoe rabbit; they resembled snowshoe tracks, because of the long fur on its feet; and the tiny tracks of mice and their tunnels in the snow; where rabbits had played and a squirrel had left a cone. There were tracks of willow ptarmigan; of a little "crying hare"; and the splay footprints of a wolverine, called "Mountain Devil" by the Indians, because of its meanness and wonderful cunning.

But our work in the forest was brought to a sudden close by my narrow escape from death. Little Creek and I were felling together a large spruce. He was chopping on one side and I on the other. When the tree began to fall, I saw it coming my way and jumped for a place of safety. But the top unexpectedly struck a leaning tree, throwing the butt of our tree into the air; and then it came rolling down towards us. It narrowly missed Little Creek. I heard him give a mighty yell; but there was no escape for me. The trunk of the tree hurled me to one side, and then the light went out.

When I opened my eyes, Little Creek was bending over me. I thought my end had come; I could not breathe, neither could I move. Then my breath slowly returned. I sat up and tried my limbs; to my surprise I could move them all. But my clothes were torn and soaked with blood. The jagged butt of the great tree had struck me as it rushed past, making a ragged wound six inches long in my side; and that scar I shall always carry. If I had been a few inches nearer the tree, I would have been crushed.

CHAPTER XVII

THE BLIZZARD

THAT fall the good weather lasted until late on the plains. The days passed clear and calm, as if waiting for a wind to bring the change.

One morning in November, I left my lodge at Mad Wolf's home in the valley, to ride after stray horses and cattle. The day was mild for so late in the year. As I rode northward along the foot of the mountains, a warm wind came from the east and clouds gathered over the Rocky Mountain range from north to south. But overhead the sky was still clear.

At midday I stopped to eat beside a small stream about twenty miles from the ranch, letting my horse, Kutenai, graze in a meadow. While stretched on the grass, I saw a great halo unusually bright, of orange tinged with blue, appear around the sun; with large sun dogs showing on both sides; and dull gray clouds, like a leaden roof, spread over the entire sky. These were bad weather signs. So I saddled my horse and started for home at a gallop.

The sky in the north became as black as ink, with bands of mist hanging low. I felt a blast of cold air and drops of rain, and saw dark clouds coming down from the north. They had a strange and ominous look, rolling over and over, spreading out and trailing along the plain and reaching upwards toward the zenith.

Then the blizzard came, straight from the north, with wind and cold and snow. In the blinding storm I lost all sense of direction. In vain I looked for landmarks — ridges, coulees, buttes, or streams — something familiar to mark my course. My heart sank and I felt in a panic. In the thickness of the storm, everything looked strange. I lost my way, going eastward toward the open plains instead of south. Then I recognized a familiar rock pile on a butte; and came finally to a broad table-land, an exposed plateau, which I knew was ten miles north of the ranch. It stretched from the foot of the mountains to the open plains, and south to Mad Wolf's home in the valley. Across its level surface the wind had an unbroken sweep from the north.

Through deep snow my horse climbed to the summit of the plateau. And all the time the wind was blowing a gale from the north with squalls of hurricane force, bearing stinging sleet and snow in blinding clouds.

By this time Kutenai looked like a snow horse. He was covered with white hoar-frost from head to foot, having holes for his eyes and nose. Long icicles hung from his muzzle and from his sides and matted his tail. He struggled through the deepening snow, losing courage and going more and more slowly. He belonged to a mild country across the mountains, and was a stranger to the plains and blizzards.

Then to save his strength and to warm my chilled hands and feet, I dismounted and tried leading him. But he acted strangely, as if blind. He reared and plunged and lay down in the snow. So I mounted again; with whip and spurs I forced him to move forward.

Night came on, with the snow above the knees of my horse. The sky was banked in darkness and the pitiless snow pelted me fiercely with every blast. People who have not felt a winter blizzard on the northern plains can never know what that struggle was.

I had strange sensations, as though I could not breathe; I felt suffocated, as if smothered by the snow. It blew down my neck and sifted through my clothes; it filled my eyes and mouth. A dense white pall was about me. There was nothing to see — not a patch of grass, nor a stone, only a dense whiteness. I thought I was going blind; my head swam. So I began to shout, just to hear the sound of my own voice. Suddenly I felt tired and lost hope. I thought how good it would be to lie down in the snow; it was useless to fight that blizzard.

I was roused by my horse floundering deep in a snowdrift. He struggled a moment; then lay still and began to groan. I struck him with my whip and tried to drag him out by the reins; I seized him by the neck and pushed him to and fro, trying to work him loose; I shouted and prodded him with my spurs.

Roused by my rough treatment, he no longer groaned. He grunted and tried hard to free himself. And with my help, he finally struggled from the drift, shook himself, whinnied, sneezed several times to recover his composure, and was ready to move on. From that moment he was a different horse.

At last came a lull in the storm. The wind went down and the snow ceased. Overhead the moon shone through low-flying clouds and gave me the right course. During that lull I crossed the plateau — just in time; the blizzard came from the northeast with greater force. But we were safe in the river valley, protected from the wind by high cutbanks, groves of big trees and thickets of willows. I knew my way and came safely back to Mad Wolf's ranch.

Throughout that night the blizzard raged. But my lodge with its inside fire was a safe refuge. In my warm blankets I felt a delicious surrender to fatigue; I fell asleep listening to the roar of the wind, the beating of snow and sleet.

Next day, when I looked out, drifts were piled around the lodge, with the ground swept clear in spots. Dense clouds of snow were being driven by the gale and whirled high into the air; sky and plain were merged in a vast expanse of whiteness.

During those long days of storm, my Indian father and his friends passed their time by the lodge-fire, telling legends and stories of adventure. They gossiped about friends and neighbors; talked of their daily life — horses and cattle, hunting, and religious ceremonies.

The women amused themselves by gambling with four bones, which they threw upon the ground and called by name. Men used four hiding-sticks of bone, one marked with a black ring. They had two sides, each with a leader who was an expert in handling the bones. The side with the bones drummed with sticks on the lodge-poles; they sang songs while they played, and made jibes and tried to rattle the guessers. These gambling songs were sung with spirit and a marked rhythm, beginning in a low tone and increasing in volume, until it reached a high pitch; then sank again to a low pass, alternately rising and falling and gradually died away. In this way the play went on until one side lost all the counting-sticks. The players wagered weapons, horses, saddles, sometimes their tepees and everything they possessed.

Children liked to coast on snowdrifts down the steep slopes of the valley, on a sort of toboggan made of animal ribs lashed to cross-sticks; or they sat on pieces of rawhide and held up the front with their hands.

Boys spun wooden tops in the soft snow, driving them over the surface with whips having lashes of buckskin or bark. They also played a game on the ice, using smooth stones like tops. They played in pairs, spinning the stones by whipping and driving them together. The top which spun the longest was the winner. They used pebble tops on hard snow, making them jump while spinning across the holes, by striking them with their whips.

On a stormy night, I sat with the Mad Wolf family around a comfortable lodge-fire, listening to the beating of snow and sleet. It was just the night for ghosts. In the roar of the storm, everything sounded strange and mysterious. The singing of burning wood in our fire was like far-off voices. The bawling of the frightened cattle and barking of our dogs seemed faint and far away.

Suddenly a violent squall shook the tepee and the door blew open. The old woman Gives-to-the-Sun cried out:

"A ghost came in! I felt its cold touch! See the smoke whirl! And the dogs gave the ghost-bark."

Said Strikes-on-Both-Sides, my Indian sister:

"Of late many ghosts have been around. They do not like the Sand Hills. They are restless and come back to visit their old haunts. The night we camped on Two Medicine, the ghost of our old friend Running Rabbit came from a clump of trees and frightened our horses. His ghost was so near we feared he might touch us."

"And why were you afraid of that?" I asked.

"It is sure death to be touched by a ghost," said my Indian sister. "I remember after Running Rabbit died, his ghost came back and took his wife to the Spirit World. She and her daughter were on their way to the home of Bull Calf. The mother felt a cold touch and turned to look. Suddenly she fell to the ground and lay as if dead. When her spirit came back, she said to her daughter: 'Your father came and touched me. He wants me to go back with him.'

"Soon after that the old woman died; and her relatives believe that Running Rabbit took her. The ghost of that old man has been bothering many people who live on Two Medicine. Strange he should become so mean. He was so good and kind when alive."

"There are many ghosts in Two Medicine Valley," said Gives-to-the-Sun. "People talk all the time of seeing them. Not long ago, Old Person was riding down the river to the home of Little Plume. The night was dark. When he came to the grove of cottonwoods, where the body of White Quiver lies in the branches of a tree, his horse jumped and snorted. As he rode away, he heard a queer voice from the tree say:

"'Old Person, why are you so long in coming to the Spirit World? I am still waiting for you.'

"Soon after that Old Person became ill and died. I heard of another ghost that bothered the families of Big Wolf and Buffalo Hide. It kept them awake all night. It came from the trees and roused the dogs. They gave the ghost-bark; they growled and sniffed the air. That ghost cried like an owl and pulled their door open. Next morning they found the reason. They saw a dead body in a tree close to their camp. It was the unhappy spirit of a man who was murdered by his jealous brother."

Then Mad Wolf told of an experience he once had with a ghost:

"When I was a young man, I went off to sleep alone. I walked all day and fasted. I wanted to have a dream and to get power. At night I came to a forest on the mountains and made a shelter of branches. As I lay alone in the dark, I thought of many things—of wild animals and of ghosts, the evil kind, which twist the mouths of people and make them crooked; they pull their tongues back into their throats and kill them, and shoot with their finger nails. I lay awake and heard strange noises—coughing and laughing and whistling by ghosts. Finally a ghost came near. I begged it to pity me and offered it my pipe to smoke. Then I fell asleep; and in my dream that ghost gave me power to doctor the sick."

Another stormy evening a lively crowd of Indians came into my lodge and sat around the fire. Two Guns, son of the head-chief White Calf, with his wife and family were there, also the family of Mad Wolf. Two Guns and his wife were great talkers and fond of repartee. He was in a good humor that night and said, to make the others laugh:

"I see your lodge has a black top like a stormy sky. It must be a bad-weather-lodge and the cause of this big storm."

"That cannot be," I replied. "We have often used it when there were no clouds and the country was dry."

Said Two Guns: "Is it because you come from the smoky-city that your tepee smokes so badly?" At this joke the crowd all laughed, and he said: "White Weasel, tell us what the medicine of your tepee forbids your doing."

I replied: "There are so many things I could not begin to tell."

At this every one was pleased. They all liked the repartee. The young wife of Two Guns was preparing her pipe for a smoke, so I offered her my tobacco bag. Her husband said:

"Look out! White Weasel! If you mix any love-medicine with that tobacco, I may lose my wife."

I told him it was already too late. He laughed and said:

"If your love-medicine acts that quickly, I shall probably lose her before we get home."

That night by the lodge-fire, Mad Wolf told us about the origin of his Winter, or Snow Tepee. He said:

Legend of the Snow Tepee

"There was once an Indian who hunted in winter, far out on the open plains. He saw a person running on foot from the north, shooting his arrows, and after him came the blizzard. After that the Indians knew that Bad-Old-Man brings the winter; also that Good-Old-Man brings the warm wind. When the chinook blows in winter, we say: 'Good-Old-Man is running down from the mountains with the warm wind.'

"Good-Old-Man and Bad-Old-Man keep chasing each other backwards and forwards throughout the winter. But in spring Good-Old-Man has the victory.

"The Supernatural Person who makes the winter storms and blizzards gave us the Snow Tepee. It is not often seen in our summer camps, because it is a bad-weather-lodge and has power to bring storms. It came to our people many years ago during a big storm; in this same moon — the beginning of winter.

"The ducks and geese had gone south; the last of their flocks had disappeared many days before. It was time for winter, but the air was still warm. A band of hunters went on the open plains to hunt buffalo. An Indian named Sacred Otter and his young son had good luck. After they had killed many buffalo they started to skin them. They were hard at work on the carcass of a big bull and had taken off the hide, when Sacred Otter saw black clouds coming towards them, spreading out and rolling over and over. He knew it was a Charge Storm — a terrible blizzard — and there was no time to get away. So he made a rude shelter with the green hide and carcass of the bull. They both got inside; the snow quickly covered them; and in spite of the bitter cold, they were warm and comfortable under a huge drift.

"Then Sacred Otter fell asleep and dreamed he was traveling on the plains. He came to a large tepee decorated with strange pictures. The top was yellow, for the color of the sky at sunset; a cluster of seven green discs was on the north side to represent the constellation of the Great Bear — the direction the blizzards come from; at the back a red disc for the Sun, from the center of which hung a buffalo tail; around the bottom was a yellow band with green discs, the color of holes in ice and snowdrifts, and the peaks of the Rocky Mountains. At the tips of the ear poles were bunches of crow feathers with small bells, which tinkled in the wind; and over the door a buffalo head in red, with green eyes — the ice color.

"While Sacred Otter was looking at these pictures, he heard a voice say:

"'Who is it that stands outside my tepee? Why don't you come in?'

"He opened the door and saw a large fine-looking man seated at the back, smoking a pipe of black stone. His hair was white and he wore a long white robe. The stranger directed Sacred Otter to a seat near the door and continued smoking in silence. His face was painted yellow, with a red line across the mouth and another across the eyes. He had a black feather in his hair; round his waist an otter-skin with small bells attached, and on his breast a minkskin. Finaliy the stranger spoke, saying:

"'I am the Maker-of-Cold-Weather and this is my Snow Tepee. It is I who send the blizzards, the snow and cold from the north. For the sake of your young son who was caught with you in the blizzard, I am going to pity you and spare your life. I give you my Snow Tepee with its pictures; also this black stone pipe, and my supernatural power goes with it. When you get safely back to your camp, make a new lodge and paint it with pictures like those you see on mine.'

"The Cold Maker taught Sacred Otter the songs and prayers that went with the ceremony of the Snow Tepee, which should be used for the healing of the sick. He also instructed him to place horse tails on both sides of the door for good luck — to keep his own horses and to get more from his enemies; and to wear a minkskin as a charm when he went to war, to keep him from being injured.

"Then Sacred Otter awoke. He saw that the blizzard was going down and knew the Cold Maker would keep his promise. As soon as he got back to his camp, he made a model of the Snow Tepee with its pictures and decorations — just as he saw it in his dream. And, when spring came, the time the Indians make their new lodges, Sacred Otter made and painted the first Snow Tepee. Since that time we have always believed in its power — to heal those who are ill and to protect its inmates from sickness and danger."

CHAPTER XVIII

SNOW-BOUND

THE scout and his family were snow-bound at the Agency and could not get back to their ranch. The prairies were impassable with deep drifts; high winds blew day after day from the north. Meanwhile with Yellow Bird I looked after their live stock, and rounded up the cattle and horses which wandered in the storm.

Then, another terrible blizzard came in the night. The roar of the wind in the cottonwoods sounded like ocean surf in a heavy storm. When I awoke in the morning, the light in the cabin was strangely dim. With a sense of foreboding I opened the door. A heavy snow was falling, coming straight down. It covered the fences and lay on a level with the cabin windows. The great depth of the snow showed on the roofs of the low-lying sheds and on the rounded banks of the river. A swift current was running, with an ice gorge against the foot log, which backed up the water and covered the meadow with a small lake.

First we opened a path to the sheds, and fed hay to the cows and calves. Then we dug a log from the snow and sawed it into blocks for firewood. The air was thick with falling snow and it was growing colder. So we made ready to hunt for cattle on the plains where they were exposed to the full force of the storm.

Yellow Bird rode his big roan horse, I a powerful sorrel. I wore a beaver-skin cap with the hood pulled down, a woolen scarf about neck and face, coyote-skin gloves, leather coat and felt boots; only my eyes were exposed.

When we were ready, our horses stood all humped up because of the cold. They were in a bad humor, ready to make us pay dear for riding them. As I leaped into the saddle, my horse was off like a flash, running with head down and back arched; he bucked in a series of high leaps, landing stiff-legged on all fours. Blinded by the whirling snow, I shut my eyes and held tight by the grip of my knees. Yellow Bird's horse followed bucking; but he shouted with delight and struck him with his quirt after every jump.

We found some cattle huddled together in the deep snow, and drove them from the open plains to the river valley, to the shelter of willow thickets. Then, because of the rising storm, we hurried back to the ranch.

Through that long night, I could not sleep because of the cold. The terrible chill in the air pierced to the marrow of my bones. I held my face under the blankets, and hands against my body to keep them from freezing. I lay listening to the wind; and towards morning fell into a restless doze.

When I awoke, a dull gray light was in the room. The roar of the wind sounded distant and far away. I waited, but it grew no lighter. A heavy frost covered the windows, the knob and latch of the door. The cracks in the window near my bed were stuffed with hay to keep out the wind; but the gale drove the fine snow through crevices and made drifts on the floor.

After sunrise the wind went down; and the temperature fell to forty degrees below zero Fahrenheit. But the sky was clear and the sun shone undimmed through the frosty air. Loud reports like rifle shots came from breaking ice in the river. The roof of our cabin cracked as though it would burst.

Outside it was hard to move about, because of the deep snow; but I made my way to a ridge near the pasture. I saw no tracks, no animals, nor birds; not even wolves nor ravens had yet ventured forth. Not a tree could be seen, nor the smallest bush, nothing to break the monotony of that dreary wind-swept waste.

Sometimes Yellow Bird and I did not speak for hours at a stretch; we only talked when we felt like it. On those long days of storm he was restless and morose. He loved excitement and hated regular work, and the monotony of ranch life in winter.

Finally the sun rose in a clear sky. The plains were dazzling, the sky a broad expanse of blue. The clouds rolled away from the Rockies, revealing the great range from north to south — a mass of snow and ice. Glaciers on the high peaks glowed and sparkled in the sunlight. The green forests were covered with a blanket of white. Tall pines held masses of snow, which reflected the sun's rays from myriads of small icicles. The icy covering of the river smoked; and the bare cottonwoods along its shores were covered with white hoar-frost.

Then Yellow Bird said that we had better saddle our horses and drive the cattle back to the ranch; if we did not feed them hay they would die. We found a big herd by their tracks, scattered among thickets of willows. We worked fast in the intense cold, rounding up and heading off. Our horses went at a gallop along the ice-covered trails; but they were agile and sure-footed and did not fall.

We drove the cattle from their hiding places, gathering them together. Then headed them towards the ranch; and, with shouting and firing of guns, drove them bellowing, their rough coats covered with white hoar-frost from the vapor of their steaming hides.

At the ford of the river a swift current overflowed the ice. The steers in the lead balked; they stood and smelled the ice. The cattle in the rear crowded forward. They ran along the shore, bellowing and with clouds of steam rising from their nostrils. A big steer led the way and the others followed.

They broke through the ice and struggled in a mass. Some were carried down-stream by the swift current and lodged against an ice-jam; but all got safely across.

Then came an accident to Yellow Bird. At our cabin he jumped from his horse and landed on the sharp edge of an axe unturned in the snow. To stop his foot from bleeding, I used a compress made tight with a stick; I dressed it with an antiseptic and bandaged the wound. Yellow Bird was now helpless and took to his bed.

The herd of famished cattle crowded bellowing about the cabin. I opened the door and saw them pushing and struggling; mad with hunger, fences could not stop them; to hold them at the ranch, they must be fed with hay that night.

When I went outside, the dry snow crackled and made a grinding sound underfoot. After the violent "low" of the blizzard, the barometer was now high; the temperature had fallen to fifty degrees below zero. But the air was dry and the sky cloudless. On a rude ladder I climbed to the ridge of the haystack and cleared away the deep covering of snow and ice. With an axe I chopped the top hay frozen into a mass. Then cut it into chunks and fed it to the starving cattle. This heavy work made me sweat freely in spite of the cold. But, when I loosened my skin cap, hair and eyelashes were quickly covered with ice; and I had the strange sensation of my eyelids freezing so tight I had to pull them apart.

The night was strangely clear. A moon nearly full rose over the plains, flooding that vast whiteness with its cold light. I saw clearly the snow-banked cabin and low-lying sheds and the struggling cattle. The heavens were of a marvelous purity and depth, with many wondrous stars.

Venus, like a great light in the west, was sinking over the snow-covered mountains. East was the burning Sirius, in the constellation of Orion with belt and sword, Gemini with its twins, Auriga made beautiful by Capella, and Taurus with the Pleiades and Hyades.

Even after the lapse of so many years, I remember that winter night as yesterday — the air, the moon, and the evening star over the shining mountains, like the vision of another world — the realm of the spirit.

CHAPTER XIX

THE MAD INDIAN

NEXT morning there was a below-zero temperature inside the cabin. The stove was as cold as ice; and the kettle, which was boiling when I went to bed, was frozen solid. I built a fire and cooked breakfast — bacon, potatoes, and rutabagas. The wounded Yellow Bird lay gloomily in bed. Then I fed the cows and calves in the sheds. Many of the chickens were frozen in their snug house underground. The cats, which lived in the cattle-sheds, were like savage beasts. When I drew off my gloves to feed them, a cat sprang at my hand and fastened its teeth in my thumb. They fought over the meat and tore it with snarls.

I found our two dogs in a deep hole under the haystack. One named Red Rover showed his fangs and slunk away. He was wild and suspicious by nature; his father was a coyote and while young he ran with a coyote pack. But after I fed him, he watched for my coming. He was no longer afraid and became my faithful friend.

Kutenai, my saddle horse, I kept in the cattle-shed. Every day he liked to play in the corral, trying to escape me by running, until I swung myself on his bare back and we went for a swift gallop in the pasture, where the snow had been trampled by the cattle.

From early morning until night I was busy, feeding the crippled Yellow Bird and the live stock and chopping wood for the hungry stove. I cooked three meals a day and washed the dishes; baked bread and swept the cabin; shoveled snow and kept the ford at the river open for horses and cattle to drink.

Every afternoon near sunset, I fed the big cattle herd,

chopping hay from the frozen stack and carrying it to them in the pasture. I had narrow escapes on foot from wild steers trying to kick the hay from my fork; and from cows with calves — sometimes they drove me on a run to the fence.

I tried to save time in the feeding, by scattering the hay in long windrows near the stack. But this only gave me more trouble. When the hungry cattle saw me spreading hay on the other side of the fence, they began to bellow and paw the snow. A steer tried to get over the fence, but stuck in the middle; another followed; and then the entire herd made a rush through the fence. I had to saddle my horse to drive them away from the stack.

One cold night, when Yellow Bird and I sat smoking with our feet against the stove, we heard a strange thumping against the cabin wall, at the back of the kitchen. Yellow Bird was afraid and showed it. He had a superstitious dread of the mysterious, of big storms and of going about in the dark. I was not superstitious by nature; yet I had a queer feeling when that mysterious sound began again.

Something struck the cabin and was followed by a rhythmic beating against the outside wall. The weather was cold, but windless. When the sound died away there was silence. I got up and peered through the frost-covered window. Yellow Bird quickly blew out the light. At that moment the same thought came to both of us — it was the Mad Indian. He had come to get a shot at us. People were afraid on both sides of the line, in Alberta and Montana. Ever since the fall we had been hearing blood-curdling tales. He came silently in the dark and shot people who stood in the light; outside he stabbed them with a long knife.

We got our rifles and held them ready, standing in the shadow, away from the glow of the fire, expecting any moment to hear a shot, to feel the sting of a bullet, or to see a wild face at the window. But nothing happened and we got tired of waiting; we hung blankets over the windows and went to bed.

Then came another blow that shook the cabin. I sat up to listen; Yellow Bird made no sound; he did not move in his bed. After the mysterious beating had died away, I was no longer afraid; even a mad Indian would not wait so long in the snow and bitter cold.

So I put on my heavy socks and coat and, taking my rifle, went cautiously to the door and waited. When the sound came again, I opened the door and ran to the back of the cabin. An animal, the size of a large cat, bounded away in the dark. It went so fast I had no time to shoot. Then, under the roof and hanging from the outside cabin-wall, I found the mangled body of a goose, which we had left there forgotten. Beneath the goose hung a long timber-saw. When the starving cat jumped at the carcass, it clung with teeth and claws and struggled, thus moving the big saw, which made the rhythmical beating.

A mounted policeman, an Indian named Many Guns, came to our cabin for shelter from the blizzard. He entered without a word and for a while sat silently by the fire. Then he said abruptly, "I came from the north. I had a bad trip."

We gave him food, and after a smoke he spoke again:

"My horse is worn out and my arm is frozen. Yesterday I crossed the Hudson Bay Divide; the snow lies in terrible drifts. My horse broke through the ice in crossing a river. I nearly froze to death. But some Indians helped me. Out there they starve; their food is nearly gone."

That night Many Guns, one of the Indian Mounted Police, told us about his north journey. He said:

Story of the Mad Indian

"In the autumn, I went across the line to hunt Opiowan, a Blood Indian. He killed many people, both Indian and white. He was once a peaceful man who lived with his two wives. The youngest, Pretty Wolverine, was his favorite. They were happy until a former lover of the youngest wife came to their lodge. Then Opiowan was jealous. He warned the man to stay away.

"One day the husband told his wives he was going away on a journey. But he did not go far. He hid and watched his tepee. He saw the lover and his youngest wife go together into the woods. The husband followed and caught them. He killed that rival and mutilated him with his knife; but he did not harm the woman. He told her to go home; and then he went on his journey. Soon the body of the lover was found by the North-West Mounted Police; but no one knew the murderer.

"Then Opiowan came home and lived with his wives as formerly. But he was afraid and did not want to see any one.

"And what was the cause of his fear?" I asked

"He was afraid of everything," said Many Guns. "At night he kept seeing the face of the man he killed and could not sleep. He believed every one was against him; he trembled at every sound — the barking of a dog, a running horse. He was afraid of the police, and whenever he heard the sound of hoofs near his tepee, he wanted to hide. He thought he was going mad; he no longer cared to live. Then he made a vow, that he would kill as many people as he could before he died. He told his wives he would die fighting like a brave warrior.

"One night he went to the cabin of a white man. He shot him through the window as he stood in the light. He saw him fall; he sang his war-song and danced; he painted his face and started on the warpath; he was ready to die.

"He made his wives take down their tepee and they fled to the mountains. From a cliff he saw the Mounted Police who had come to take him. He escaped with both his wives and they hid in the forest. They went north along the mountains.

Whenever they got hungry, Opiowan took all the food he wanted from Indian camps. One night he stole into a white settlement near the foot of the mountains. He shot a white man and took all the ammunition he could get. The police followed his trail, but he escaped into the hills.

"By this time it was the end of autumn, and winter came quickly with cold and deep snow. But Opiowan was always on the move. He had a way of shooting people through cabin windows, as they stood in the light. He was like a myth. He was said to be in many places at the same time, and to travel miraculous distances.

"But, one night a heavy snow fell in the mountains and his wives left him. They fled to an Indian camp on the plains. Then Opiowan was driven from the mountains by cold and hunger. He came to the tepee of his brother in the Blood camp. His brother took him in and tried to hide him. But the Mounted Police trailed the murderer and surrounded the camp. Then Opiowan the Mad Indian killed himself. He cut his wrists with an awl and bled to death; and that is the end of my story."

Not till then was the feeling of dread removed from the people both Indian and white who lived near the border-line, on the lonely prairies and in the foothills of the Rocky Mountains. The tales about him may have been exaggerated but the story of the Mounted Policeman proved that the Mad Indian was not a myth.

CHAPTER XX

COMING OF THE CHINOOK

AFTER many days the scout came back alone to his ranch, and we rode together on the open plains to look for missing cattle. We found cows and calves dying without food or drink, and a young steer that had fallen through the ice, frozen in the river. We hauled it ashore with our lariats and, after dragging the carcass back to the cabin, skinned and butchered it; the way Indians used to cut up buffalo. We took out the tongue, short-ribs, boss-ribs, shoulders and hams, briskets and belly-pieces. There was no waste; we used the entrails for eating, saving the hide for tanning, also the brains and liver; the tissue was used for sinew.

Then another blizzard came with more snow, intense cold, and a gale from the north. That night as we sat by the stove, the side of our bodies towards the fire was warm, the other numb with cold. Whenever we opened the door, the cold air formed a cloud of steam, which shot along the floor and made a fall of snow on the threshold. Then the roof began to crack, and loud reports came from ice in the river. I heard the booming of a bursting tree, and then of a water-filled hollow. The scout said:

"Those are signs of more bad weather. My friend Bear Paw, who lives near the mountains, says it is over forty years since we had a moon with such bad storms. Before they came, he saw a mysterious ball of fire hang over the forest. Bear Paw keeps tribal records on buffalo skins: deaths of chiefs, cold winters, summers of drought and of plenty."

It was a dreary time when our oil gave out; I could neither read nor write. There were only six hours of daylight, with darkness for the remaining eighteen.

Big gray wolves and packs of coyotes driven by hunger came close to the ranch. One night I heard them feasting on the carcass of a cow not far from our cabin. Finally they became so bold we made baits of poisoned meat and placed them on the hills, dragging the bloody head of the steer behind our horses to lead them to the baits.

I saw sun dogs in the sky, shining dimly, like great crosses of light near the sun. Then shadows appeared over the Rocky Mountains, strange "snow banners," or cloud-shaped drifts in the sky, stretching out from the summits of the high peaks, waving and shimmering in the rays of the sun — a sign that a powerful norther was raging over the mountains. The light dry snowdust, being driven by the wind up the flanks of the high peaks, was carried over them and into the sky, each peak having its own snow banner, all pointing the same way, all gleaming and waving against the blue sky.

That night a nor'wester came roaring over the plains, with a whirling wind that sought to lift the roof and terrible gusts, which struck the walls like a battering-ram, until the cabin swayed and trembled.

The scout sat dejected by the fire. He was filled with gloom; and when I wakened towards midnight he was still there, with his head bowed. I heard him pray earnestly and in a low voice to the Sun:

> "Father, have pity and help us.
> I am praying for my people.
> The Indians starve and are cold.
> Break up the clouds and shine upon us.
> Take what I say and send the Chinook.
> Father, the Sun, have pity and help my people."

At last came a day with signs of better weather. At dawn the sky was vivid green with clouds of pink and gold; and at midday water was dripping from the roof and the thick frost melted from the windows.

Then on Kutenai I went forth to hunt, following the tops

of the ridges. I saw tracks of a wolf pack, and the large round footprints of a pair of Rocky Mountain lions, with marks where their long tails dragged in the snow. But I had no luck. The traveling was bad; the low places and gullies were choked with snow, and the plains covered with huge drifts, following one another like billows of the ocean, with smaller waves on top. The bright sun was blinding on the white surface snow, and the air filled with particles of floating ice. My horse's hoofs rang on the icy crust; sometimes it bore our weight; at others his feet broke through. One moment his hind quarters were down, at another he seemed to be standing on his head. Once he slipped on an ice-covered hill and turned a complete somersault. I flew over his head and landed safely in a snowdrift. The only game I saw was a bunch of antelope. But they were feeding on the bare summit of a ridge with no cover near, and I had no way of stalking them. After that I turned back because the sun was getting low.

I remember well how the cabin looked that night, after my trip on the snowy wastes. Our table was covered with a cloth of bright red; the steam rising from a bountiful supper of rib-roast; the glow of the firelight over all, and the glistening of frost-covered windows.

Then the south wind rose and the river was covered with mist. Misty clouds hung along the horizon, and I saw two rainbows at a distance from the sun. Banks of heavy clouds settled low over the Rocky Mountains, with another great bank higher up. In the west the sky became as black as ink and the color of indigo at the zenith. The wind went down and there came a strange stillness.

Suddenly, from out of the west I heard a dull roar, like the roll of distant thunder. "Listen!" cried the scout. "The Chinook! At last! Good-Old-Man comes from the mountains to run out over the plains."

I looked towards the Rockies and saw dense clouds of snow

swept into the air by the force of a mighty wind. It passed the foothills and came swiftly over the plains, like banks of driven fog. Then the gale struck us carrying masses of melting snow, which covered us from head to foot. In a few minutes the temperature rose forty degrees.

A Chinook wind occurs on the east side of the Rocky Mountains, whenever a well-developed cyclonic storm passes over the northern part of the United States. It blows from the direction of the country occupied by the Chinook Indians. It is not a wind from the Japanese Current of the Pacific Ocean, as is commonly believed. It is a "descending wind" that flows over the Rocky Mountains, following the low pressure on the eastern side, which draws it down the mountains to the plains. Thus the wind is compressed and has capacity for holding heat. When the Chinook blows, precipitation ceases, clouds disappear and the air is dry.

That Chinook blew for three days. It went down in the evening after the sun, but came again in the morning, melting the snow as if by magic. In a few hours as much snow had melted as by a gentle thaw of many days.

Our river was a wonderful sight. It became a raging torrent that whirled and foamed and burst its icy covering. The huge drifts of snow that filled the valleys and were piled along the river banks looked yellow and shrunken and lost their graceful curves. The cowhouse and other sheds were flooded. In the night the air was filled with strange sounds — the running and dripping of water, the slipping and sliding of melting snow and ice.

For days we were storm-bound, because oi tne floods and the force of that mighty wind. Finally the grass-covered summits of the ridges appeared — the first time in many weeks. Then we gave cattle and horses their last feed of hay at the ranch, and drove them forth to pasture on the hills.

CHAPTER XXI

BEGINNING OF SPRING

THE end of winter I was camped with my friends Onesta and Nitana, near the log cabin of Little Creek and his wife Strikes-on-Both-Sides, my Indian sister. The heavy snow had melted from the prairie, but drifts still lay under the summits of high ridges. The air was mild with mists over the valleys; streams overflowing their banks and with soft ice running. I saw the first flocks of white geese returning from the south, also ducks and whistling swans, all pressing northward on warm sunny days when the wind was in the south. And then the big storm, which Indians say comes every year, "when horses begin to shed their winter hair." It began in the night, coming straight from the north. Then veered to all points of the compass.

During the worst days, we stayed in our lodges and slept. But I was strangely contented and happy. My mind seemed to have reverted to the state of a savage. I was alive to everything and alert. Things about me interested me — the life and simple pleasures of the Indians, the habits of birds and wild animals, the flowers and trees.

The cabin of Little Creek had one small room, where he lived with his wife and children, two dogs, a snowshoe rabbit, pet hawk, and a black ground squirrel. Strikes-on-Both-Sides found it on Sun River. She rescued it from a band of yellow ground squirrels, which were trying to kill it because it was black.

On stormy nights I liked to sit by my cosy inside fire, listening to the wind as it rose and fell, whistling through the lodge-poles and humming against the ropes, the hissing of whirling snow and beating of rain and sleet. Sometimes I felt uplifted by a good and controlling spirit. I wanted to do something to make people happy that they might have time to think and dream, and be able to enjoy the world of nature. And, as I lay on my couch of robes and blankets, looking into the flames of my small lodge-fire, I dreamed of Indian chiefs and medicine men before the white race came. There was something very lofty and noble about these aboriginal Americans; deep in their natures, they had qualities hidden, which white men in their literature have ever failed to reach.

After being storm-bound many days, I wakened one morning to the musical song of a lark sparrow seated overhead, on top of one of my lodge-poles. The clouds had rolled away and the sun shone in a sky of deepest blue. It was the beginning of spring.

Then we took down our lodges and traveled southward along the Rockies, until we came to the valley of Two Medicine River. How good it was to enter that warm and sunny valley after the bleak and wintry plains; we were protected from cold winds by high cutbanks, groves of big cottonwood trees and thickest of poplars and willows.

It was one of those rare days in spring, when all nature awakes and becomes radiant with beauty. Everything was new — grass, leaves, and the scent of wild flowers. Some of the thickets had small green leaves. Buds were bursting on the cottonwood trees; balsam poplars had young leaves in a lovely shade of yellow-green; through every opening in the trees I saw the deep blue sky. Blue violets grew along the river bank. In the meadows were daisies, yellow violets, and blue forget-me-nots. The sun was hot, bringing forth the fragrance of wild flowers, leaves and buds. Butterflies and bees were abroad. Birds sang in thickets of alder and willows, in sloughs and water-meadows. All nature was busy and alive to the joy of living.

ONESTA

In a suit of soft-tanned deerskin decorated with colored quills and bordered with strips of ermine

We made camp in a meadow; and then I went with Little Creek to explore the valley. On a rocky cliff, surrounded by sharp pinnacles, the place where an eagle would build its nest, we found the graves of two women, one a young wife who died in childbirth, the other killed by a jealous lover. Their graves were placed on the other side of the valley from their former home, in the belief that ghosts would not cross a river to bother the living.

We saw the grave of an aged medicine woman in a big cottonwood tree. The body rested on a rude scaffold of poles among the branches, surrounded with utensils and articles of clothing for use in the spirit world. In another tree were the bodies of two Blood women from Canada, who had died while on a visit to relatives. From the branches hung ornaments of beadwork — sacrifices by women who mourned.

On the north side of the valley was a high cliff, over which Indians of long ago drove herds of buffalo, in the days before they had horses or firearms. From the top of the precipice a level plain stretched away to the grass-land of open prairies, with two ancient and overgrown fences of stones, which had been used by the Indians as guides in buffalo drives. Near by were signs of an ancient camp — eight circles of large stones, deeply imbedded in the soil and overgrown with grass, where eight skin lodges once stood.

That night we sat by our tiny camp-fire and talked about those ancient hunters and how they chased the buffalo. Onesta said:

"In those days of long ago, summer was the time of plenty. Then our people used flint knives and arrow-points instead of guns. They had pots of stone, and bone-scrapers for tanning skins. Dogs were their beasts of burden instead of horses, and people carried things on their backs. They killed buffalo in great numbers by driving them over cliffs. When the herds moved in from the grass-land, they followed our stone fences; they ran over a cliff and were killed; the wounded were caught in a corral at the bottom.

"The chief picked a strong runner to lead the buffalo. On the day of the run, that man rose early and went forth before sunrise. He covered himself with a robe and wore horns on his head. He kept moving about until the buffalo herd saw him and stood looking. Then he led them between the stone piles; and Indians lying hidden rose up; they waved their robes and shouted; they stampeded the buffalo, which ran over the cliff and were killed.

"Then the women came to cut up the carcasses. They used the skins of old animals for lodges and those of young ones for robes. They carried the meat on dog travois back to their tepees, spreading it on poles to dry in the sun; making pemmican and mixing it with marrowfat and dried berries, which they kept in rawhide cases for use in winter."

Thus Onesta talked that night.

We stayed in Two Medicine Valley, until our horses were through shedding their hair and became fat on the new grass. Then we broke camp and moved up towards the Rocky Mountains. It was an Indian custom to go every spring to the forests on the mountains, to cut new lodge-poles for their summer camps and to gather roots and wild vegetables for both eating and healing.

We followed the valley westward, riding through grassy meadows with gardens of wild flowers. Masses of loco weed were in bloom, growing in dense spikes of brilliant pink, purple and blue, clusters of gaillardia with radiant yellow blossoms, and fields of phacelia, a rich carpet of white and blue, flaming Indian paint-brush, drooping bluebells, and shooting stars.

Along the banks of the river were thickets of peach-leaf willows, fragrant balsam poplars, and cottonwood trees, with their cottony tufts of seeds. Lark sparrows were singing, and willow thrushes with mellow flutelike notes. A little bird called "black-breast" by the Indians (horned lark) ran along the ground ahead of our horses. It sang at all times, through the heat of midday and even at night. On the prairie he would spring from the grass and soar into the air. Then extending his wings he would sink slowly to the ground, always against the wind, hovering like a butterfly and singing his cheerful rippling song like that of the English linnet.

But the most wonderful of all the birds was the soaring song of the Missouri skylark. At first I could not see them. They sang so high in the air, they were like specks in the blue sky. Their sweet strains came from overhead like a song from heaven. When several skylarks were singing, the air was filled with the tender strains. Then, after hovering awhile, they closed their wings and pitched to the ground to hide themselves in the long grass.

CHAPTER XXII

OUR CAMP IN THE MOUNTAINS

We camped in a broad and sunny valley, with lovely grassy meadows, groups of firs and tapering spruces; where clear streams of ice-cold water wound their way through thickets of alder and willows. Across a lake was a snow-capped peak, with foaming cataracts falling over timbered cliffs, and a hanging valley where the slopes of two mountains met in a massive rock wall.

That evening the fish were rising in the lake. After picketing my horse, I lost no time in getting out my rod and fly-book to fish the outlet, where the current was broad and swift. From a high bank at the mouth I made my first cast. The water was clear and many fish in sight, darting hither and thither over a bottom of clean sand and gravel, with pebbles of many shapes and colors shining in the sunlight.

Soon I had a strike. My line tightened and there came a holding back, a palpitation of the rod. Then a big tail flashed in the sunlight and thrashed the surface. It was an open river with good going along the shore. I gave my fish plenty of line and held him in the current. Before long I had a four-pound Dolly Varden flopping on the pebbly shore. I caught several Dolly Vardens, and then a double catch of brook trout, a two-pound and a one-pound fish. My largest brook trout weighed three pounds.

We pitched our lodges near the lake, in a meadow where wild geranium and blue camas were in bloom. Little Creek and his wife were in one of the tepees, Onesta and Nitana and their small daughter Yellow Mink in the other. I slept outside under a pine tree and on the shore of the lake. Overhead were the feathery arms of the tree, with clusters of cones at the ends of the branches. The ground was covered with fragrant pine needles, piles of cone scales and shells where the squirrels had been feasting.

From my bed I watched the stars come slowly out above the dark battlements of the mountains. Overhead the night-hawks were feeding, pitching about and diving with a rushing sound of their wings. I saw a flock of ducks on the lake and a solitary beaver swimming in the twilight. After dark the night wind began to blow, sighing through the branches of my pine tree. I heard the lapping of water along the sandy shore, roar of an avalanche, and the distant thunder of cataracts wind-borne across the lake.

There is no sweeter chorus than the songs of birds in the early northern dawn. I heard thrushes and purple finches in the willows and Western yellow-throats and evening grosbeaks in groves of quaking aspen. Along the lake-shore the dominant singers were the white-crowned sparrows with sweet and uplifted melody.

After sunrise I had a swim luxuriously cold. I dove deep and gazed through the depths of the clear green water, while little bubbles floated around my body; then came up into the sunlight and floated on my back, gazing into a sky of deepest blue. For a moment I lay still and my body seemed to leave me; then swam into the lake, cutting through the clear cold water until I landed on a sandy beach, where the sun felt hot on my back and I tingled from head to foot.

My Indian friends never burdened themselves with work. They lay in the sun for hours and did not work until they felt like it. We cut the straight and slender trees of lodge-pole pine for tepee poles, peeling off the bark and standing them in the sun to dry. The women also gathered plants and herbs in meadow and forest, both for eating and healing; and they helped me make a botanical collection [1] of my own.

[1] Medicinal and Useful Plants of the Blackfoot Indians. See Appendix.

For vegetables they gathered wild onions, wild potatoes, cow parsnip, bitterroot and prairie turnip. But the camas was their favorite vegetable. It had a root like a small potato and had a sweet flavor. They roasted the stalks of the cow parsnip, when they were tender and juicy in the spring; and dried the leaves of bearberry for tobacco, also pipsissewa or princess pine. They used a lichen that grows on pine trees as yellow dye, a pore fungus for cleaning buckskin, and yellow orthocarpus for dyeing skins. For eye inflammation they used the blossoms of horsemint, the long plumed avens for coughs, Oregon grape for stomach trouble, and gum plant for the liver.

One day I went with Little Creek for a hunting trip on the mountains. He took his rifle and I my camera for pictures. Little Creek was a good guide. He had the instinct of an Indian for traveling in the forest and a wonderful memory for landmarks. He was a fountain of shrewd wisdom and something of a philosopher.

We crossed a valley to the base of a mountain; then went slowly up the steep slope, stopping to rest and smoke and listen to the birds, to see the trees and flowers and look for signs of game. I heard a Gambel sparrow singing among the spruces. It closely resembles the white-crowned sparrow and is related to our Eastern white-throat. But its song has only three notes which are of different tones, like the sounding of clear bells. Many squirrels chattered at our approach and ceased from hiding cones to watch us pass. We raised some blue grouse, saw signs of wapiti and moose and the splay footprints of a wolverine, called "Mountain Devil" by the Indians, because of its meanness and wonderful cunning.

We went through a chain of meadows with masses of wild flowers of many shades and colors, crimson, yellow, pink and blue, growing luxuriantly among the tall grasses. A warm wind swept across their faces, bearing a delicious fragrance that reminded me of the sweet clover fields of our Eastern States in June.

Deep down in the soft grass were anemones and lady's-slipper, and along streams masses of pink wild heliotrope, bluebells, and shooting stars — vivid little red flowers that held their pointed yellow noses downward towards the ground. In the woods were tiny twin flowers, golden arnica growing high above the forest floor, and clematis with lovely purple blossoms, festooning with its vines the shrubs and logs and lower branches of trees. The Indian called clematis "Ghost's Lariat," because it catches people and trips them up in the dark.

In the forest the largest trees were Engelmann spruce and Douglas fir, growing in scattered groups, some one hundred feet in height. But the chief tree was the lodge-pole pine, tall, slender, and clean-shafted.

Near timber-line many trees were broken, having been thrown by the southwest wind. The forest became open and the trees shorter, till we passed from the cover and came to battered and storm-twisted "limber-pines." Some of them were centuries old, undersized and imperfect, with trunks only a foot in diameter and several feet in height; some trailed on the ground, like serpents and long-bodied animals; others, in exposed places on the mountain side, looked like tattered and wind-torn banners, with branches all flung out on one side of the trunk.

On the high slopes it was still early spring; the flowers followed close upon retreating snowdrifts. There the growing season is so brief, the spring and autumn flora bloom together. High up I saw blossoms in all their vernal freshness, that had long ago faded on the prairies.

Along the borders of streams and in mossy bogs, the swamp laurel was in flower, its blossoms rosy pink, also snow buttercups and the Western globeflower. Close by a snowbank, I saw a carpet of yellow snow lilies, a belt of solid gold, false forget-me-nots and chalice cups of cream-white blossoms and fluffy gold-green centers.

We followed an old game trail across an upland meadow, through a carpet of heath and heather with delicate pink flowers. On the rocks were colored lichens; dainty wind-flowers bloomed in every sheltered nook. In crevices of cliffs were maidenhair ferns, and in moist meadows the fragrant alpine lady fern.

Little Creek was a tireless climber and as sure-footed as a mountain goat. We crossed snowdrifts, ledges, broken rock and treacherous shale, climbing along frowning red precipices where I dared not look down, but kept my eyes on the sky and rock wall. Finally, we gained the summit and stood at the edge of a cliff, where the mountain fell abruptly a thousand feet. Far below in the valley lay our miniature camp, with its white lodges on the lake-shore. Everywhere were snow-clad peaks and glistening glaciers, rock-strewn ridges and gorges with rushing streams, forest slopes and valley lakes of emerald and blue. Far off the green ocean of the prairie stretched into the eastern horizon and hundreds of miles beyond.

About us was a wilderness of solitude and silence, not a sound of bird or beast, only the rushing of the summit wind. Dark blue was the sky; the air pine-scented, clear and luminous, uplifting the soul and attuning it to the majesty of our surroundings.

Pointing to a mountain that overlooked the plains, Little Creek said: "That is the place where Swift Eagle died."

"How did he come to die there?" I asked.

"He was wounded in a fight with the Flathead Indians," replied Little Creek. "He was the leader of a band of warriors. Early one summer they crossed the mountains after horses. They came to a Flathead camp in a park, which was surrounded by forest. That night, when they were ready to make off with the horses of the Flatheads, Swift Eagle came upon an Indian of the Nez Percé tribe, who was after the same horses. He was a famous chief named Crazy-Cut-Top-Knot, but Swift Eagle did not know this.

"The Nez Percé saw the Blackfoot chief and rushed at him with his war club. They fought hand-to-hand. Swift Eagle struck the stranger with his knife. But before he died, the Nez Percé swung his terrible war club and hit Swift Eagle.

"It was night, and the Blackfoot warriors found their chief lying beside the body of the Nez Percé. They recognized the war club. It was made from the huge antler of a bull elk and was different from all others. They knew it belonged to the famous chief, Crazy-Cut-Top-Knot.

"Then they made a litter of poles and carried Swift Eagle across the mountains. After they had passed the summit, he opened his eyes. His warriors told him he would soon be home. But he said:

"'My children, it is useless to carry me farther. Before I started on this trip I had a strong dream that I would never come back alive.'

"He told them to take him to a high cliff on that mountain. He died there and his followers left beside him the war club of the Nez Percé chief."

After the story we sat awhile on the summit to look out over the plains, and then descended into a basin, a beautiful amphitheater with a peaceful little lake, clusters of pines and a moist green meadow with a sheep-lick. In the meadow were golden snow lilies, sky-blue forget-me-nots, and the rose-red monkey flower, growing close to a cold brook that came leaping down the mountain. At the head of the basin was a lofty rock wall, with silvery waterfalls and a great gray glacier, close to the saw-tooth cliffs of the Continental Divide.

Then we lay silently behind some stunted spruces and watched the sheep-lick for game. We saw some conies on the slide-rock, a timid little rabbit-people who live among the rocks at timber-line. They scampered about, squeaking and running back and forth with grass and flowers in their mouths. From a rock-cliff a hoary marmot came waddling across a barren slope to his feeding grounds on the green turf. He was gray in color, with short legs and heavy body and a white band round his nose.

The only sound was the singing of a waterfall at the head of the lake, and of the brook flowing softly through the grass. Suddenly a stone came tumbling down, followed by a rattling of shale; a small ram came into view, making his way leisurely along the mountain, stopping now and then to take a bite of grass. The spot where he had chosen to feed was beyond our range and without cover to approach. But the wind was favorable. Then Little Creek crawled among the rocks to get near enough for a shot. Finally I saw him lie flat, and with elbows resting on the ground, he took aim and fired. The ram leaped into the air and started up the mountain with wonderful speed. At several more shots it scarcely seemed to touch the ground, but bounded along and disappeared among the high cliffs.

Then we left the basin and followed the gorge of a mountain torrent, which descended into the valley. We came down through a series of parks and meadows with many kinds of grasses, the brightest greens I have ever seen; and an open forest of alpine firs, with long-pointed crowns and blue-green leaves and bark so pale and smooth their trunks seemed carved from stone.

We came upon two black-tail deer, a buck and a doe, and, as we had the wind in our favor, we approached under cover of the forest to within one hundred yards. Little Creek rested his rifle in a forked tree and fired. At the shot the buck stretched out his limbs and bounded away, running in a zigzag course, then round and round until he fell dead. And, after cutting up the carcass, we took the meat back to camp.

By our camp-fire my Indian friends talked about a trip to Canada. Nomads by nature, they loved to wander and were happier on the move. They liked trips of all kinds, to hunt and fish and visit friends; but most of all to go among their northern relatives, the Bloods, North Piegans and North Blackfoot.

Said my Indian sister: "We should start right away; the weather is warm and clear; this is the best time of year to travel."

"But we cannot get a permit from our Agent," replied Onesta. "And besides the North-West Mounted Police would stop us at the Line. I know Indians who tried to cross into Canada and were stopped. The police turned them back and they had to come home."

For a moment there was silence; and then I said: "Your Agent is my friend. From him I have a pass to go whither I please. You can all come with me and we will make the north trip together."

Then Onesta was glad and said: "We will take you to our friends and relatives among the Blood Indians, to the tribe of the North Piegans and camp of Brings-down-the-Sun. He is my uncle and I shall ask him to help you. He lives with his children and grandchildren in a camp on Old Man's River. He is the wisest of all our medicine men; and knows more than any one about our legends and worship of the Sun."

"Let us go at once," I replied. "I want to visit that uncle of yours."

Then were all happy and like children they showed it. They wanted to start next morning at the rising of the sun.

CHAPTER XXIII

OUR NORTH EXPEDITION

We brought in our horses at daybreak and were on our way to Canada soon after sunrise, following an old Indian trail northward over the prairie; winding along the benches of round-topped ridges and down their long slopes, through wide grassy valleys and across streams and blue-gray rivers, clear and icy cold, always following the best grade like an old buffalo trail.

The first day we traveled far; we did not stop until evening shadows were touching the rounded summits of the grass-covered hills, camping for the night at an old Indian ground thickly strewn with buffalo bones from former feasts. Broken tepee poles were scattered about, bare frames of old sweat-lodges and blackened stones of camp-fires.

On the summit of a high ridge stood a pile of stones, sharp and clear against the sky of evening, like the solitary figure of a sentinel, marking the grave of a chief named Red Blanket.

That night Onesta told me to picket my saddle horse close to camp because of a ghost. He warned me, saying:

"Old Red Blanket, who is buried on yonder hill, was a good man and kind; but his ghost is mean. It does not like people to camp here and drives away their horses in the night. That hill was his favorite haunt when he was alive. For many years he went there to meditate and dream. When he was dying he asked his family to place his body there."

We did not heed Onesta's warning and turned our horses loose to feed in the night. Strangely enough they were all gone in the morning — driven by the ghost, Onesta said. We had to walk a long distance to find them.

Our next camp was on the open prairie east of Divide

Mountain, a triangular peak of the Rockies, where two great watersheds meet — the Hudson Bay Divide, a smooth ridge running east and west, and the Rocky Mountain chain extending north and south.

That evening our women had time to prepare the meat for our journey, boiling the boss-ribs in a kettle; the rest was cut into strips and stretched on poles to dry over a fire.

In the meantime with Little Creek I went to the camp of a widow named Katoya. The bodies of her husband and children were on a hill near her home. The lonely old woman welcomed us to her lodge and was glad to tell about the past. In our talk with her she said:

"How happy we used to be at this time of year, the beginning of summer, when our hunters came home with plenty of meat. Then I said to my husband: 'Invite now our friends; this night we shall have a feast.'

"Then he would ask some of the old people in for a smoke. Near the time of the first big snow in the autumn, we hastened to move away from the mountains and camp on the prairie. We went down a river, stopping to camp at our favorite camp-grounds and waiting for buffalo to come near. We were careful to choose the best place for our long winter camp. In those days we were happy. There were no white men and we wandered where we pleased. The buffalo were plentiful; the antelope of the prairies were fat and made good eating.

"After my husband killed some buffalo, we brought in the hides. I tanned the skins, stretching them on the ground to dry in the sun; I oiled them with the brains and liver and made them soft by working them. Some of the skins I used for making clothes, and others for parfleches and berry-bags. After I had finished tanning our robes for winter, I had nothing to worry about. My husband and children had plenty to eat; they all slept warm on the coldest nights."

Then we left the old woman and returned to our own camp. Instead of taking time to pitch our tepees, the women made an ingenious shelter by stretching a canvas sheet over a wagon tongue for a ridge pole and fastened it to the ground on both sides. I made my bed outside, on the grassy bank of a small stream, where the night wind blew fresh from the mountains, bearing the fragrance of pine forests and flowery meadows.

That night we sat by our camp-fire and talked about ghosts. Because of the near-by graves on the hill, the Indians thought that spirits were near. Onesta said:

"The worst kind of ghosts are the 'haunting spirits.' I have always been afraid of them. They prowl around at night and try to harm people. They are unhappy in the spirit world and envy the living. They are the ones who use the ghost arrows, which bring sickness and death. Outside in the dark, they shoot at people. Sometimes they strike people on the head and make them crazy; they paralyze the limbs of people and make their faces crooked. Some ghosts don't like to see people eat in the night, so they punish them by pulling their mouths crooked; and sometimes they kill people that are ill.

"I have heard ghosts make a noise at night by striking the lodge-poles; sometimes they make a queer sound like whistling, overhead in the smoke-hole of the tepee, and sometimes they laugh. But they never come inside if a fire is burning; and they are always afraid of the smell of burning hair."

Here Onesta stopped abruptly. Just outside the bright circle of our firelight, we heard something moving through the grass. It sounded like an animal walking stealthily. Little Creek seized his rifle and was ready to shoot. This "thing" glided slowly along and into a thicket of willows. Onesta said it sounded like a cougar. But Strikes-on-Both-Sides said it acted like an Indian who came to watch our camp. Then they all agreed it was a ghost. And next morning, when we went back to see the widow, Katoya, in her tepee, she confirmed that belief. For she said:

"Last night I could not sleep. I lay awake thinking of the happy days of the past. Just before dawn, the ghost of my dead son came to see me. He has been my protector for many years and often visits me at night. Last night he was hungry. After I gave him food, he said: 'Mother, there are strangers here. Be not afraid; they are good people and will do you no harm. This night I watched their camp. I saw Little Creek, Onesta, and White Weasel. They were seated beside a fire. I went too close and they heard me. Little Creek was going to shoot. I was afraid this might frighten you, so I came away. Then I met the ghost of my father coming down the hill from his grave. He said he was coming to watch over you because of strangers. But I told him to go back to his grave and rest in peace. I promised him no harm would come to you.'"

After that the old woman bowed her head and sat in silence. So we went away and left her to the companionship of her ghostly dead.

Then came one of those violent changes in the weather, which are common on the high plateau country of the northwest. Dark clouds came down from the north and settled over prairies and mountains. We broke camp in a hurry, and got under way before the storm set in. A bank of angry clouds advanced rapidly over the prairie; from it extended curving black streaks, moving in waves downwards toward the earth — the sign of a severe hail storm.

When the temperature fell, we stopped and unhitched our horses, tying them with long ropes to the wheels, while we got under the wagons — just in time. The sky became dark and we heard the distant roar of falling hail. Then the storm broke with lightning and thunder, and a deluge of hail that covered the ground.

Heavy clouds enveloped us all the way to the summit of the Hudson Bay Divide. But on the other side, the northern slope, it was a glorious day with the sun shining in a clear sky. Before us lay a vast expanse of grass-covered prairie, level to the horizon; west was the main range of the Rocky Mountains, peak after peak, snow-capped and snow-mantled, stretching northward out of sight.

Descending from the divide, we entered a broad and fertile valley, where our trail led along a shallow stream. At the head of this valley rose the sharp peak of Chief Mountain, 4000 feet above the surrounding plain, and an altitude of 9056 feet above the sea. It is a lone citadel of rock, an eastern spur of the Rocky Mountains, a landmark of the international boundary line between Canada and the United States. The Indians named it "Chief," because they could see it so far from the plains. It overlooked the Old North Trail of the Indians, which ran north and south along the foot of the Rockies. In those days of long ago, what sights could have been seen from the precipitous slopes of Chief Mountain — great herds of buffalo and graceful antelope, deer, wapiti and moose, and bands of primitive red men moving north and south over the broad plateaus and along the foothills of the Rocky Mountains.

We came that night to a broad stream called Green Banks by the Indians (St. Mary's River), and camped near the lodge of an old medicine man named Spotted Eagle, a friend of Mad Wolf, my Indian father.

He had a wrinkled, merry old face, with gray hair which was separated into braids over his shoulders by bands of otter-skin. I found him lying on a couch of robes and blankets fanning himself with the wing of an eagle. The day was warm and he was naked except for a loin-cloth.

When I entered, he gave an odd exclamation of surprise, intended to be humorous. Then he sat up, and made his toilet, shaving by pulling the straggling gray hairs from his wrinkled face with a pair of small tweezers, and combing his hair with the bristly tail of a porcupine; and all the time he talked.

He liked to joke and had a reputation as a wit. After each of his jokes he laughed and winked. At the barking of a dog or neighing of a horse, he would give a startled cry as if frightened; and made a grimace. He did this as a joke and to make me laugh, which I always did to please him. He loved funny stories, especially of Old Man (Napi), a strange and mythical character known to many Indian tribes. He was a sort of creator and teacher, but at the same time a trickster who played evil pranks. Some of the tales about him were brutal and obscene. But Indians, both old and young, always liked the Old Man Stories, because of their power to entertain and make people laugh. Spotted Eagle told them to me, as he would tell fairy tales. He enjoyed them because of his keen sense of humor.

After dark by his lodge-fire, when the air had the chill it always takes after sunset near the foot of the Rockies, Spotted Eagle told me the story of

Old Man and the Squirrels

"Old Man was always on the move; he never stayed long in one place. He could talk with the birds and animals, and often conversed with them on his travels. One time he came to a place where some squirrel-people were having a game. They were running around a fire, squealing and having a big time, all chasing one squirrel. As soon as that squirrel was caught, they would bury him in the ashes near a fire until he squealed; then they threw him out in a hurry. After that another squirrel ran until he was caught and was buried in the ashes. But, as soon as it got hot and he squealed, they always dug him out.

"Old Man watched them for a while and then said: 'Let me do that too.'

"The leader of the squirrels replied: 'Come on, elder brother, we will bury you first.'

"Old Man was careful to squeal as soon as the squirrels covered him with ashes; and they quickly dug him out.

"Then he said: 'Now younger brothers it is your turn; since there are so many of you, I shall bury you all at once.'

"So the squirrels lay down together, and Old Man covered them with hot ashes. But he told a mother squirrel that stood to one side of the fire: 'Just go away from here, so that there may be some young squirrels for the future.'

"Soon the ashes got too hot and the squirrels squealed to be taken out. But Old Man heaped on them all the ashes he could. He did not pull them out until all the squirrels were cooked. Then he sat down and ate his fill. There were so many he could not eat them all. He put the rest on poles and lay down to sleep, telling his hind-end, which always watched for him, to waken him if anything came near.

"Old Man was asleep only a little while, when he heard a noise. He jumped up and looked around; but he saw only a crow sitting in a tree. This made him angry, and he said:

"'Is it for that bird you make such a noise?'

"He went to sleep again and a lynx came around, but Old Man slept on. When he woke up at last and looked for the squirrels, they were all gone. The lynx had eaten them up.

"Then Old Man followed that lynx and found him asleep after eating all the squirrels. Old Man seized him and shouted: 'I have you now.' He took him by the ears and banged his nose against a rock and made it flat. He stood him on his hind legs and stretched out his body and his legs to make them long. He broke off most of his tail and left only a stump. Then he took some hair and stuck it on his nose for whiskers, and said:

"'You bob-cats will always look like that. You will have flat faces, long bodies and long legs and a stump of a tail; and you will be so short-winded you cannot run far.'

"Old Man was so angry with his own hind-end for not waking him, that he struck it with a fire-stick. And when the burned place began to hurt, he held it towards the wind to cool it off and shouted: 'Let the wind blow harder and harder.'

"Then the wind came so hard Old Man was blown away. He felt himself going and caught hold of anything within reach; he tore up trees and bushes by the roots. At last he held to some birch trees, and they did not break.

"After the wind went down, Old Man got up and shouted:

"'Mean old birches! You spoiled all my fun. I was having a good time being blown by the wind, until you stopped me.'

"He grabbed the birches and slashed them with his knife; all up and down the trees he cut, until they were covered with slashes. 'Now you will always look like that,' he cried. 'And forever, all the birches shall have these same cuts.' They came from the slashes Old Man made long ago with his knife."

By this time it was late, and the old medicine man ended by saying: "Now the dogs are scratching the ground, having had their evening meal." An Indian way of saying: "My story-telling is finished."

CHAPTER XXIV

ONESTA AND HIS SACRED BEAR SPEAR

ONESTA was an older man than Little Creek. He was religious, fond of rituals, inactive and inclined to sit by the fire. But he had a good mind and liked to lead ceremonies. It gave him a prominent social position in the tribe. He was a good story-teller, but only talked when he felt in the mood, and that did not happen often. He was reserved and adroit in hiding under an air of candor what he did not want to discuss; then he had a sort of mask to cover his feelings. Although he lacked a sense of humor, he was fond of jokes when he felt in the mood; but he was inclined to be religious and serious rather than pleasure-loving.

He disliked being questioned, and in all my dealings with him he never asked me a question and never went directly to the point. He was moody, as sensitive as a child and easily offended. I never felt sure of him. To get on with him, it was necessary to gain his confidence. If I treated him familiarly, it put him on his guard and hurt his pride. He did not reason, but acted from impulse. Sometimes he got offended for no apparent reason. Then no explanation would satisfy. It was better to take no notice, to joke and be friendly and make him forget. Then his mood would suddenly change and he would feel light-hearted and happy. He had a certain kind of sentiment. He liked to talk over the good times we had together, and camps where he had been happy with his friends.

Onesta was the owner of a sacred bundle called the Bear Spear. On our travels he always kept it near him and attended to it first, whenever we came into camp. By day it

NITANA

hung from a tripod in the sunlight; but he always took it inside the tepee at night. He never exposed it to storm, nor let it lie on the ground. Once, when he went away from camp, he asked me to look after the Spear. He said his wife could not attend to it, because women were not allowed to handle the Bear Spear.

The day before we came into the country of the Blood Indians, Onesta and his wife Nitana gave a ceremony over the sacred Spear. They said it was necessary to do this, before approaching a strange camp, to protect our party from danger and to guard against any "bad medicine." They put on their ceremonial clothes of yellow, the color sacred to the Spear. Nitana washed their small daughter, Yellow Mink, and dressed her in yellow. They sang chants together and burned sweet grass as incense and prayed for a safe and successful journey. I helped them with their songs, because Onesta said my voice added power to their prayers.

Then he brought forth a minkskin and had another ceremony. He prayed over it and burned dried seeds for incense, which he got from the tops of the narrow-leaved puccoon. They painted their faces, and Onesta said to me: "Brother, you had better let me paint your face too, that the Bloods may know you have become an Indian; the paint will also so protect your white skin from the hot sun."

Nitana decorated my moccasins with paint, the way they did their own; it made them look better, she said.

She was a good-natured woman and easy-going, but liked to bully her husband. Naturally timid and shy and inclined to stoutness, she lacked energy. But she had great respect for my Indian sister Strikes-on-Both-Sides and always followed her lead.

That evening by our camp-fire, Onesta was in the mood for talking. He told us about the origin of his Bear Spear.

Legend of the Bear Spear

"The things I now tell you happened long ago, in the days when our people used dogs instead of horses to carry their baggage. One evening, when a band of Indians came into camp, the chief announced that one of his travois dogs was lost. No one remembered seeing the dog, so Little Mink, youngest son of the chief, asked his father to let him go back to look for the missing dog. He said:

"'I am old enough to make the trip alone. I shall go straight to our old camp-ground.'

"At first the father refused, he thought his son was too young to make such a long trip alone. But the boy was so eager, he was allowed to go.

"Little Mink followed the trail back to their last camp-ground, which was close to the foot of the Rocky Mountains. First he went to the place where his father's lodge had stood; he thought the dog might still be there. Then he walked around the deserted camp-circle, watching the ground for tracks.

"At last he found a single dog track going towards the mountains. It led him into a well-worn trail through a rocky ravine, to a cave whose mouth was hidden by service-berry and chokecherry bushes. And there he saw the missing travois, but the dog was gone.

"While Little Mink was looking at the travois and wondering what had become of their dog, he heard a loud roar; and a big grizzly bear rushed from the cave. Raising himself on his hind legs, he seized the boy in his arms and carried him into the dark cave. When Little Mink's eyes became accustomed to the dark, and he saw the enormous size of the bear that held him, he fainted. After a while he wakened and found himself lying on the floor of the cave, so close to the mouth of the big grizzly he could feel his hot breath. When he tried to move, the bear thrust out his long sharp claws and held him tight. After that the boy lay very still; he scarcely even moved, but gazed straight ahead. At last the bear said:

"'My son, be not afraid, for I shall do you no harm. I am the chief of the bears and my power is very great. It was my power that brought you to this cave. If you are willing to remain here with me while the snows are deep, I will help you. Before you leave my den in the spring, I will bestow my power upon you. You will become a great chief and can help your people.'

"Then the grizzly stood upon his hind legs; he was so big his head almost touched the roof. First he walked round and round; and showed the boy a pile of green branches with different kinds of berries. He said:

"'You will have plenty of berries for food. The bear eats them branches and all, but you can pick off the berries.'

"After that the bear took him to the other side of the cave and showed him a pile of buffalo chips. He changed these into pemmican through his supernatural power, dancing around the cave and holding them in his paws.

"All that winter Little Mink stayed in the cave with the bear, acting just as he did. His eyes became so accustomed to the dark, he could see as well as the bear himself. While the snow was deep, the bear lay on one side, he did not even move. But, when the warm winds of spring began to blow, he began to get restless and move about. One day the bear rolled over on his back and lay for a long time with his legs in the air. He sat up and began to yawn. Then he rose to his feet and walked round and round the cave, and finally stopped to look outside.

"He said that spring had come and it was time to leave the cave. He took the boy to the door and told him to look out. A warm wind was blowing and the snow was melting from the hills. But, before they left the den, the grizzly bestowed some of his supernatural power upon Little Mink.

"He took a stick and raised himself on his hind legs, holding out his arms and extending his long claws. He tossed up his huge head and snorted and rolled back his lips; he showed his sharp teeth and chanted:

> "'Behold my nose with its keen scent,
> My claws and teeth, they are my weapons.
> Everything that lives fears the grizzly bear.'

And then the bear said to Little Mink:

"'When you get back to your tribe, make a Bear Spear. Take a sharp stone and fasten it to a long shaft. Fasten bear's teeth to the handle, also the nose of a bear, because the nose and teeth should go together. Cover the staff with bearskin and decorate it with red paint. Tie grizzly claws to the handle; they will rattle and sound like a grizzly does when he runs. Whenever you go to war, wear the claw of a grizzly bear fastened in your hair; and my power will go with you. Make a nose like a grizzly bear when you charge in battle; and your enemies will run, because everything that lives fears the power of a grizzly bear.'

"The bear taught Little Mink how to heal the sick. He showed him the ceremony to use; how to paint his face and body and the marks to use for the 'bear face.' He told him that the Spear was sacred and should be used only on important occasions. If any one were ill, a relative could make a vow to the Bear Spear. After that the ceremony should be given, and the sick would be restored.

"Then Little Mink left the grizzly and returned to his father's camp. The chief was proud of his son. He gave a big feast and invited the head men to meet him. After they had feasted and smoked, Little Mink told them how he spent the winter in the den of the chief of the grizzly bears and showed his Bear Spear."

CHAPTER XXV

CAMP OF THE BLOOD INDIANS

AFTER fording the St. Mary's River, we crossed the international line into the Province of Alberta, a country of rolling prairies with black soil and luxuriant grass, stretching away in gentle slopes to the horizon.

We saw many "fairy rings," both large and small, made by a species of fungus. Onesta believed they were overgrown trails made years before by buffalo going in circles. But Little Creek who was more practical said they were the remains of old buffalo wallows. They are identical with the mushroom growths common in the fields of our Eastern States, where they are popularly known as "fairy rings" or "fairy dances."

On the journey, our Indian women were always on the lookout for herbs and plants. They gathered them wherever we went and dried them in the sun or by the camp-fire at night. Some were used for seasoning meats and stews, others for hair tonic, sore throat and pain in the stomach.

We made a special collection for the medicine man, Brings-Down-the-Sun, whom we were going to visit — certain herbs he was known to use in doctoring the sick. The women also kept adding to my botanical collection,[1] showing me rare plants and telling their Indian names and uses. We made a collection of the perfumes they used — braids of sweet grass, dried blossoms of dog fennel and meadow rue, balsam fir, red cedar, punk from the cottonwood tree, buds from the balsam poplar, beaver musk and ringbone of a horse.

At last we saw the white lodges of the Bloods in the valley of Belly River. I rode in advance of our party and was the first to enter their camp. It was a hot day, and many of the

[1] Medicinal and Useful Plants of the Blackfoot Indians. See Appendix.

lodges had their doors open and the sides raised for ventilation. Soon a horseman came to meet me. He wore a headdress of curving horns and a deerskin suit covered with colored beads and ermine tails. He addressed me in the sign language, raising his right hand and moving it to and fro to say: "Who are you and from whence do you come?"

I signed back: "A friend, I travel with a party of South Piegans." To express this, I clasped my hands as though shaking hands; then pointed to the rest of my party and made the sign for Piegan by closing my right hand, holding it to the lower part of my right cheek and moving it in a small circle.

The Blood grunted and nodded that he understood, looking at me all the while with the steady gaze and keen observation of an Indian. He took in every detail of myself and my horse. Meanwhile the rest of our party came up. After a short parley with the Blood, he led us through the camp to the lodge of One Spot and his wife Snake Woman, who were relatives of Little Creek.

They were hospitable and invited us to share their tepee. But we made camp on the shore of the river, in a place sheltered from the wind by groves of poplars and cottonwood trees. Before we had time to unpack our wagons, some Blood women came with presents of food, according to the Indian custom of showing hospitality to visitors. The wife of One Spot brought dried meat and service berries — the first of the season for our Indians. So they made an offering to the Sun, before eating any of the berries. They all waited while Onesta held a berry toward the Sun with a prayer for plenty; then planted it in the ground, with another prayer to the Underground Spirits. Then the women of our party carried a supply of tobacco and food to the Blood camp, in return for their gifts.

Just before dark, a band of Cree Indians arrived from the

north and went into camp near us on the bank of the river. Soon they had their shelters ready for the night and camp-fires burning. In the meadows many horses were feeding, watched by young herders who galloped back and forth, driving them in bands to drink at the river and making ready for the night. The evening quiet of the prairies was broken by the barking of many dogs, neighing of horses, and songs of the herders. I heard the mournful wailing of an aged woman who stood alone on a hill near our camp. The Cree Indians brought her the sad news that her only son had died while on a visit to a distant camp of the North Blackfoot.

That night was sultry and warm. Lying in my blanket-bed on the ground, I watched the heavy clouds rolling up in the north and west in lofty thunderheads, giving forth brilliant flashes of silver lightning over the entire sky and deep rumbling peals of thunder. But not a drop of rain fell.

Sometime in the night I was wakened by groans, which came at regular intervals from a thicket near my bed. I straightway thought of my saddle horse, Kutenai, being strangled by his picket rope. Black clouds covered the sky and the darkness was intense. But I could not lie and hear those terrible groans. On hands and knees, I groped my way. When I came near the edge of the thicket, the groaning ceased. I threw sticks and stones, but nothing moved; there was not a sound. Careful not to lose my direction in the dark, I crawled back to bed. No sooner was I comfortably settled in my blankets, than the groaning began again. After that I gave up the mystery. And I never did find out whether the sufferer was a person or some animal.

Next morning we went to the lodge of One Spot. The day was warm with brilliant sunlight, and the sides of the lodge were raised from the ground to allow the breeze to sweep through. First we smoked a pipe together; and then One Spot told me the following story:

Red Head

"A girl once lived in one of our camps who had three brothers. They went to war against the Crow Indians and were all killed by a chief named Red Head.

"In the same camp with the girl was a good-looking young man; he was her lover and wanted to marry her. One day he said to his sweetheart: 'Let us stay together.' And she answered:

"'I promise to live with you if you kill Red Head, the Crow chief.'

"Then the young man mourned, for he knew that Red Head was a warrior of great power. He went off alone and fasted. He prayed to the animals and birds and was pitied by wolverines. They gave him their supernatural power with a sharp elk bone, which the young man carried hidden in his clothes as a weapon.

"After that he went into the country of the Crow Indians and looked everywhere for the lodge of Red Head.

"Now it happened that Red Head always camped alone; he pitched his lodge far away from other people. He lived with his aged mother; they had no other relatives. But he kept a flock of pet crows, which sat on top of the lodge-poles and watched for enemies. For this reason Red Head could not be killed. His crows warned him of all danger.

"One day when the Crow chief was away on a hunt and his old mother was alone in the lodge, a good-looking young woman came to her and said: 'Mother, I want to marry your son.'

"'My son will not marry,' replied the old woman; 'his pets always warn him. But I promise to help you. I am getting so old he ought to have a wife.' And she kept the young woman in the lodge.

"That evening, when Red Head came home from the hunt, his pet crows flew to meet him, and kept saying:

"'Master, look out! Here is a woman with a man's eyes and a man's legs. Kill him.'

"Then his mother went to meet him and said: 'Listen, my son! There is a girl here; she has come to marry you. You need a wife, because I am old and get tired.'

"Red Head went into the lodge and saw that the stranger was young and good-looking. He seated himself and the girl came to him; she put her arms round his neck and kissed him; she gave him presents of dried meat and moccasins, and said:

"'They treated me badly in the Blackfoot camp, so I ran away. I want to marry you; I will work and take good care of your tepee.' And all this time the pet crows sat overhead on the lodge-poles. They warned Red Head over and over, saying:

"'Look out, master! She is cheating you. She has a man's eyes and a man's legs.'

"But Red Head wanted the woman. He paid no attention to the warnings of his pets. He liked to have her near and made her sit beside him. He ate the dried meat she gave him and wore her moccasins. At last the pet crows got tired sitting on the lodge-poles. They flew away to watch for other enemies.

"Then Red Head wanted the woman to go with him into the forest. They sat under a tree and the chief put his head in her lap. She took the sharp weapon, which she carried hidden in her clothes, and drove it into his ear. She hammered it with a stone and killed him; she took his scalp and went away.

"Then that young warrior came back to the Blackfoot camp. He told his sweetheart how he killed Red Head and showed her the scalp. He married the girl and became one of the head men of the tribe."

CHAPTER XXVI

COUNTRY OF THE NORTH PIEGANS

WE stayed several days in the camp of the Bloods, to rest our tired horses and to visit the family of One Spot. The Bloods were fine-looking Indians, both men and women. But they were not popular with other tribes. They were proud and considered themselves the aristocrats of the plains.

The night before we left their camp we picketed our horses close and made ready for an early start. In hot summer weather, early morning is the best time to travel on the plains.

We broke camp before sunrise and followed the shore of the river, looking for a place to ford. The crossing of a broad, swift river is always hazardous, because of washouts, hidden boulders, and stumbling horses. We rode through thickets of poplars and willows. Under the trees lay the golden light of early morning, with purple shadows. Light mists floated along the banks of the river. From the grass and bushes hung countless gems of sparkling dew. Everything was fresh and blooming, the buds and leaves, flowers and perfumes. The fragrant breath of the morning came through thickets, with odors of balsam poplar and wild flowers. Butterflies rested on the first wild roses, bees hummed in the air. Fragrant primroses were in blossom, wild hollyhocks, purple fleabane and the large-flowered agoseris.

When we forded the river, I did not hurry my horse, but let him take his time, holding his head a little upstream, to avoid the full force of the rushing water, bending my body to help him in his balance and fixing my eyes on the top of his head, to keep from getting dizzy in the rapid current.

Out on the open prairie the birds were calling; near and far the air was filled with their songs. Chestnut-collared longspurs were climbing high into the blue sky, then fluttering slowly to the ground, always against the wind, singing their cheerful rippling song. I heard the calls of ducks and the choruses of prairie chickens, repeating it over and over, the strange cries of cranes as they soared high overhead, and the voices of curlew, killdeer, and Western meadow-larks.

Then we climbed to the summit of a ridge and saw before us a great table-land, bounded on the north and west by high hills and distant mountains. It was part in light and part in shadow, with the golden sun rising over a bank of clouds in the east and shining on the snowy peaks of the Rockies in the west — a wide expanse and without any sign of life.

We took an old Indian trail, which was known to Onesta. It led us across a plateau and into a hill country, where the sun shone in a clear sky and the heat was intense. As the day advanced, the sun beat down with ever-increasing heat. My thermometer registered ninety-eight degrees in the shade and a hundred and thirty in the sun.

At mid-day we stopped on the shore of a lake, to let our horses feed on the rich grass. The women made a shelter from the sun by spreading canvas over a tripod of poles, with the sides raised for the wind to blow through.

As we rested under our comfortable shelter, Onesta called my attention to swallows hovering over our horses to get hairs for lining their nests, and to grasshoppers flying high in the air, saying:

"Their wings have no color until they fly into the sunlight; it makes them red, yellow, and black."

He taught me a song by which he made some sandpipers dance on the shore of the lake. He clapped his hands and sang:

"Ik-sis-a-kuyi! Ik-sis-a-kuyi!" (Meat! Meat!)

He showed me a wild rose bush that was covered with the

webs of tent caterpillars; and made them dance by beating time with his hands and singing:

"Ko-me-os-cha! Ko-me-os-cha!" (Worms! Worms!)

At first the caterpillars lay perfectly still. But, after he sang a few moments, they began to wake up and move slowly. Then they all stood up and waved their heads to and fro, dancing as long as Onesta continued his song.

When the heat had passed, we harnessed our horses and moved on, following a trail that led upwards toward the mountains. While making our way slowly, Onesta and Nitana began chanting a religious song in unison. I rode closer and joined them in their song.

Then Onesta explained that it was customary to sing on entering a strange country, as a prayer to the Sun for a safe journey and for protection against the magical arts of its people. On this occasion, he said they were also praying for my success among the North Piegans.

Finally, we gained the summit of a massive ridge of the prairie, which overlooked the country of the North Piegans — a broad river valley with green meadows and groves of cottonwood trees. On the undulating hillsides herds of cattle and horses were feeding. And, as far as the eye could reach, the river rolled eastward from the base of the Rockies, gleaming in the sunlight like a ribbon of silver.

Nestled among the groves of green trees in the valley, I saw a number of white Indian tepees, with blue smoke rising from their tops. North lay the Porcupine Hills covered with forests of pine; west, the snow peaks of the mountains. Onesta said the hills were called "Porcupine," because the bristling trees on their ridges look like the quills on a porcupine's back.

He pointed to some rocks on the prairie and said: "A big grizzly once lived in a cave there. Now many kinds of berries grow around it, from the seeds carried there by that bear."

THE COUNTRY OF THE NORTH PIEGANS
The Rocky Mountains in the distance

He showed me a mountain in the main range of the Rockies, with a great landslide on its eastern slope, and said:

"We call it 'Lodge-Lining-Mountain,' because it looks like the inside lining of a lodge. The river that rises there is named after Old Man; and in the mountains near its source is Old Man's sliding place and the place where he gambled." On our way down from the summit, we met some young men of the North Piegans, who were watching over their tribal herds of horses and cattle. One of them, the son of Crow Eagle, a famous chief, rode with us. He was hospitable and invited us to his camp. But Onesta told him we were going to visit Brings-Down-the-Sun, the medicine man. Before the young chief left us, he pointed out the camp we were seeking, among some big trees on the north side of the river.

Then we crossed a table-land, which rose gradually from the river, and descended into the valley. On the face of the hills and in little ravines were clusters of chokecherry bushes, bearing a fruit like a wild cherry, only larger and better flavored. I saw a coyote standing motionless in a ravine, but it was only for a moment; because of his protective coloring, I quickly lost sight of him.

The river valley, with its fragrant masses of flowers, thickets, and shady trees, seemed like a Promised Land, after the heat and dust of the plains. A soft wind blew over the meadows, bearing odors of wild flowers and ripened grasses. Wild roses were in bloom, sky-blue forget-me-nots, purple geraniums, yellow clusters of puccoon and rose-colored heads of horsemint, called "manekape" (young man) by the Blackfoot. They used its blossoms for inflammation of the eyes.

We followed a trail through rich meadows, and thickets of aspen and willows; and then entered one of those beautiful groves of cottonwood timber, that are sometimes found along the larger rivers of the prairies. Finally we stopped in an open meadow densely sheltered by poplars and willows and canopied by wide-spreading cottonwood trees. Through the thick foliage I saw the gleam of white Indian tepees. It was the camp of Brings-Down-the-Sun, the medicine man, and the end of our journey. Here he lived surrounded by his children, grandchildren, and great-grandchildren.

I saw a group of women and children on a high cliff overlooking the valley. They had been watching our approach, their figures sharply outlined against the deep blue sky. Onesta recognized one of the women as Long Hair, favorite daughter of Brings-Down-the-Sun. Her long black hair was flying in the wind; she had a baby on her back and a group of children clinging to her skirts.

Then the venerable figure of the patriarch chieftain came from one of the lodges. With hand shading his eyes, he stood under a cottonwood tree and gazed intently at our outfit. He recognized his nephew, Onesta, and welcomed us saying:

"My children, I am glad in my heart that you have come to visit my camp."

I went closer and saw that he was an old man, with long gray hair falling in waves over his shoulders. He had high cheek bones, and clean-cut Indian features. In his face were deep lines, as though he were burdened with care and responsibility. He wore a bright-colored blanket wrapped closely around him, a red band across his forehead and encircling his head. His tall figure was bent with age; but he had a keen and penetrating gaze, and the dignified bearing of a chief who was accustomed to command.

He stood a moment without speaking, and then he said:

"You may pitch your lodges close to mine if you wish. But the best place to camp is in the open meadow. Sometimes heavy winds come, which break the big trees. If you should be camped underneath in a storm, some of the branches might fall and do you harm. Take your horses to feed on the hills beyond the valley, where the grass is more nourishing. You will find a cold spring on the north side of the meadow with good water to drink."

Thus he spoke and disappeared into his tepee, while we made ready to camp, choosing a place among the big trees, near the camp of the old medicine man; and there we unloaded our wagons.

Soon the women of the North Piegans, Bird, the wife of Brings-Down-the-Sun, with her daughter, Long Hair, and daughters-in-law, came bearing presents. It was always interesting to watch the exchange of presents by the women. On this occasion, Nitana received an old pot, a bag of dried beans, a big knife, and a copper kettle. She gave in return two blankets, two pairs of moccasins, and some mineral paints. Such articles, which might seem of little value to white men, were cherished by Indian women.

That evening we had an invitation from Brings-Down-the-Sun to eat with him in his tepee. So at sunset, in company with Little Creek and Onesta, I walked along a well-worn trail that led among the cottonwoods to the camp of the North Piegans. Near the lodge of the chief, we came upon a charming picture of a happy and contented Indian family.

A bright fire burned under the big trees, sending a shower of golden sparks into the air, lighting up the white lodges with their clusters of tapering poles and shining on the massive trunks and green foliage of the cottonwoods. Gathered round the fire were women and girls dressed in bright colors, busily at work, cooking, making moccasins and clothes; groups of children were at play — all were merry and lighthearted.

A baby hammock was stretched between two trees, the mother rocking it gently and singing a cradle song. But the approach of a strange white man changed this peaceful scene abruptly. A barking dog rushed suddenly out, and a woman shouted:

"Puks-i-put! Kops-ksisse!" (Come back! Swollen Nose!)

For a moment the merry throng was silent; and then quickly vanished.

CHAPTER XXVII

CAMP OF BRINGS-DOWN-THE-SUN

THE chief was waiting inside his lodge. He directed Onesta to a place on his right, Little Creek and myself to a couch on his left. It was covered with robes and blankets and had comfortable back-rests, which were made of small willow sticks bound on both ends with rawhide. The tepee was scrupulously neat and clean; a small wood fire burned in the center, surrounded by a circle of smooth round stones; cooking utensils were near the door; provisions and clothing stored in painted rawhide cases. At the head of the chief's couch hung a sacred medicine case with long fringe hanging down; and from the lodge-poles articles of clothing decorated with needlework, beads, and colored quills.

For a while we smoked in silence. I listened to the last songs of the birds and the evening wind in the tree tops. Then Bird, the wife of the chief, entered the lodge. She was small and slender. From the smile she gave me and her kindly expression, I knew she had a good heart. She straightway began to work, and soon set before us a meal of service berries, dried meat, and hot tea. After we had eaten, we smoked again. Then Onesta said to Brings-Down-the-Sun:

"We have come a long distance with this white man to see you. Mad Wolf adopted him as his son and gave him the name of White Weasel; and he is now a member of our tribe. On our journey we told every one we were taking White Weasel to visit you. Now I want you to tell him Indian legends, and our ancient customs and religion. This white man is our friend; and you are my kinsman; I ask you to do this."

But the aged chief was strangely cold and silent. For a

while he sat calmly smoking, gazing into the fire. Finally he turned toward me, and, looking intently into my face, said with spirit:

"This man comes from a race that has always cheated and told us lies. This spring I made a vow to have nothing more to do with white men. They have taken away our freedom, our country, and our means of support. Now they try to take away our religion. They have forbidden us to give our ceremony that is sacred to the Sun; and for this they give no reason. The white men have no right to take away our religion. It was given to us by the Sun and Moon, and as long as the Sun and Moon are in the sky, I shall continue to worship them. We struggle to keep up our religion, that our people may lead good lives and be happy; as they were in the days of the past before the white men came into our country.

"This spring the white men shut off my rations. They refused to let me have food for my children, because I was making ready to give the Sun Dance. I had to give the ceremony to save the life of a child that was dying; its mother had already made her vow to the Sun. Now my heart is bitter against all white men; I do not want to make known any of my knowledge to a white man. But Onesta, you are my relative, and have made a long journey. This white man can remain in my camp for a few days to rest; and during that time we may get to know each other better."

Then a slender, pretty girl, dressed in soft-tanned deerskin, came into the lodge. She was the youngest daughter of the chief and was named "Whistling-All-Night," because she was born in the moon, "when the jack rabbit whistles at night in calling its mate."

Said Brings-Down-the-Sun to Onesta and Little Creek: "My family comes every summer to gather wild berries in this valley; and we are glad to have you come too. Berries are plentiful this summer; you had better gather a supply and dry them for winter, as we are accustomed to do. But I ask you to be careful of our berry bushes. Do not break the branches, or injure any of our big trees. I am looking ahead for the good of my people. I want to preserve the trees and berry bushes for future generations. I am accustomed to warn my fellow tribesmen not to be shortsighted like the Blood Indians. They once had big trees like ours, but they cut them all down for firewood. Now their country is bare and they have few berry bushes. I told my people to haul their firewood from the forests on the mountains. They have followed my advice, and we still have our big-leaf-trees (cottonwoods). The trees with long leaves we call spear-leaf-trees (balsam poplar); we have also round-leaf-trees (quaking aspen), and thickets of brush-sticks (willows). We call the big trees 'the-old-time-trees,' and the small ones 'young-people-trees.'"

So they talked until darkness settled over valley and Indian camp. I saw the pale light of the rising moon shining on the tepee walls. And, while I sat watching this venerable medicine man, I thought: "How strange that he, of a savage race, an untaught son of the wilderness, should have the wisdom and foresight of a statesman in trying to husband their natural resources of big trees and berry bushes; and, although he had just cause for hating the white race, yet he treated me with kindness and generosity."

As I was leaving the tepee, I made presents to all his family — a silk handkerchief of bright colors to Brings-Down-the-Sun, a blanket to his wife, and a bracelet of shining white shells to his daughter, Whistling-All-Night.

That night came the first heavy thunder of the season for the North Piegans. So, next day, it was necessary for owners of Medicine Pipes to give a ceremony and distribute tobacco. A messenger came inviting us to a ceremony at the lodge of Running Antelope. I went with Onesta and Nitana and some of the members of Brings-Down-the-Sun's family.

When we arrived, the tepee was already crowded with Indians. But they made room for us because we were strangers. As soon as I entered, I recognized the leader of the ceremony. He was Bull Plume, a medicine man who had visited the camp of my Indian father. When I took my seat in front of him, he gazed at me in astonishment. He stopped in the midddle of a song and announced to the assembled Indians, that I was the adopted son of Chief Mad Wolf and my name was Á-pe-ech-e-ken. He asked me to sit beside him and help him in the songs. He said my voice would add power to their prayers. So the singers made room for me and I joined in their chants.

After a number of songs and prayers, Bull Plume took up the Medicine Pipe, which lay before him, and carried it out-of-doors. He held it up towards the Sun and prayed for all the people who were present; that none of them might be killed that year by the Thunder.

Then they had a feast of service-berry soup; and some of the tobacco from the Pipe Bundle was given to every one. To possess this consecrated tobacco and to smoke it, was believed to bring a person into the good will of the Thunder.

After the Medicine Pipe Ceremony, the wife of Running Antelope got Bull Plume to help her with another ceremony over a sacred headdress. This was necessary because of a vow she had made in behalf of her son who was so ill they thought he would die.

That afternoon I went to explore the valley about our camp. I came upon groups of North Piegan children, like wild sprites of the woods slyly peeping through the trees, curious to see the feared white man. At first they fled in terror, but their fear quickly vanished when I gave them presents of crackers and sweet chocolate, which they took without thanks and disappeared among the trees and bushes.

I followed a well-worn trail through the woods, leading past the lodge of Brings-Down-the-Sun to a pool in the river, where he took his morning bath. It was a lovely spot — a still-water where the deep current flowed gently; the grassy banks were lined with birch and berry bushes, fragrant thickets, and leafy arches overhead. Along the trail were bright yellow flowers of gaillardia, drooping bluebells, Canada violets, and scarlet Indian paint-brush.

I saw Long Hair, daughter of the chief, come from the river with her water pails; and Nitana on the shore bathing her small daughter, Yellow Mink. A young girl was riding on a rude raft of poles, which stuck fast in midstream. I refrained from going to her assistance, because of the talk it would cause in the camp. But I took her picture with my camera. She wore white-shell ear-rings, a long necklace of blue service berries, and leggings and moccasins decorated with colored beads. Her deerskin dress was bound at the waist with a girdle of colored beads; Indian fashion, it had no sleeves, but was cut into a fringed cape across the shoulders and hung freely over her bare arms.

In the woods many birds were singing, yellow-throat, goldfinch, catbird, white-crown sparrow and many varieties of warblers. I found the spring of cold water which the chief had recommended. Around it were beds of delicious red strawberries, wild cherries, and wonderful service-berry bushes; they reached high above the ground and were covered with ripe fruit.

In the soft mud of the river bank were the marks of a family of beavers — large tracks of old beavers and the tiny footprints of their children. I saw poplars freshly cut by them, also the stumps of trees they had felled many years ago. When I told Onesta about them, he said:

"That family of beavers has lived here many years; the Indians have never disturbed them. Beaver are like people.

Some are restless and keep on the move; they are never satisfied in one place. But this beaver family is content to stay here, happy in their good home; they have a sandy beach, mud bottom, and plenty of food."

I came upon some children of the North Piegans, playing with dolls in an open glade. They had a miniature camp with little play-tepees, men and women dolls dressed in skin costumes, with real hair, little belts, and moccasins and leggings to match the clothes. In the center of the camp, which was in the form of a circle, was a tepee for the head-chief; it had diminutive back-rests and painted rawhide cases, little tanning tools, knife sheaths and squirrel-skins for robes.

The children had a lively game, like our "catcher," in which all the players tried to get away from one of their number, at whom they sang derisively:

(You are an old skunk with no hair along your mangey backbone)

Boys played a rough game of kicking each other from two opposing sides, to see which would give way first; and a game called "playing bear," that was popular while swimming. They caught one of their number and tossed him into deep water and scampered away. When he got ashore he ran after them until he caught another boy, and then they all joined in tossing him into the water.

The boys also had a curious arrow game, in which they shot at a stake, trying to hit it, or to come as near as possible. If the second in turn were doubtful whether he could shoot better than the first, he went to the stake and danced for power to win, beating time with his arrow on the stake and singing: "I am the one who can hit the stake arrow first."

If the second player made a good shot, the third danced at the stake to beat him, and so on.

Women had a game of throwing arrows at a target, also a four-stick gambling game, using marked buffalo bones.

The favorite gambling game with young men was to roll a small wheel over a smooth stretch of ground. Two players followed it, trying to throw, so that the wheel would not fall on their arrows. Their comrades held the stakes and kept score. Whenever a play was finished one side would shout: "Give us one point"; or the other side: "We get two points." If a player gambled away all his possessions, he was said "to walk the prairie."

Near sunset I left the valley and climbed Lookout Butte, a high hill where Brings-Down-the-Sun was accustomed to go to meditate and dream. Its summit was covered with wiry grass in bunches, and creeping cedar which grew in great clumps, forming mats with branches growing close to the ground.

From the top of the butte I had a broad view of the Rocky Mountains, the pine forests on the Porcupine Hills in the north, and the surrounding plains for miles. There I waited for the sun to set.

Soon vapors formed along the river valley and shadows extended over the plains. The air was so clear it was long after sunset before darkness fell and the stars came out. In the valley at the foot of the butte were clusters of white Indian tepees, nestled among the trees and glowing with firelight. The night wind from the mountains, blowing softly over the valley, brought the faint tinkling of horse-bells and the rhythmic beating of an Indian drum.

As I sat on that solitary hill and felt the deep peace that comes from close communion with nature, a doubt came into my mind, whether white men with all their striving, their wealth, and material success, have attained as high an average of happiness, contentment, and loyalty to community interest, as was attained under the simple and natural life of the average Indian family before the coming of the white man. One could look in vain among Indian camps near the foot of the Rockies and by the streams and rivers of the plains for the misery and discontent, which involve masses of people in our great industrial cities.

CHAPTER XXVIII

ONESTA GIVES HIS CROW WATER CEREMONY

OUR camp-ground under the cottonwood trees was covered with a deposit of sand and fine loam, which got into our food, our blankets and clothes. The Indians noticed me scratching and had a joke at my expense. Little Creek said to Onesta, so that I could overhear:

"During the past few days I have been feeling itchy; I believe we have become lousy from sitting on the blankets of these North Piegans." Onesta replied without a smile: "I have had the same trouble, but got rid of mine by bathing in the river."

I had my own suspicions as to the cause of our discomfort, but, after this conversation, I imagined that lice were crawling in my hair and all over my body. To the joy of the entire camp, I hastened to the river, where I discovered sand as the real cause of my affliction.

Onesta told me afterwards that few of the Blackfoot were troubled with vermin, but it was among the Crees and Gros Ventres. He said it made him feel uncomfortable to even go near the Crees.

We had no regular hours for meals. The women cooked when it was convenient. It was customary for Indians to have only two meals a day, morning and evening. When we were on the road, we ate before sunrise and in the evening after our journey. In a permanent camp the morning meal might not come until noon; and if the women did not feel in the mood for cooking, they would omit it entirely. The time for our evening meal varied from five until nine; sometimes an entire day went by without any cooking. I adopted the Indian custom of eating dried meat or pemmican, whenever

I felt hungry. Meat was their chief article of diet — boiled, roasted, or dried. They were especially fond of soups and meat stews.

Their vegetables were generally roasted or baked. They peeled and split the stalks of wild parsnip, roasting them over the hot coals to bring out the juice. They baked the prairie turnip, also camas roots, which they put in a long hole three feet deep, in layers with grass and leaves between, and hot stones at the bottom. Then the hole was covered and a fire kept burning over it for two days and two nights.

The women of our camp were continually at work, gathering wild berries and firewood, cooking, dressing skins, and making clothes. They had an ingenious way of getting dry branches for firewood, when they were out of reach on the big trees, breaking them off with a long pole with a crook at one end, which they called a "limb-catcher."

In gathering wild berries, a crowd of women and children generally went together. They struck the bushes with sticks and caught the berries in blankets, putting them into bags made from the whole skins of small animals or unborn calves. On hot days, they worked in the open, seated together under a large cowskin, which was spread over a tripod of poles as a sun shelter, making clothes, parfleches, and lodge covers.

The day Onesta gave his Crow Water Ceremony, he asked me to help him in the singing. He began his drumming before sunrise to waken the people of the North Piegan camp; and made our women get up early to prepare the feast, which they cooked in a large kettle over an outside fire.

Then they pitched a large lodge, which was loaned for the occasion by Brings-Down-the-Sun. It was decorated with symbolic pictures; a band of dusty stars and mountain peaks at the bottom represented the earth; round the center were four red bands, representing the trails of the Thunder Bird

ONESTA ENTERING THE THUNDER TEPEE WITH HIS SACRED BUNDLES

THE CROW WATER CEREMONY OF ONESTA IN THE THUNDER TEPEE

or lightning; the top was black for a cloudy sky at night, with a cross at the back for the Butterfly, or Bringer-of-Dreams. They called it the Thunder Tepee.

The Crow Water Ceremony came to the Blackfoot tribe in recent years from the Crow Indians. It was a society of both men and women for singing and dancing. It was believed to have power to make its members wealthy, to fulfill their desires, and to cure the sick. The women did most of the singing, while the men beat drums and helped in the songs.

When it was time for the ceremony to begin, Onesta carried his sacred bundles to the Thunder Tepee, beating on his drum as a signal for the Indians to assemble. Many came from the near-by camps and from a distance — men, women, and children. The Crow Water Ceremony was new to the North Piegans; they were eager to hear the songs and see the dances.

Onesta as leader sat in the place of honor at the back of the lodge, surrounded by sacred bundles. His face was painted yellow and he had a long eagle plume in his hair. On both sides of him sat men with painted medicine drums who helped in the ceremony. The women who took part were seated on his left. They arose from time to time and danced to the singing and drumming. The leader made motions with the skin of a bird or animal; and the women dancers imitated him with their hands.

I saw a visiting Indian who came for the ceremony, holding himself aloof. Instead of entering the tepee with his family, he sat at a distance, near the edge of the woods. His mother-in-law had already arrived and it would be a breach of etiquette for him to go into her presence. If she met him face-to-face she would feel outraged and he must make her a fine present.

Brings-Down-the-Sun attended with his family. They all

sat outside and did not mingle with the crowd. He was a religious leader and his wife one of the wise women. They had their position to maintain; and must be careful of their actions in public, so as not to be criticized.

When the ceremony finally came to an end, Onesta burned sweet grass on one side of the fire; and the berry soup was distributed among the people. But before eating, each person took a berry and held it up with a prayer. Then they all held their dishes of food over their heads; and, after setting them down again, began to eat.

Onesta asked me to spend that night in the Thunder Tepee as it was against the rules of its medicine to leave it unoccupied. He urged me, saying:

"If no one sleeps there, trouble is sure to come. But if you stay in the sacred tepee, you may have a wonderful dream, like one of our medicine men."

I agreed, and straightway made preparations for the night, by carrying my blankets inside and gathering a plentiful supply of firewood.

That evening many people came to see me in the Thunder Tepee; the Indians of our party and North Piegans, too. They were a jolly crowd, as light-hearted and happy as children. After the feast of that day they were in a merry mood, chaffing each other good-naturedly and finding fun in everything — their old clothes and the holes in their moccasins, the children and dogs, and their own talk; they laughed and joked until they were tired.

Then they asked me to sing Indian songs. I agreed, on condition that Running Wolf, the oldest son of the North Piegan chief, would sing a song for every one of mine. Quickly the news of our song contest spread through the camp and more Indians crowded into the Thunder Tepee. But Brings-Down-the-Sun did not come. He still held himself aloof.

I was the first to sing and chose a night song — one used

by young men and their sweethearts, when they rode together at night.

In his turn, Running Wolf sang a song of war. He said: "In the old times our people had a custom. Youths who wanted to become warriors had to prove their bravery. They stood naked round a burning pine tree, holding hands and singing. Two warriors with long poles scraped the burning bark, making showers of sparks, which fell on the bare skin of the dancers. Those who had brave hearts kept on dancing and singing in spite of their burns."

After my dance song, Running Wolf gave a song used in an old game. He said:

"Long ago our people played a game by going in single file. They followed a leader who carried two burning brands, holding each other and singing while he led them, his brands striking together and throwing off showers of sparks. They had to keep in line in spite of the sparks."

Then I sang a love song, which interested the women; they asked for it over and over. I learned it in the camp of my Indian father, from a young brave whom I heard singing

to his sweetheart. Strikes-on-Both-Sides recognized the song and made known the name of the lover to the North Piegan women. Then the youngest daughter of Brings-Down-the-Sun came late, and they made me sing the love song again for her.

Running Wolf sang the song of a maiden who was disappointed in love, with the words:

> "My lover looked like an eagle,
> When I saw him at a distance.
> But, alas! He came near,
> And I found he was nothing but a buzzard."

It was after midnight when that merry crowd broke up. Before Onesta left, he warned me of certain taboos for the Thunder Tepee — things to be avoided, lest they bring me bad luck. He said:

"Be careful not to leave the door open, nor to lean a pole against the tepee; neither should you blow on the fire, or allow any dogs to come inside; keep the fire burning throughout the night; don't let it die out. If you should neglect any of these things, trouble is sure to come."

Running Wolf said with grim humor: "A skunk may visit you in the early morning. He generally comes here, just before daybreak. But if you lie still, he is not likely to bother you."

By this time the evening constellations had swept far into the west. Already the Great Dipper, that clock of the night-sky, had its handle pointed downward to the horizon; day would soon dawn. I built up the fire and lay on my couch, listening to the sound of the river rapids and the wind in the tree tops. I thought about my Indian friends and their close communion with nature, their feeling of brotherhood with the birds and wild animals of the prairies and mountains. As I gazed into the dying fire, the pictures on my tepee walls took weird shapes. I thought of a large eagle that I had seen soaring over the camp. In my dream he came to my lodge; he stood by my side; he communed with me and gave me a message to the Indians of the North Piegans.

When I awoke, the bright rays of the sun were shining through the trees and the open door of my Thunder Tepee. How glorious are the first rays of the morning sun! The high summits of the Rocky Mountains looked like islands in a sea of fire. The women of our camp were already cooking breakfast. I saw the blue smoke rising slowly on the still air, curling gracefully from the tops of our lodges under the cottonwoods.

After I had a swim in the river, Onesta asked me whether anything had happened in the night. I said, "Yes," and remained silent.

When we were all seated by our fire after breakfast, Onesta asked me again if I had any dream. I replied:

"Just before daybreak I had a strong dream. An eagle came and stood by my side, saying:

"'My son, I am chief of all the eagles. I am going to help you, because you are alone and among strange people. Good luck will come to you in the camp of the North Piegans, and to any one who helps you.'"

Then I stopped and looked around the circle of my Indian friends. I was serious and did not smile; I counted on their sense of humor and not in vain. They laughed and told my dream to the North Piegans. Soon it was repeated throughout all their camps. The people were not fooled, nor did I expect them to be. Nevertheless, after my night in the Thunder Tepee, I was in high favor among the North Piegans, and from that time all went well.

CHAPTER XXIX

THE RIVAL MEDICINE MEN

HUMAN nature is the same the world over. Bull Plume, the medicine man, was jealous of Brings-Down-the-Sun because I was in his camp. Bull Plume was of humble descent, ambitious for power and social position. On the other hand, Brings-Down-the-Sun came from a famous line of chiefs — one of the best families in the tribe. The older medicine man was revered by all the people for his noble character and kindness of heart, his wisdom and knowledge of their ceremonies.

On the day of Onesta's ceremony, I had my first public recognition from Brings-Down-the-Sun. I was outside the Thunder Tepee, where I could watch both dancers and the crowd of spectators. In the midst of the ceremony, Brings-Down-the-Sun left his family and took a seat by my side.

This straightway roused the jealousy of Bull Plume, which he did not try to hide. He was seated next to Onesta and said so that any one could hear:

"White Weasel has not come to visit my camp. He was my friend before he came into this part of the country. Now I know who has turned him against me."

Next morning Bull Plume came to our camp. He was a fine looking Indian of over six feet, muscular and well-proportioned, with a roman nose and high cheek bones. His voice was strong and resonant and of a quality well suited for leading ceremonies. When he talked he had a nervous habit of tossing his head and throwing back a long lock of hair which fell over his forehead.

On this occasion I knew that Bull Plume had something on his mind. He was morose and ill at ease. We talked for a while, but soon fell into a gloomy silence. Then he said:

"My heart is heavy because you are in the camp of another. You were once my friend, but now you do not come to see me."

I was loth to offend him and began to make excuses. But he said abruptly:

"I ask you to come to my lodge now. It is not far, on the other side of the river. I have tribal records to show you. Some of them are very old; they are picture records made on buffalo hides, which were handed down from my grandfather. If you come with me to-day, I will allow you to copy these old records."

I assured him I wanted to see his records, but again made excuses for that day, because our horses were feeding on the hills and there was no way for me to cross the river to his tepee.

Then Bull Plume was angry. He arose and drawing his blanket around him, stalked from our camp. That was the last I ever saw of him. He took down his tepee and left the country.

As soon as Brings-Down-the-Sun heard of the visit of Bull Plume, he came to our camp for the first time. He seated himself by our fire. After smoking awhile in silence, he said slowly and deliberately:

"If you would rather go to the camp of Bull Plume than remain here with me, I will not stand in your way."

"But I have no idea of going," I replied. "I would rather stay with you."

Said Brings-Down-the-Sun: "I would prefer to have you stay here. Ever since the day Onesta brought you to my lodge, I have been preparing myself; now I have many things ready to tell you."

Again I assured him that I wanted to remain in his camp, saying:

"We made this long journey on purpose to see you; Onesta told me about you. He said you were the wisest of all the medicine men; that you could tell more than all the others. I do not want to go to Bull Plume; I want to learn from you alone."

Then Brings-Down-the-Sun said with deep feeling:

"For a long time I have borne in silence many things from Bull Plume; but now it is time for me to speak plainly. He told you about the tribal records handed down from his grandfather. He got that information from me. No one knows who his grandfather was. I can remember him as a small boy, barefoot and poor; he walked behind the travois when our tribe moved camp. Not until he became a man did he gather information for the records of which he boasts. He lied to you, but you were not deceived."

For a moment Brings-Down-the-Sun was silent. Then he turned and said earnestly:

"I can read a man's character in his eyes and by the look I see in his face. I now take you for my son. From this time forth, I shall be your Indian father in the north; and the people of my tribe shall be your brothers and sisters. Now I give myself up to you; and will tell you anything you want to know. Your relatives who live far away towards the rising sun, I take as my friends; my heart feels warm towards them; I shake hands with all of them."

Then he pointed reverently towards the sun, which was setting over the mountains, and said:

"Behold! Our Father, the Sun. He looks down upon us here together and hears everything we say. I am going to tell you many stories and legends, about our religious ceremonies and ancient customs before the white men came. Before the Sun, I promise to tell you nothing but the truth."

After that, the old chief came regularly to our camp. He had a fine mind and a wonderful memory. He talked day after day and filled my notebooks with information and stories — the way they had been handed down from father to son through many generations of ancestors.

CHAPTER XXX

BRINGS-DOWN-THE-SUN TELLS ABOUT HIS FATHER

WHEN Brings-Down-the-Sun came to our camp the following evening, he took a seat by the fire. For a while he meditated, smoking his everyday pipe in silence, and then he began:

"There is a trail we call 'The Old North Trail.' It runs along the Rocky Mountains outside the foothills. It is so old no one knows how long it was used. The horse trail and travois tracks were worn deep into the ground by many generations of Indians.

"My father told me that this old trail was started ages ago by an Indian tribe coming down from the north; and other tribes followed in their tracks. I have followed the Old North Trail so often I know every mountain, stream, and river of its course. It ran from the Barren Lands in the north to the south country, where people have dark skins and long hair over their faces (Mexico)."

By this time it was growing dark and the fire burned low. No one spoke until the silence was broken by the mournful howling of a wolf in the near-by hills. Then Brings-Down-the-Sun continued:

"The wolf is our friend and we do him no harm. The Indians have a saying, 'The gun that shoots a wolf or coyote will never again shoot straight.'

"I never heard of a wolf that did not wander. They raise their young in one place and then move on to another. They like to run all over the country.

"My father's first name was Running Wolf. His father, Little Mountain, gave him that name, because a wolf appeared in a dream and advised him, saying:

"'I am the head-chief of all the wolves and my name is

BRINGS-DOWN-THE-SUN AND THE AUTHOR

Running Wolf. You often hear my voice; my tracks are everywhere and I shall always continue to wander. Name one of your sons after me; and if he has a son, let that name be handed down; all of your descendants who bear my name will have long life and good luck.'

"I have now the wolf-nature, because my father bestowed the name of Running Wolf upon me. Like the wolf I wander over the plains and through the mountains; I never like to stay long in one place.

"Now I am going to tell you more about my father — how my grandfather, Little Mountain, happened to honor him with the name of Running Wolf, although he had two older brothers.

"One day in early summer, when my father was only a boy, he saw a band of warriors gather near my grandfather's lodge; he was then head-chief of the tribe. They were dressed for war and had their horses painted with war signs. They stood in a circle, holding a big rawhide between them, upon which they beat with sticks like a drum and sang a wolf song. They marched singing through the camp, saying farewell to friends and relatives; and then started south on a war expedition.

"Now this was very exciting to my father; his two older brothers were among the warriors. He wanted to go too. But he knew they would not take him because he was too young.

"After the expedition had gone, the boy ran into the lodge and took a bow and arrows. He told his father, the head-chief, he was going for a hunt; but he rode fast and overtook the war party. They tried to send him back. But one of his brothers said:

"'If he is so eager, let him come; he can look after one of the pack horses.' Thus it happened that my father went with that war party.

"One night, after they crossed the Yellowstone River,

the boy was wakened by a noise. He scouted around and saw a band of hostile Indians coming into camp. They were some of the Snakes and he gave the alarm. The Blackfoot warriors made ready to attack, but waited until just before dawn.

"In the fight my father made a wonderful shot and killed a Snake Indian. It was the only scalp they took on that trip. When the warriors came back to the Blackfoot camp, they waited on the summit of a hill, until a big crowd came out to meet them.

"Then they made known to the people how the boy was the only one to kill an enemy. They showed the Snake scalp and the head-chief was proud of his son. He tied that scalp to a long pole and told the boy to hold it aloft, and to shout as they rode triumphantly through the camp: 'My name is Running Wolf; I am the youngest of the war party and the only one to kill an enemy. Behold! Here is the scalp.' Thus it happened that my father got the name of Running Wolf.

"When my father was head-chief of the tribe, he went by the name of Iron Shirt, because he was accustomed to wear a shirt which was decorated with shining pieces of metal. He was also head man of the band of Grease Melters. He was a large and muscular man, with fine mind and a wonderful memory. He knew all the legends and lore of his tribe. He could tell the age of a horse by its whinny and of a man by the sound of his voice. He kept 'winter-counts' by making pictures on buffalo robes. He recorded important events in the history of the tribe — places of tribal camps, battles and the names of war chiefs, years of smallpox, summers of drought and winters when snows were deep and food scarce. He kept count of the winter when many of our people died from the cough-sickness, the winter when the children broke through the ice, when some moose came into our camp, also the winter when we had to eat dogs to keep from starving, the time a herd of antelope broke through the ice, when we caught some antelope in the deep snow, when buffalo were scarce, and the time we made the first treaty with white men.

"Sixty-one winters have passed since we had our first great sickness of smallpox (1836); forty-two, since we had the big camp on the Yellowstone River (1855), the time eight Indian tribes came together and our head-chiefs were Little Dog, Big Snake, and Lame Bull; twenty-seven winters since the coming of the North-West Mounted Police (1870), and twenty-one since the bad winter, when many of our horses were frozen to death (1876).

"I was born in the spring, the year the first white men appeared in our country. And I was still a young boy when my father became the owner of his first Medicine Pipe. This happened in one of our tribal camps, which was being held in mid-summer. Wolf Child was the owner of a Pipe and chose my father as his successor. He told the medicine pipe men he wanted them to take my father.

"Now it happened that my father was a 'bear-man'—that is, his power came from the grizzly bear. He had a sacred bearskin inside his lodge, which he kept hanging from the lodge-poles, just over his couch. The word 'bear' must never be spoken in the presence of a Medicine Pipe; it has an evil influence. For this reason the medicine pipe men were always afraid to offer a Pipe to my father, with the sacred bearskin so near.

"But Wolf Child, the owner of this Pipe, advised there was no danger from the skin. He said my father had great power; besides it was possible for them to drive away the evil by burning sweet pine as incense.

"Thus Wolf Child persuaded his friends and overcame their fears. It was after midnight, when I heard the medicine pipe men stealthily enter our lodge. Wolf Child came first, with the sacred Pipe hidden under his robe. They caught my father asleep; and, when he woke up, they offered him the Pipe. He took it in both hands and they all began to drum and sing. After that my father smoked the Pipe and said:

"'I am the owner of many horses, which of them do you want?'

"Wolf Child answered: 'Your black buffalo-horse.' Now this was the most valued horse in my father's herds. He was a famous race horse, the fastest in the tribe; he was so high-spirited it took three rawhide bridles to hold him.

"But my father did not hesitate. He answered quickly: 'Take him, he is yours.' So Wolf Child got the horse and my father became the owner of a Medicine Pipe. It was an honor to be chosen, although the Pipe was a great burden. But my father could not refuse; no one ever dares to turn down a Medicine Pipe. I know of an Indian who tried it, because he did not want to give up a valuable horse. Misfortune came upon him. His father-in-law died, then the horse; and finally the man died himself. All because he refused to take over a Medicine Pipe when it was offered to him."

Origin of his Father's Thunder Pipe

"Once I was camped with my father and grandfather on the St. Mary's River. We were near the mountains after beaver, which were plentiful then. One day my father went alone on a hunt, following the trail of some elk to Chief Mountain. At timber-line he came upon a band of mountain sheep and trailed them towards the summit. Near the top of the mountain, he came upon bad-smelling smoke coming from a deep hole. Into it he rolled a stone. He waited to hear it fall. But no sound came back; only a cloud of smoke so dense he could hardly breathe. Then he saw a thunder cloud coming down the mountain and started to run. There came a crash and he fell to the ground. A woman stood over him; her face was painted black and she had red zigzag streaks for lightning below her eyes. Behind her stood a man with a huge weapon. My father heard him say:

"'I told you to kill him quickly, but you stand there and pity him.'

"He heard the woman chant: 'When it rains, the sound of the Thunder is my medicine.'

"Then the man sang and fired his big weapon; it sounded like the crashing of thunder, and my father saw lightning coming from the hole in the mountain. Suddenly he found himself inside a cave; he could not speak, neither could he raise his head. He heard a voice say:

"'This is the person who threw the stone into our fireplace.'

"He heard some one beating a drum; and after the fourth beating, he was able to sit up and look around. He was in the home of the Thunder. He saw the Thunder Chief in the form of a huge bird, with his wife and children around him. They all had drums painted with the claws of the Thunder Bird, and its beak from which came streaks of lightning.

"Whenever the Thunder Chief smoked his Pipe, he blew two whiffs towards the sky, then two to the earth; and after each whiff the thunder crashed. Finally the Thunder Chief said to my father:

"'I am the Thunder Maker and my name is "Many Drums." You have seen my great power and can now go in safety. As soon as you return to your camp, make a Pipe just like the one you see me smoking. When you hear the first thunder in the spring, you will know I have come from my cave. Then it is time for you to take out your Pipe and hold it up. If you are ever in a bad thunderstorm and feel afraid, pray to me saying:

"'Pity me! Many Drums, for the sake of your youngest child,' and no harm will come to you.

"Thus it happened that my father became the owner of a Thunder Pipe. When he knew he was going to die, he gave this Pipe into my care. He said it was a 'long-time-pipe' and must not be buried with him. I still have the Thunder Pipe and smoke it only on important occasions.

"My father was skilled in the catching of eagles. He taught me how to take eagles alive, and for many years the catching of eagles has helped to support my family. But it was a hard and dangerous calling. I had to go to a solitary place near the foot of the mountains and dig a hole in the ground deep enough for me to stand in. I killed a coyote and stretched the hide on sticks, laying raw meat along the sides, to look as if it were freshly killed. I entered the pit before daylight, in order that no eagle could see; and covered it over with branches and leaves. The coyote bait lay on top, just over my head. I stood in that pit all day without food or drink. I could not even smoke, lest the eagles might get the scent. Throughout the day I chanted the coyote song, 'I want the eagles to eat my body,' because it had the power to attract eagles to my bait.

"The Long Tails (magpies) generally came first. They walked around the meat, chattering and saying to each other over and over, 'Long Tails go ahead and hang your sack upon a tree.'

"After a while an eagle would see the magpies eating the bait and come near. At first he would be suspicious. When he walked upon the blind and started to eat, I thrust both hands through the branches and seized him by the legs. I drew him quickly into the pit and killed him by breaking his neck with my foot, so that the wings fell to both sides and the feathers were not injured.

"Golden eagles were the most profitable to catch; the Indians wanted them because of their white tail feathers with black tips which they used for headdresses and sacred bundles. Bald eagles were scarce and hard to catch. Some of them were so powerful they almost dragged me from the pit.

"In those days eagle-catching was a dangerous occupation, because of grizzly bears. I remember an Indian, who held fast to his bait when a big grizzly started to drag it away. The bear pulled off the branches and saw the man in the pit. He pulled him out and tore him to pieces. When his relatives came, there was nothing left but his bones.

"My father did not die in battle, nor of sickness, but of old age. After his death, I became interested in religious things and came north to live. One night I slept alone on a high hill of the prairies. I had a strong dream. The Sun God came to me and said:

"'My son, be not afraid. I give you my power and will guard you through life.'

"I took an interest in the Sun Dance and became one of its leaders. From that time, I was no longer called Running Wolf. People called me Brings-Down-the-Sun (Natósinnépe-e), because I had the power of the Sun.

"I have nine children living, four sons and five daughters. The names of my sons are, Running Wolf, Iron Shirt, Double Walker, and Three Eagles. The girls are, Long Hair, Turns-Back-the-Herd-Alone, Good Kill, Double-Gun-Woman, and Whistling-All-Night.

"Towards the north lies the highest summit of the Porcupine Hills. No trail leads to it and it is surrounded by a dense forest. The top is steep and is covered with stunted pines. From that direction come our hardest storms. When my oldest son died I went to that lonely summit. I did not want to see any one. I stayed there night and day and fasted. Then I had a dream. The Spirit of the Mountain came to me and gave me a Medicine Robe;[1] and with it went supernatu-

[1] This Medicine Robe of Brings-Down-the-Sun is now in the Blackfoot Collection, American Museum of Natural History, New York City.

ral power—power to heal the sick. This wonderful Robe had many skins of birds and wild animals attached. There were marks to represent the Sun and Morning Star, also the constellations of the Bunch Stars and the Seven Persons. I wore it in the ceremony of the Sun Dance, when I stood before the people; and it gave me power to doctor the sick.

"That Spirit of the Mountain warned me to give up using the sweat-lodge, lest more of my children die; and to wash daily in the river. Since that time I have always bathed in the river every morning, even in winter when I have to break the ice. I tell my sons to bathe regularly; and after they finish, the women go in. I believe sickness can be warded off by keeping the body clean and using sweet smoke for incense."

CHAPTER XXXI

BRINGS-DOWN-THE-SUN TELLS ABOUT MEN'S SOCIETIES

THE BRAVES

"I AM a member of the Society of Braves. It was started long ago by an Indian. He had a strong dream in which he saw a band of dogs and the way they acted. The Braves ruled the camp and helped our chiefs to keep order. We punished men and women who quarreled; we sometimes killed people who disobeyed our orders.

"When it was time for our tribe to move camp, we marched with the beating of drums and singing, each member carrying a knife and a bow and quiver full of arrows. We went to the center of camp and spent the night curled up on the ground like dogs. The day our tribe moved, we stayed behind and acted like dogs, eating all the food that was left; like dogs we followed slowly and entered camp after all the lodges were pitched.

"We placed our big lodge in the center of camp, taking possession early, on the morning we danced. Our leader wore a coyote skin for a headdress with the tail hanging down behind. He was called Wolf-Skin-Man and carried a short lance, which was decorated with feathers. The next in rank carried a willow branch. He wore a robe with buffalo hoofs attached, which rattled when he danced.

"On the left of our leader sat the 'white braves,' with white painted lances stuck into the ground in front of their seats. Their bodies were painted white; and they had yellow stripes across nose and eyes. Two other members called 'water braves' were painted black; they carried bladders on their backs for water pails and bags for back-fat and pemmican. There were also 'black braves' carrying black lances, with bodies painted black and black stripes across their faces; and 'red braves' with red lances and red painted bodies.

"Two other braves carried bows and arrows instead of lances. They had their faces painted to impress the spectators; their bodies were covered with red and on their faces was the bear sign — black streaks down over the eyes and at each corner of the mouth. They wore their front hair short and made it stand straight up by covering it with paint. They had fringed shirts made from the smoked tops of old lodge covers, belts of bearskin and arm-bands of bearskin with bear claws attached; for headdresses they had strips of skin with bear ears and two claws attached to look like double ears.

"Whenever we danced outside our society lodge, we sat in an open circle with four drummers in the center, our lances stuck into the ground with points down. Wolf-Skin-Man as leader was at the head of our circle, opposite the opening, with the two bear braves outside. They covered themselves with robes, as if they were bears lying in a den.

"Our leader, Wolf-Skin-Man, danced first, blowing his bone whistle as a signal for the others to follow. Then we dropped our robes and followed him, blowing whistles and bearing our lances. We danced slowly in a circle, leaning forward and holding our lances near the ground and acting like dogs looking for places to lie down. The white-painted braves drove the others before them with their lances, but stopped as soon as the two water braves appeared. Then came the brave with the willow branch, who could not stop dancing until the two grizzly bears appeared.

"The bears only danced when they felt like it. They lay in their den and did as they pleased. Sometimes the spectators threw things at them to make them dance. When they were ready they got up slowly, holding their hands the way bears do their paws. They danced leaning over, hopping along in short jumps with their feet together, as bears are accustomed to do. They aimed with bows and arrows, and drove the other dancers back to their seats.

"When we wanted to bring our dance to a close, the two bears pretended they were going to shoot at the spectators with sharp-pointed arrows; but they changed quickly to painted arrows without points and shot them over the heads of the people. Then we ran over the prairie, in the direction the arrows flew, taking off our moccasins and throwing them away.

"We marched through camp singing our society song and shouted our orders to the people. It was our custom to take anything we wanted, even food from the kettle, as dogs do. We stopped to dance at the lodges of prominent chiefs, who were expected to give us presents of food and clothes. If any people bothered us or held us back, the bears shot at them with their arrows.

"If our leader told us to allow no one to chase buffalo, then we were the watchmen of the herds. If the buffalo were frightened and ran away, scared by some one who chased secretly, we followed that man and took away his horse and weapons; we tore off his clothes and whipped him; we sent him back to camp naked and on foot. We alone could look for buffalo; and, when we found plenty of them, we moved the tribe that way. We also punished women who picked berries against our orders by tearing their lodges to pieces.

"Men who joined the Society of Braves had to face danger whenever it came; they could not turn away. When we decided it was time to change our camping place, we made a feast in our society lodge and invited the head-chief. After we had eaten and were smoking together, our head-chief would say:

"'My children, why have you asked me to come here? What is it that you want'?

"And our leader would answer: 'Grass is scarce for the horses; the water is poor and the ground no longer clean; it is time for us to move to another place.'

"Then the head-chief would reply: 'In the morning we shall break camp; it is too late to-day. Tell the people to bring in their horses from the hills and to picket them close to their lodges; we shall start at the rising of the sun.'"

The Society of Mosquitoes

"This society was formed many years ago by an Indian who hunted in a place where there were great numbers of mosquitoes. They came in swarms and bit him all over; he lay on the ground and lost all feeling; he heard strange voices singing:

> '"Mosquitoes, mosquitoes, get together, get together.
> Mosquitoes, get together,
> Our friend is nearly dead.'

"And then he saw mosquitoes beginning to dance. Some were red and others yellow. They had claws attached to their wrists and long plumes hanging from their hair. They sat in a circle and sang; they jumped up and down, springing this way and that, always dancing in the direction of the sun. He heard a voice say:

"'Brother, because you were generous and let us drink freely from your body, we give you our society of mosquitoes; we make you the leader.'

"Then that man came safely home and started the Society of Mosquitoes. Its members wore buffalo robes with the hair side out. Some painted themselves red and others yellow, with stripes across nose and eyes. They wore plumes in their hair and eagle claws attached to their wrists to represent the bills of mosquitoes.

"When the mosquito society gave their dance, they sat in a circle around the drummers; the leader was at the head, with yellow mosquitoes on both sides. After each song, they held down their heads and made a buzzing noise in imitation of mosquitoes. After repeating this dance four times, they scattered and went through the camp. Any person they met, they scratched with their eagle-claws, and said: 'Now I shall take blood from you.'

"Any one who resisted or tried to run away, they caught and scratched hard. But those who offered themselves freely, and invited them to take their fill, they did not hurt. Because, if a mosquito is left alone, its bite does no harm."

The Society of Kit Foxes

"This was one of the oldest of all our societies. It was started by an Indian named Elk Tongue, who dreamed about a kit fox. It invited him into its den. And there he saw the chief of the foxes with many foxes seated around him. Before he left their den, the fox chief said:

"'When you return to your tribe, take a foxskin for your medicine; wear it always on your back and my power will go with you. Form a Society of Kit Foxes. Gather together some young men and show them how to dress and to dance. Tell them, if they do these things and never kill any foxes, they will have benefit. But it will be bad luck for them to harm a fox.'

"After Elk Tongue came home he started the Society of Kit Foxes. The members had great power. The ceremony was secret and the people were afraid; it was dangerous to talk about it. Elk Tongue was their leader. He alone knew the secrets and told the other members what to do. Before he died he taught the ceremony to his son and told him all the secrets. After that the power of the foxskin was handed down from father to son through many years; and the members of that society taught their children never to harm a fox.

"When the Kit Foxes gave their ceremony, they opened up two lodges and made them into one. For four days and four nights they sat inside, painting and dressing themselves, singing and making ready, only appearing outside their dance lodge at night.

"But, on the fifth day, they came out and marched through the camp. Their leader wore the foxskin with its head in front, the ears on top, and the skin itself, with small bells attached to the tail, hanging down his back. He carried a bow and arrows, which were painted green; his body was also painted red, his face green, to look as frightful as possible and to make people afraid.

"The second in rank, called the white-circle-man, carried a long lance, with one end bent into the form of a hook; it was covered with white swan's-down and had white eagle feathers attached at regular intervals along its staff.

"The next in rank had a long lance in the form of a hook, which was wrapped with otter-skin and had black and red feathers attached. The other members carried pointed lances decorated with feathers, and small pipes painted red. They all painted their faces and wore eagle feathers in their back hair. Around their legs were wide bands of otter-skin with small bells attached.

"When the Kit Foxes marched through the camp, they formed in the shape of a fox head. The chief went first to represent the nose; behind him were the second and third men for the eyes; then came the other members in a group, all together representing the head of a fox. The two second men, as the eyes, watched the chief who was the nose, or leader; they acted as he directed and the rest followed after.

"For their dance, they sat in lines, with the regular members in the first line. If any were withdrawing from the society

— giving up their lances to new candidates — they sat in a second line; and the wives of the members sat behind.

"As soon as the drums began, the leader started the dance; and the two circle-men with white lances followed. After them came the other members with plain spears. They danced in pairs, the way Kit Foxes run together. They gave short, even jumps with feet close together, imitating the movements of a fox. They barked and moved about, first in one direction, then in another, just as a fox is accustomed to do. The two circle-men (eyes), barking and swinging their spears, danced between the two lines. They did not move in a straight line, because a fox never goes straight; his tail always seems to guide him. When the white-circle-men shouted, 'It is enough,' the dance stopped and the members returned to their seats. But, after a short rest, they began again. And that is what I know about our societies."

CHAPTER XXXII

BRINGS-DOWN-THE-SUN TELLS ABOUT THE BIRDS AND THE STARS

WE were seated by our camp-fire with the old chief and his family. My Indian sister, Strikes-on-Both-Sides, and Long Hair delighted the children, making whistles from cottonwood bark and toy lodges from leaves of the balsam poplar, winding them around their fingers into the shape of little tepees and fastening them together with twigs. They set them up like real lodges and made them into a big camp in the form of a circle.

Then we gave Brings-Down-the-Sun the collection of roots and herbs we gathered especially for him; and a rare medicinal root called "sharp vine" by the Indians, one of his favorite remedies for breaks and sprains. He was so glad to get it that he chanted and prayed over it. After putting our present carefully in an old medicine sack, he seated himself apart from the others, and with dignity waited for the women and children to become quiet.

From his manner I knew he was ready for his Indian stories and hastened to prepare notebooks and writing equipment. The old chief was watching, for he said with a smile:

"My white son there reminds me of a squirrel; he runs in one direction as if to steal something, then darts quickly in another; he never sits still a moment; he is always on the move."

At that moment a woodpecker with red-crested head called from a tree top. Brings-Down-the-Sun pointed to the bird and said: "He calls to the worms and bugs to stick out their heads; he is hungry and wants to eat them."

I asked the chief to tell about other birds and their songs. He replied:

"We called the yellow-breast (Western meadow-lark) 'big-rump-bird,' because he is so broad across the back. He is one of the first birds to come in the spring. We are always glad to see him; when he comes we know that summer is near. He has different songs: 'Good whistler (his wife) is a selfish woman'; also, 'Your sister has a black skin.'

"The black breast (horned lark) sings in the air: 'Spread out your blanket and I will light upon it.'

"Summer bringers (white-throats) sing: 'The leaves are budding and summer is coming.'

"We call the bird that chatters among the bushes, when women are gathering berries, 'stingy-with-their-berries' (kingbird). A bird with long legs and black breast (spotted sandpiper) we call 'shadow-in-the-water,' because it stands in shallow water and looks at its own shadow.

"My father taught me how to read the future, by watching the flights of birds and the habits of wild animals. Of all the birds, we look upon the raven as the wisest. When I see one soaring over our camp, I know a messenger is coming from a distance. If two ravens sit near a trail with their heads close together, it is a sign an enemy is near. On a hunt, if I see a flock of ravens playing together, I go in that direction and am sure to find game.

"My father told me how to read the signs in the sky — if the sun paints his face (sun dogs), a big storm is coming; when the 'fires of the northmen' (aurora) show in the sky, a heavy wind is coming; a 'feeding star' (comet), is a sign of famine and sickness; and if the sun hides his face (eclipse), a great chief is about to die. The rainbow is the 'lariat'; it is the Thunder roping the rain; and the storm will slow up."

Calendar of Moons

"The first moon of winter (November) is the 'wind-moon,' or 'time of the first big snow.'

"Last of December and early January, 'moon of the first warm wind' (chinook).

"January, 'moon when the jack rabbit whistles at night.'

"February, 'moon of heavy snows,' or 'when buffalo calves are black.'

"March, 'moon of sore eyes,' or 'moon when the geese fly north.'

"April, 'moon when ice breaks up in the rivers.'

The spring moon has different names — 'time when the trees are budding,' 'when buffalo calves are yellow,' 'when the buffalo plant is in flower,' 'when the grass begins to grow.'

"May, 'moon when the leaves come out.'

"June, 'moon of high water.'

"Late June and July, 'moon of flowers,' 'when strawberries get ripe.'

"We call August, 'home days.'

"September, 'moon when the leaves turn yellow.'

"October, 'moon when the leaves fall.'

"Last of October and early November, 'moon when the geese fly south.'

"My father used to sit by the lodge-fire on long winter evenings and tell us stories and the wonderful things that happened in his life. He told about the Stars and the Sun and the Moon, saying:

The Bunched Stars

"There is a family of small stars in the sky; we call them Bunched Stars. They are some children that got lost from an Indian camp on the plains long ago.

"This happened in the spring, the moon when the buffalo

calves are yellow. Some hunters were driving buffalo over a cliff. When they went back to camp, they gave the little yellow skins of the buffalo calves to their children, who wore them in playing.

"There was a poor family in the camp, whose children did not get any of the calfskins; and the others made fun of them.

"Then the poor children were ashamed, because they were not dressed like the others. They ran away from the camp and got lost on the plains. They had no place to go, so they went up to the sky. We know they are the Bunched Stars (Pleiades), because they never show themselves in the spring — the time buffalo calves are yellow. But, in the fall, when the calves are brown, you can see the Bunched Stars in the sky every night."

THE SEVEN STARS (*Ursa Major*)

"There is a constellation in the north sky we call the Seven Stars. They belonged to a family of nine children, two girls and seven boys. The oldest girl had many suitors, but she would not marry. She went every day into the forest to gather wood.

"One day her little sister followed; and when they were in the forest together, the older girl left her and went off alone. She stayed a long while and came back with her clothes covered with earth and leaves. The younger girl said to herself: 'There is something my sister does when she goes alone; and now I shall find out.' Next day she followed secretly; she saw her sister having a good time with a big grizzly bear; and came home and told her father.

"Then the father was angry. He said to his oldest daughter: 'Now I know why you do not marry any of our young men; you have a grizzly bear for your lover.'

"He went through the camp and called to the people: 'I have a grizzly bear for a son-in-law; he waits near by in the forest; let us all go forth and kill him.' So they went out and killed him.

"Then the girl stood by the body of her bear lover and mourned. His spirit came to her in a dream and bestowed his supernatural power upon her. After that she wore a piece of his skin for a charm and could do wonderful things.

"One day she suddenly changed herself into a big grizzly bear. She went through the camp and killed all the people; she spared only her little brother and sister. And the three of them lived together. But all this time the six older brothers were away on the warpath.

"One day the little sister went to the river with her water pails and met the brothers coming home from war. She told them about Bear-Skin-Woman — how she had killed all the people and would surely kill them too.

"Then the brothers planned to save their little brother and sister. They gathered prickly pears and scattered them in the dark, leaving only a narrow path from the tepee. That night the two children ran away in the dark and joined their waiting brothers by the river.

"As soon as Bear-Skin-Woman knew they had gone, she turned herself into a grizzly bear and followed them. But the prickly pears got into her feet and she had to stop to pull them out.

"It turned out that the little brother, whose name was Body Chief, was a medicine man with great power. He carried a bow with magical arrows and wore an eagle feather in his hair. When he heard their bear sister coming, he took his feather and made a lake between them and the bear; again he made a thicket to hold her back; and another time they all climbed into a tree.

"When the bear came to the tree, she said: 'Now where can you go? I am going to kill all of you.'

"She climbed into the tree and knocked six of the brothers

down; only Body Chief and his little sister were left. Then a little bird lighted in the tree near Body Chief and sang:

> "'Shoot her in the top-knot.
> Shoot her in the top-knot.
> You must shoot the top of her head.'

"By this time the bear was near Body Chief, so he took one of his magical arrows and shot her. She fell dead, and Body Chief came down from the tree.

"Now six of the brothers were dead. But Body Chief shot six of his arrows into the air. Each time he brought a brother back to life, until they were all alive again.

"Then Body Chief said: 'Now what shall we do? Our relatives and friends are all dead and we have no place to go.'

"The oldest brother said: 'Let us go to the sky and become seven stars in the north. Then people will always know that the morning comes from us.'

"So Body Chief took one of his eagle feathers. He waved it over his head, and the brothers went up to the sky one after the other. They took the same places they had in the tree, with the four oldest at the bottom. Body Chief, the medicine man, is the end star in the constellation, and their little sister the small star at one side. Every night you can see the brothers move around the sky, until their heads are up in the morning. And that is how the Seven Stars (*Ursa Major*) came to be."

Then Brings-Down-the-Sun arose and pointing to the bright constellation in the north, said: "Behold! The last brother is pointing down towards the prairie and the light of day will soon come."

CHAPTER XXXIII

LEGENDS OF STAR BOY AND SCARFACE

OUR last evening in the North Piegan camp many Indians came to visit. So we gathered logs and built up the fire, until the flames lighted up our white tepees and the surrounding woods.

Brings-Down-the-Sun took his customary seat on a log by our fire and silently smoked his redstone pipe. The fire burned low and there came a silence. I heard the last birds chirping in the thickets and frogs croaking in a near-by swamp. Finally I asked the old chief to tell about two bright stars (Venus and Jupiter) then in conjunction; they rose in the early morning before the sun. He knocked the ashes from his pipe, and for a moment gazed meditatively into the fire. Then he said:

"The things I am going to tell you happened long ago, long before we had the Sun Dance; when our people used stone weapons and had dogs instead of horses for beasts of burden.

STAR BOY

"It was a night in early summer. The sky was clear and a warm wind blew over the prairies. Two sisters were sleeping on the grass outside their father's lodge. The youngest, whose name was Feather Woman, wakened before daybreak and saw Morning Star rising from the prairie. For a while she watched this wonderful star; and she talked to him as if he were her lover. At last she woke her sister and said: 'See Morning Star! He is beautiful and must be very wise. I want him for my husband.'

"This happened in the spring. In the 'moon when leaves

were turning yellow,' the sister who loved the star found herself with child. The people learned her secret and taunted her until she wanted to die.

"One day, at the time when geese were flying south, Feather Woman went alone to the river for water. On her way back to camp, a young man met her in the trail. He stood in her way and she said:

"'Why do you want to head me off? None of the young men have ever bothered me before.'

"And he answered: 'I am Morning Star. One night in spring you took me for your husband. Now I have come from the sky to take you to the lodge of my father and mother, the Sun and Moon. We shall be together and you will have no more trouble.'

"Then the girl remembered that night in the early summer and knew Morning Star was the father of her child. He wore a yellow plume in his hair and held a juniper branch with a spider-web hanging from one end. He was tall and straight and his hair was long and shining. His beautiful clothes were of soft-tanned skins; and had a fragrance of pine and sweet grass.

"She wanted to tell her father and mother; but Morning Star allowed her to speak to no one. He fastened his plume in her hair and told her to close her eyes. He gave her the branch with the spider-web to hold; and thus she was drawn up to the sky. When she opened her eyes, she was standing with Morning Star before a large lodge. He said: 'This is the home of my father and mother, the Sun and Moon.'

"It was daytime and the Sun was away on his long journey, but the Moon was at home. Morning Star said to his mother: 'I saw this girl asleep on the prairie; I loved her and she is now my wife.'

"Then the Moon was glad and took the girl into their lodge. She gave her a dress of soft-tanned deerskin, trimmed with elk teeth, wristlets of elk teeth, and an elkskin robe, and said: 'I give you these because you married our son.'

"So Feather Woman lived with Morning Star in the home of the Sun. She was happy and learned many wonderful things. When her child was born, they called him Star Boy; then the Moon gave her a sacred root-digger, saying:

"'It is used only by good women; with it you can dig all kinds of roots; but do not dig up the big turnip that grows near the home of the Spider Man.'

"Everywhere Feather Woman went, she carried the root-digger and Star Boy. She often looked at the big turnip, but was afraid to touch it. But one day she felt curious to see what was underneath; she thought how strange was the warning of her mother-in-law, the Moon.

"She laid Star Boy on the ground and started to dig; but the root-digger stuck fast. Two large cranes came flying from the east; and she called on them for help. The man-crane stood on one side, his wife on the other. He took the turnip in his long bill and moved it slowly backwards and forwards. They chanted four songs in the four directions. Then they pulled up the turnip; and Feather Woman saw a hole in the sky.

"She looked down to the earth, and saw the prairies and rivers, the meadows and lodges of her people. For a long time she sat watching the familiar scenes; women tanning skins and making lodges, gathering berries on the hills and crossing the meadows to and fro for water. It made her unhappy and she began to cry. She felt lonely and wanted to go back to her own people on the prairies.

"Then Feather Woman returned to the lodge of the Sun. As soon as she entered, Morning Star saw she was unhappy and said:

"'Alas! You have dug up the sacred turnip.' And, when

she made no reply, the Moon said: 'I warned you, because I did not want to lose Star Boy.'

"Nothing more was said, because the Sun Chief was still away on his long journey through the sky. In the evening when he came home, he said:

"'What is the matter with my daughter-in-law? She looks unhappy and must be in trouble.'

"Feather Woman answered: 'Yes, I looked down to the earth and feel homesick for my people.'

"Then the Sun God was angry and said to Morning Star: 'She has disobeyed and must go back to the earth. She can no longer be happy with us.'

"After that Morning Star took Feather Woman to the home of the Spider Man, whose long web had drawn her up to the sky. He laid Star Boy on her breast and wrapped them both in the elkskin robe; he bade them farewell and let them down to the earth.

"This happened in midsummer, the time 'when berries were ripe.' In the Blackfoot camp many people were outside their lodges, watching a crowd of young men play a game of rolling the wheel. Suddenly they beheld something coming down from the sky. And when they came to the place where the bundle lay, they saw the woman and her baby.

"They took her to her father's lodge and she lived there. But after that she was not happy. She used to go alone to the summit of a hill and mourn for her husband. One night she slept on the hill; and, at daybreak, when Morning Star rose over the prairies, she begged him to take her back.

"Before Feather Woman died, she told all these things to her father and mother. Then the grandparents of Star Boy died, and he was left alone in the camp. He was so poor he had no clothes, not even moccasins to wear. He did not play with other children; they made fun of him and stoned him. Whenever the tribe moved camp, he had to walk barefoot behind the rest of the people. He had a ridge-scar on his face; and they called him Scarface.

Scarface

"Now when Scarface became a young man he loved the daughter of a chief. She had many suitors, but refused all of them. Scarface asked her to marry him. But the chief's daughter ridiculed Scarface and said: 'I shall not marry you until your scar can be seen no more.'

"Then Scarface was ashamed and went away from the camp. He wandered alone; he fasted, and prayed to the birds and wild animals for power. Finally an eagle took him to the home of a wise old woman. She asked him why he traveled so far, and he replied: 'Because of this, my scar.'

"Then the old woman said: 'Ah, yes, I know, I understand. You must go to the place where the sun sets, beyond the mountains and down the other side, to the big water. There you must wait, for you will be near the home of the Sun. In the evening he comes home to his lodge; and before dawn his only son, the Morning Star, comes out. He will tell you how to live.'

"The old medicine woman pitied Scarface and gave him food to eat, and moccasins to wear, for his feet were torn and bleeding. Then he left her and traveled again, across the mountains and down the other side, until he came at last to the shore of the big water. There it was so hot he knew he was near the lodge of the Sun. So he lay down and waited.

"In the early morning a young man with a beautiful face came forth. It was Morning Star. He saw Scarface and said:

"'Brother, I shall hide you. Soon my father, the Sun, will appear and would kill you. In the morning he comes from his lodge and starts on his long journey through the sky.'

"So Morning Star hid Scarface. And after the Sun had gone, he took him to his mother, the Moon, and said:

"'I want this fellow for my comrade. He has come a long way and I ask you to pity him.'

"The Moon answered: 'Wait until your father comes home to-night; I am afraid he won't allow the young man to stay.'

"That evening, as soon as the Sun entered the lodge, he said to his wife: 'Whew! Old woman, I smell a human here.'

"And the Moon replied: 'Yes, your son has a chum hidden yonder.'

"Then the Sun would have killed Scarface, but the Moon interceded and saved his life. Morning Star burned juniper and sweet grass. He put Scarface in the sweet-smelling smoke; and after that the Sun allowed him to stay in the lodge.

"Thus Scarface became the comrade of Morning Star; and the two young men went everywhere together. On one of their trips, some huge birds with sharp bills attacked Morning Star. They would have killed him, but Scarface cut off all their heads and saved his life. Four of the heads he gave to the Sun and three to the Moon. Then the Sun praised Scarface. He said he was a chief and gave him a war shirt, which was trimmed with scalps and ermine and with leggings to match. On each legging the Sun made seven black lines to represent the seven enemies he had killed. Because of this our warriors have always painted their leggings with the number of enemies they kill in battle.

"The Sun asked Scarface why he traveled so far, and he replied:

"'A girl said she would not marry me until my scar was healed.'

"Then the Sun doctored Scarface in four sweat-lodges, until he and Morning Star looked alike in every way. Even the Moon could not tell them apart. When the Sun asked his wife which of the two was Morning Star, she pointed to Scarface. For this reason the Indians sometimes call him Morning-Star-by-Mistake.

"When it was time for Scarface to leave the sky and return to the earth, the Sun gave him power to heal the sick. He told him about the Sun Dance and taught him the songs and prayers, saying: 'It must be given in midsummer, when my power is greatest. If a virtuous woman makes a vow to the Sun and gives this ceremony sacred to me, the sick will be restored to health.'

"At parting, Morning Star showed Scarface the Wolf Trail (Milky Way), the short path across the sky to the earth. He gave him a magic flute and a song with which to charm the girl he loved. So Scarface left the home of the Sun and returned to the earth. He brought the Sun Dance to the Indians and power to heal the sick. Then he was taken back to the sky and became another Morning Star, just like his father."

Thus spake Brings-Down-the-Sun. And after a short silence he continued, saying:

"I remember another time years ago, when these two stars rose close together in the early morning before the sun; also when I was a boy, I remember my father waking me one morning when we were going on a journey, saying: 'Get up, my son! Morning Star and Star Boy are rising over the prairie. Day will soon dawn and it is time we were off.'

"Sometimes these two stars separate and travel alone through the sky. I have also seen them together in the evening sky, going down after the sun. Now they are together in the morning. You can see them before dawn. Scarface comes up first, his father soon after, and then his grandfather, the Sun."

When the old chief ended his talk, no one spoke for a while, because of the magic of his words and the spell of the night. Suddenly a bright meteor flashed across the heavens and burst into a shower of sparks near the horizon. Some of the Indians thought it an evil omen. But Brings-Down-the-Sun said:

"That falling star is a sign a great chief has just died — a man who had a good heart and lived a straight life. The Sun God is all-powerful; he sees everything and watches over every one.

"And now our story-telling is ended, for the dogs have separated, having had their evening meal."

After Brings-Down-the-Sun and his followers had gone and our Indians were asleep in their tepees, I lay on my blanket-bed under the cottonwoods, thinking of Star Boy and Scarface, and watching the moon, very broad and big, mount slowly into a cloudless heaven, higher and higher, until the great trees were bathed in its silvery light. I heard the night wind in the trees, the murmuring of the river, and once the mournful cry of some night bird. In the peace and quiet of that wilderness camp, my home in civilization seemed like another world.

At dawn I wakened and saw our women making a fire to cook breakfast. After a plunge in the cold river, I went to find our horses, along the wooded trail in the valley, past the silent white lodges of the North Piegans. Out on the open prairie a gentle breeze was blowing, bearing the sweet fragrance of woods and meadows.

In the east were the two bright morning stars in conjunction, Star Boy and his father, the planets Jupiter and Venus. Star Boy (Jupiter) came up first, and was followed by Morning Star.

The first birds were chirping in the thickets and from the hills came the wailing cries of bands of coyotes. Soon a rosy glow spread over the Rocky Mountains, over the snow-capped peaks and the forests of the lower slopes. By the time I found our horses, the sun itself came up and flooded the prairies with light.

When our lodges were down and wagons packed, Brings-Down-the-Sun came to say farewell, leading his favorite horse, Soks-kinne (Loud Voice).

Soks-kinne was a handsome stallion with silvery mane and tail, the fastest race horse of the North Piegans. What a chest he had! Long legs and brightest of eyes. The old chief cared for him as for an old and faithful friend. But he led his horse forth and gave him to us.

When we refused to take him, Brings-Down-the-Sun handed me his favorite pipe of redstone, and said:

"My son, I give you my 'everyday' pipe — the one I have smoked for many years. Keep it as a remembrance of your Indian father. My heart feels heavy because you are going; and I shall be lonely every time I see your deserted camp-ground. Never have I gone into another camp to talk day after day as I have with you."

Then he shook hands; and, as I turned to go, the old chief gazed towards the rising sun and prayed:

> "Father, the Sun!
> May he go safely while traveling afar!
> May we live long and continue to be friends!
> May we both meet and be happy again!"

As we left the valley for the open plains, I turned in the saddle for a last look, and saw Brings-Down-the-Sun with bowed head, going along the trail to his lodge, leading his horse and followed by his old dog, Kops-ksisse.

CHAPTER XXXIV

BEGINNING OF THE SUN DANCE

The Blackfoot Indians did not have a personal God. They looked to the Sun as the source of all power, believing he was everywhere — in the mountains, lakes and rivers, birds and wild animals. They believed that Sun Power could be transferred to man. Any one might be the favored person; an individual was powerless to gain it, but he could put himself in the way of receiving the gift.

If an Indian wanted a religious experience, or to gain supernatural power, he went alone to a remote place to fast and pray, sometimes for many days. The gift came generally through the medium of some wild animal, bird, or supernatural being, whose compassion was aroused by his fasting and by his exhausted condition; often through one of the more powerful animals — the buffalo, grizzly bear, beaver, wolf, eagle, Thunder, or the Maker of Storms and Blizzards. If the grizzly bear bestowed his power, the man who received it was believed to attain the great strength and vitality of the bear.

The tribe had many sacred bundles containing supernatural power; all had songs for their rituals, and all the songs were different. The medicine men who led the ceremonies had to know the songs of the different bundles. This required many years of patient study and was an important part in the preparation of a medicine man.

In the ceremonies of these bundles, the objects they contained were of minor importance; the songs were the means of contact with religious power. Some of the ceremonies were believed to have power to heal the sick, others to promote the welfare of the people, or to bring success in war. But each bundle was owned by an individual who, in turn, could transfer it to another.

The Sun Dance was the only ceremony in which all the people participated. It was a great tribal festival held every year at midsummer when the grass was long and food plentiful. It always had its origin in a woman's vow to the Sun generally in behalf of a relative who was dying. Some attended to fast and pray, others to fulfill vows; but most of the people came for social enjoyment, and to see the ceremonies and social dances.

Mad Wolf, my Indian father, and his wife were the givers of a Sun Dance. One day in the early summer, I rode Kutenai, my saddle horse, across the prairie to attend their opening ceremony. When I came to a long ridge-like summit that led down to his camp, I dismounted to rest and view the landscape.

In the wide and grassy valleys were herds of fat horses and cattle. Sharp against the western horizon stood the snowy peak of Divide Mountain, where two continental divides meet, and the rocky summit of a mountain called "Chief" by the Indians, because it stands apart and is higher than the other peaks. It was evening and the hills and mountains were bathed in the rosy light of sunset. On all sides I heard the sweet sounds of prairie birds — the Western meadowlark and lark sparrow and the serene and exalted song of the willow thrush.

But the dogs of Mad Wolf's camp soon broke the spell; they got wind of the approaching white man and began an incessant barking. So I leaped into the saddle and rode down to his camp.

When I entered the lodge, the chief and his wife Gives-to-the-Sun were seated together at the back, their heads bowed in prayer. He looked at me with his keen glance, then shook hands and, directing me to a seat on a couch, said:

"I am glad in my heart that you have come to our Sun Dance. Ever since you went away, I have prayed to the Sun for your safe return. Now you can see our ceremony. I shall tell you everything and you can explain it to the white men; for I believe you are straight and will tell them the truth."

I asked Mad Wolf how it happened they were giving a Sun Dance, and he replied:

"Last winter, at the time of the second big blizzard, Small Otter, our youngest grandchild, was ill. Snow lay deep over the prairie; it was cold and for many days the sun did not shine. The doctors, White Grass and Ear-Rings, came. They gave root medicines; they danced and sang and beat upon their medicine drums. But our child grew weaker; they said he was going to die.

"One evening the clouds broke and the sun shone through. My wife went outside the lodge; she looked up to the Sun and prayed:

"'Sun, have pity!
I am praying for my grandson,
The one that is dying.
May he get well!
Sun, you must listen.
I swear I am pure.
All my life I lived straight.
Sun, I promise to give your ceremony,
If our child gets well.
We shall call in all the people.
Sun, have pity and hear my prayer.'

"Then she went to the bedside of Small Otter and said: 'Rise up, my child, and get well; for your sake I have vowed to give a Sun Dance.'

"After that my wife went to see Bull Child, the medicine man, and told him of her vow. Next morning they stood together facing the rising sun; and Bull Child prayed:

"'Sun, I know this woman has led a pure life. If her sick grandchild recovers, I promise she will give the ceremony for you; she will fast before all the people and become a medicine woman.'

"The following spring, by the time the snow had melted, Small Otter was well. So when the warm winds began to blow and the grass was green, we began to save tongues and make ready to fulfill our vow to the Sun. Now we are going to prepare them for the sacred food."

Before Mad Wolf and Gives-to-the-Sun started on the tongues, they asked White Calf, the head-chief, and his wife to help and guide them in the ceremony. They were the givers of the Sun Dance the year before. So they came to our camp and went through the ceremony of painting Mad Wolf and his wife and Small Otter, for whom the vow was made. They prayed with them and sang many songs. And the two couples stood together outside the lodge, while White Calf prayed to the Sun, promising that the Sun Dance would be given. White Calf repeated this promise in the four directions, while they faced in turn, north, south, east, and west.

Then they smoked a pipe together, and White Calf and his wife promised to lead and instruct and to act as "father" and "mother" throughout the long ceremony of the Sun Dance. And from them Gives-to-the-Sun purchased a "na-tóas" (sun-dance bundle), containing a sacred headdress and other articles, which were used by the woman who made a vow to the Sun. Thus it became known throughout the tribe that the Sun Festival would be given that summer by the Mad Wolf family.

After many tongues had been gathered and dried ready for use, Mad Wolf moved his camp to another place and summoned his relatives and friends to assist him in the ceremony. Then came many well-known Indians and their families and joined the camp, White Grass, Ear-Rings, Curly Bear, Middle Calf, Double Runner, Morning Plume, and

Blessed Weasel — the men to help in the singing and prayers, the women in preparing tongues.

Throughout these long rites my Indian father gave me instruction and every facility to learn; he stopped the ceremony that I might write down the chants and prayers and make photographic records. All his friends and relatives were well-disposed and the way was open.

The consecrating of the tongues lasted several days, the same ceremony being repeated for every lot of tongues brought in. They chanted and prayed and burned incense. White Calf and his wife directed. Throughout the entire ceremony of the Sun Dance, they were known as the "father" and "mother," Mad Wolf and his wife as the "son" and "daughter."

Gives-to-the-Sun, as the medicine woman, sat directly back of the fire in the central position, with Mad Wolf on her left and the wife of White Calf on her right. Next to Mad Wolf sat the head-chief, White Calf, and the other men. The men were all together on the north side of the lodge, while the women were together on the opposite side and in the same order as their husbands.

The wife of White Calf, as the "mother," took the tongues from the cases and laid them in rows on a rawhide. It was her privilege to hand them to the other women for slicing and skinning. She gave the first one to Gives-to-the-Sun, because she made the vow to the Sun. This tongue was then painted black on one side and red on the other, to distinguish it from the others; and as soon as Gives-to-the-Sun had taken it, she renewed her vow by praying:

"Sun, I have lived a straight life.
Ever since I came to my husband,
I have been faithful to him.
Sun, help me! What I say is true.
Help me to cut this tongue without mistake."

During the preparing of the tongues, if any of the women cut themselves or made a mistake, it was taken as a sign they were not virtuous.

After the tongues were cut into slices, two women went to the river for water, carrying a kettle between them. Before starting and all through their movements, they made prayers and sang. On their way to the river they stopped four times, each time standing with bowed heads, praying earnestly to the Sun. While dipping the water, they also sang and prayed and made four pauses for prayer on their way back to the lodge.

When the women placed the kettle of tongues on the fire, they burned sweet grass as incense. And while the tongues were boiling, they chanted and prayed, burning sweet grass and throwing it into the kettle. At this time the women made vows to the Sun that they were virtuous. They recounted their temptations — the occasions when they were improperly approached by men; they made known the names of the men and told how they had resisted.

After the boiling of the tongues, the kettle was taken from the fire and held in the sweet smoke, while White Calf sang to the Sun, Moon, and Morning Star. Then they had another ceremony for drying the tongues, and still another one for placing them in cases. Thus the meat was consecrated and made ready for taking to sun-dance camp, where the entire tribe would assemble.

CHAPTER XXXV

FORMING THE GREAT CIRCLE CAMP

INDIANS with their families kept coming to Mad Wolf's camp until their lodges spread far out upon the plain. The days were warm with clear sunshine and all were eager to move to the sun-dance camp.

At last the ceremony of the tongues was finished and they were packed in parfleches. One evening, when the sun was sinking into the west, I saw Mad Wolf come from his lodge and heard his strong voice ring out over the quiet plain, saying:

"Hear, my children. The time has come to move to the circle camp. Berries are ripe and the grass is now long over the prairies. To-morrow we shall go to the big flat on Willow Creek. Bring in your horses to-night and be ready to start at the rising of the sun."

Next morning I wakened soon after dawn and went out from my lodge. Along the horizon of the prairie was the golden glow of sunrise. Smoke was already rising from some of the tepees where the women were cooking breakfast. In the meadows many larks were singing and from the hills came the wailing of coyotes.

At Mad Wolf's tepee I saw Gives-to-the-Sun seated outside, with her head bowed in prayer; she faced south, the direction the tribe would move to the circle camp. As sacred woman she could do no work; she had women assistants, the wives of White Grass, Ear-Rings, Middle Calf, and Morning Plume, who took charge of moving her tepee. The wife of White Calf, as the "mother," looked after the wants of Gives-to-the-Sun. All through the preparations for moving, she kept praying — while placing the sacred travois before the woman and loading it with the cases of tongues and the ceremonial clothes — the elkskin dress of Gives-to-the-Sun with beaded leggings and moccasins to match, her headdress and robe of soft-tanned elkskin, and juniper for the altar. She hitched Gives-to-the-Sun's own riding horse to the travois, which was painted red; also the saddle, harness, and all of her equipment. Gives-to-the-Sun was so weakened by fasting and by sitting day after day in the same position that she had to be lifted upon her horse.

When it was time to break camp, the Indians watched the lodge of Mad Wolf for the signal to move. As soon as they saw the poles being removed from his tepee, the entire camp became a scene of confusion. All the white lodges came down together; quickly they were waving and flapping in the wind, and then lay flat on the ground. The horses stood ready and were soon loaded; and the people fell into line according to their different bands.

Chief Mad Wolf mounted his horse while singing a chant. He rode a short distance with White Calf by his side, and was followed by the sacred woman and her "mother." They rode in single file to a near-by hill; and there they waited for the rest of the people to fall into line.

Then Mad Wolf and White Calf slowly led the way across the open prairie. In the procession that followed were prominent Indians with their families — White Grass the medicine man, Ear-Rings the doctor, Heavy Breast, Bull Child, Middle Calf, Double Runner, Three Bears, Morning Plume, Bear Child, Blessed Weasel, Cream Antelope, and Medicine Weasel. I rode with the Mad Wolf family and among his relatives and friends.

It was still early morning when we started. The undulating hills were glorious under a bright July sun. Western meadow-larks were singing and I saw many wild flowers — pink roses, purple asters, and yellow gaillardia with dark-brown centers. On my face the sun felt hot, but a fragrant west breeze came from the mountains.

The plain we crossed stretched many miles in every direction and swept upwards towards the mountains, with snow-capped peaks in the distance. Then we climbed to a broad table-land, which was covered with tussocks of tough wiry grass, and here and there the skulls and bleaching bones of buffalo.

When we came to a range of grass-covered hills, I left my place and rode ahead to the summit of a butte to see the line pass. That was many years ago, but in memory, I can still see clearly that primitive procession of Mad Wolf and his redskin followers, as they slowly crossed the summit, their figures sharply outlined against the deep blue sky.

Mad Wolf was in the lead, tall and erect, with head thrown proudly back. The venerable head chief, White Calf, rode by his side; he was older than Mad Wolf and was somewhat stooped, his long gray hair falling in waves over his shoulders. The women followed with the sacred travois, its poles crossed in front, high over the horse's head, and the ends dragging behind on the ground. Then came a group of women helpers in bright-colored clothing. They rode horses with beaded ornaments on heads and breasts, having saddles with deer antlers for pommels and beaded buckskin flaps for the flanks.

In the van was a group of warriors with war bonnets of eagle feathers; they carried weapons, also a sacred Lance and a Shield. Their limbs were bare, and their clean copper skins shone in the sunlight. They were a hardy lot, with lithe muscular figures, riding gracefully, with an easy careless air and the haughty military bearing of warriors.

Then came many travois laden with baggage, groups of old men and women, children and young girls. The granddaughters of Mad Wolf and White Calf, Anatapsa and

Dives-Under-Water, were both astride a pinto horse. Anatapsa rode in front, her long black hair flying in the wind; round her slender waist, a blanket of bright scarlet was fastened by a belt of colored beads. She was pretty and vivacious, continually striking the sides of their old saddle horse with her small moccasined feet. All the time the hands of both girls moved gracefully in the sign language, for Dives-Under-Water was deaf and dumb.

I saw a travois with three old squaws, drawn by an aged rawboned horse. When he refused to go farther, the old women dismounted and beat him with ropes; but it was in vain. He stood as if asleep, with eyes closed and head down, oblivious to both their blows and curses.

Our procession wound in and out among the grassy hills, until we came to the broad plain chosen by Mad Wolf for the circle camp. It was covered with rich bunch grass, still green from the rains of early summer. On the west side of the plain was Willow Creek, a small trout stream, which was lined with willows and marshy meadows. Toward the east were the open plains, south, a range of grass-covered hills, and north, a ridge with a huge rock near the center.

The Indians all waited while Mad Wolf and White Calf chose the place for the sun lodge; and then the sacred woman and her attendants dismounted. Mad Wolf and White Calf seated themselves beside the medicine bundles and smoked, while the women helpers pitched the Mad Wolf tepee over the place where the sacred bundles lay. They placed green branches against the back, also the sacred travois — a sign to the people that the fasting woman was inside and must not be disturbed.

Around the lodge of Mad Wolf, the great circle camp was formed according to bands or blood relatives. Each family knew where their lodge belonged and took their accustomed places, each band under a head man.

THREE CHIEFS, FOLLOWERS OF MAD WOLF

A LINE OF WARRIORS WITH WAR BONNETS

Mad Wolf was the head man of the "Hard-Top-Knot" band, which were on the north side of the camp. They were called Hard-Top-Knots, because of the way they wore their hair. Other bands were called — Small Robes, because of the size of their robes; Fat Melters, who liked to eat melted fat; Don't Laughs, Worm People, Skunks, Buffalo Chips, and Lone Fighters. There was a band called All Chiefs, because their men all acted like chiefs; Lone Eaters, who were selfish and ate by themselves; Eat-Before-Others, because they had their meals before others were ready.

Then Mad Wolf sent a messenger to the southern division of the tribe, who were assembled under Running Crane many miles to the south, calling on them to move to the circle camp on Willow Creek.

Now Running Crane was a venerable chief, loved and respected throughout the tribe. He was head man of the band of Fat Melters, a wise counselor and one who acted as a father to all the people. He was brave in war, yet of a gentle and benevolent spirit. He gave freely to the poor, and was always ready to help those who were in trouble. I found him simple in his manners, modest, yet full of dignity.

In the afternoon of that same day, Running Crane arrived with his followers of the southern division. Among them were the war chiefs, Little Plume and Little Dog, Bear Chief, Spotted Eagle, Big Moon, Shoots-in-the-Air, Black Bear, Flat Tail, Strangling Wolf, and other prominent chiefs with their families.

Throughout that entire day people continued to come, until two thousand Indians were gathered together in the circle camp. Families came from many other tribes of the northwest, traveling long distances to attend — Mandans and Sioux from the Dakotas, Flatheads, Pend d'Oreilles and Nez Percés from across the Rockies. From the far north came Sarcees and Crees, North Blackfoot, Bloods, and North Piegans; also Bannocks and Crows from the south.

The big camp was over a mile in circumference, with the lodges of the head men of different bands on the inside circle; the small and inferior tepees of the poorer class were relegated to the outskirts.

Near the center of the camp, and apart from the others, the powerful society of Brave Dogs had their lodges where they kept their weapons and dance clothes. In their society lodge they gathered to feast and dress for their ceremonies and social dances, which took place at all times, both day and night. They were the police of the tribal camp. The head men looked to the Brave Dogs to enforce their orders. They saw that all the tepees were in their proper places and the big camp was symmetrically formed.

CHAPTER XXXVI

LIFE IN THE CIRCLE CAMP

THE first day of the big camp, the Indians were all outside their lodges, eager to see friends and on the lookout to greet those who came from a distance.

Excitement was in the air. Packs of dogs ran barking through the camp. Men and boys galloped over the hills, shouting and singing, rounding up bands of horses and driving them to water, picketing them in the meadows and driving others to feed on the grassy hills. Women were at work cooking, stacking lodge-poles or handling unwieldy covers flapping in the wind.

My lodge was pitched in the band of the Hard-Top-Knots, near Mad Wolf's tepee, where the ceremony of the Sun Dance was taking place. I shared it with Little Creek and Strikes-on-Both-Sides, my Indian sister, and their children, also Tears-in-Her-Eyes, a niece of Mad Wolf's, a baby of six months whom Strikes-on-Both-Sides adopted, because the mother had died in childbirth.

Near by was the lodge of Morning Eagle, an aged warrior, the hero of many battles. He was so old and decrepit he had to be lifted from his horse. Every morning before sunrise, he wakened me, singing his medicine songs. He was not musical and they all sounded alike; the only variation being slight changes in the rhythm, or in the bird or animal calls, at the end of each song. On a cold and rainy day, he crawled from his tepee to drive back the storm. In spite of his age and rheumatism, he sat in the wind and rain, singing and praying to the Maker of the Storm.

Another neighbor was Little Owl, who had a large family. I watched them every day at their outside fire. His pretty young wife, Coming Running, was tall and slender, with jet-black hair, which hung in heavy braids below her waist. Strong and healthy, she was always at work, with a flock of small children about her. She had many cares — a babe in arms and a small daughter with a dangerous abscess, and two visitors to entertain from the Flathead tribe. Yet she was always smiling and in a good humor. I did not hear her complain or speak an angry word.

She had a little play-tepee for the children, made by a blanket fastened round a cluster of poles. There they kept their playthings — dolls with deerskin suits decorated with real beads and feathers, dolls in baby cases, also little robes and blankets and cooking utensils. The boys had bows and arrows, and stilts made of cottonwood, crooked sticks for hobbyhorses and wooden tops.

At the tepee of Running Fisher, I saw a pet coyote puppy, and at another place a tame magpie sitting on top of a lodge-pole. In former days these Indians had many pets — hawks, eagles and cranes, beavers, wolves and antelope. A chief had two grizzly bears for pets. They were so well trained he could make them lie down with noses between their paws.

Another Indian had a pet crane, which followed him everywhere, and was said to be very wise. The man and the crane went so much together the people called them father and son. Whenever he left the crane behind, it mourned and was unhappy, going through the camp, even into tepees, until it found its master and stood beside him.

I met an elderly man from the north, whose name was Natosin (Sun Chief). He was over six feet in height and had long gray hair falling over his shoulders. He was venerable in appearance and his face had a kindly expression. He occupied a small traveling-lodge and had two travois to carry his baggage, one with a wicker frame of green branches built over the seat, to shield him and his aged wife from the sun. When I asked him how it happened they came so far to attend a Sun Dance, he said:

"Last winter I was very ill; the doctors said I was going to die. But I made a vow to the Sun; if I recovered I would attend the next Sun Dance, wherever it might be. In the spring I heard that Mad Wolf and his wife were giving the ceremony, so I came from the north to fulfill my vow and eat one of the sacred tongues."

I saw two women tanning a deerhide stretched on the ground, hair-side down, and held in place by wooden stakes. They raked it with large tools of bone sharpened at one end. Then they used an adzelike tool, removing the surface of the hide in chips, and made it of uniform thickness. When they had finished the flesh side, they turned the hide over and scraped off the hair and left it to bleach and cure in the sun.

At another lodge, I saw an aged woman with snow-white hair seated in the doorway, soft-tanning a skin by sawing it back and forth through a loop of twisted sinew fastened to a pole. Then she whitened it by rubbing it with a piece of fungus and the skin was ready for use.

The wife of Running Fisher was making decorated parfleches at the Otter Tepee, to be used as cases for packing with horses. And at the Buffalo Tepee of Wolf Plume, I saw a group of women at work, sewing a large lodge cover, which was spread between them on the ground. They enjoyed their work, smoking, gossiping, and feasting. The lodge covers were so large one woman could not handle them alone. It was the custom for a number of women to coöperate, making it a social affair with light refreshments. When the women finished at one lodge, they moved on to another.

A marked feature of Indian life was the superiority of the women in all household arts; they were trained in them from childhood. Though women performed most of the menial work and men were the providers and defenders, the women were not dissatisfied. A mother trained her daughter from childhood in tanning skins and making them into clothes and shelter; also in the knowledge of herbs and wild vegetables, which were used for eating and healing. Women considered this their special vocation and allowed no interference from the men, who were unfitted for the work.

In front of the War Tepee of Running Rabbit were two women drying and curing meat. They cut it into thin slices and smoked it, hanging it on a scaffold of poles and left it to cure in sun and wind. They made pemmican from choice pieces of dried meat, pounding it with stone hammers and mixing with crushed wild cherries, together with marrowfat and tallow. For the marrow, they boiled cracked bones and skimmed off the fat. They split tongues the long way and dried them in the sun. The tongues were a great delicacy together with beaver tails.

Meat was the chief article of diet for the Blackfoot; they were unhappy without it. In former years, when wild game was plentiful, they lived mostly on the flesh of buffalo and the deer species, but of late years on cattle. Their favorite way of preparing meat was by boiling, or in the form of soup. Sometimes they ate dogs at ceremonial feasts; but this was not a common custom.

In the circle camp, I saw preparations for a dog feast by a band of visiting Assiniboine Indians. Near our lodge was Eagle Child, who owned a litter of fat puppies. He had a miniature tepee for them, where they slept and had shelter from the hot sun. I saw them playing daily before my door. One night all of the puppies mysteriously disappeared; Eagle Child and none of his neighbors knew what had become of them. But I finally solved the mystery. While walking among the lodges of the Assiniboines, who were on the out-

DRYING AND SOFTENING A SKIN

FLESHING A HIDE

skirts of the big camp, I saw their women cooking over an outside fire. In the hot ashes were the remains of my puppy neighbors with their hair singed off, while some were boiling in a kettle. Nothing was wasted. At one side was a pile of little puppy legs and paws to be used for soup.

CHAPTER XXXVII

PAINTED TEPEES AND PICTURE WRITING

THE circle camp, on the prairies at the foot of the Rocky Mountains, had a strange and fascinating interest. Even after many years, the scenes are still fresh in my mind. Night and day there was generally something going on. Morning was the quietest time, when few people were stirring. Never did the meadows look fresher or lovelier than in the golden sunlight of a July morning. Flowers and grass were hung with sparkling lace and shining gems of dew.

On my way to the stream for my morning bath, I waded through masses of golden sunflowers and blue and purple vetches up to my knees. Dim on the eastern horizon, where the sun was rising, were the blue outlines of the Sweet Grass Hills; and in the west the mighty frontier range of the Rockies, with glistening glaciers and snowfields. In the long grass I saw a prairie hare, a pair of kit foxes, and ground squirrels running about, chirping in the sunlight. Along the shore of the lake were killdeer, long-billed curlew, and spotted sandpipers.

All the birds were singing, robins, yellow-throats, and lovely mountain bluebirds; horned larks were fluttering and trilling, hovering like butterflies against the deep blue sky. Along the stream were thickets of willows and snowberry bushes in flower, and in marshy places blue flags, scarlet painted-cups, and blue-eyed grasses.

After a plunge in the cold water of the brook, I went back to my lodge and had breakfast; looked after my horses, watered them and changed their picket places, then sat outside in the sunlight.

Health is a wonderful thing. On lovely summer mornings,

when nature was at her best over the prairie, my heart felt light and I was happy; the civilized world was easily forgotten. With my horses, cameras, and notebooks, I could always occupy myself and had plenty of work to do.

In the circle camp I counted three hundred and fifty lodges — thirty of them were Painted Tepees with symbolic decorations. They belonged to the head men of different bands and were pitched in prominent places on the inner circle. The owners were proud of them. The ceremonies that went with them gave a social prestige and a good standing in the tribe.

At first it was hard to find out anything about the Painted Tepees — about their symbolic declarations, ceremonies, and the legends of their origin. The owner believed that the divulging of the secrets weakened their supernatural power. Each Painted Tepee had a sacred bundle and a separate ceremony. The pictures on the tepee cover and the ceremony that went with them could not be separated. They came originally through a dream and belonged exclusively to the founder, who might transfer them to another; but no one could copy them. They were believed to have protective power for the owners and their families. Both men and women made vows to them in time of danger and in behalf of the sick. If the tepee cover with its decorations wore out, a new one with the same pictures took its place. But the old one was sacrificed to the Sun — destroyed by spreading upon the surface of a lake and sinking it under the water.

I learned about an Otter Tepee by living in one for a week, watching the owner in his ceremonies and his care of it. The supernatural power came to the founder in a dream, when he visited the home of an otter. The top of this Otter Tepee was painted black, with a yellow cross at the back for the Morning Star. Round the center were four male and four female otters; above the otters red bands representing ripples on the surface of the water, which an otter makes while swimming; and at the bottom of the tepee, a broad red band for the earth, surmounted by triangular figures for mountains.

The owner had a large otter-skin, which he sometimes took from his sacred bundle and hung from a pole over the tepee, to float in the wind like a flag, also a drum and a number of bird and animal skins. These he kept in a rawhide case, which hung from a tripod outside the tepee in good weather, but were always brought inside at night, or during a storm.

For the ceremony, he held the sacred bundle in the smoke of burning sweet grass, then laid it on the grass. When he opened his bundle and took out the contents, he sang songs and prayed. He painted his body yellow to represent the shore of a lake, with red marks for otter trails and tracks in the soft earth. A circle on his forehead stood for the home of the otter, another on his breast for a hole in the river bank through which the otter passes.

In the tribal camp, I counted five different Otter Tepees; also two Crow Tepees, two Eagle, and one each of the Snake, Water Animal, Big Rock, Deer, Elk, Mountain Sheep, Antelope, Horse, Rainbow, Thunder, Snow, Pine Tree, Bear, Buffalo Head, beside many others.

The owners of Painted Tepees guarded them jealously, because of their supernatual power and value to the tribe. It was long before I could purchase one. But I finally secured an Otter Tepee, because the owner lost faith in it. His wife and children had all died and he no longer believed in its protective power.

I saw Wolf Tail, a son of the head-chief White Calf, take over the Big-Stripe Tepee. He made a vow to purchase it during the winter. At the time of the circle camp, he went to Wipes-His-Eyes, the owner, and made known his vow. Now Wipes-His-Eyes did not want to sell; and his wife and children were sorry to give up their comfortable home. But

CIRCLE CAMP OF THE BLACKFOOT
It was more than a mile in circumference

because of the vow, they dared not refuse. So Wolf Tail took down their tepee and pitched it in another place in the circle camp.

The first lodge I owned had no pictures on the cover. Then I knew nothing about Painted Tepees — their rules and regulations. I wanted mine decorated, so I went to Medicine Weasel, a friend of Mad Wolf; he had a reputation as an artist and was willing to do the work. But, when I told him to paint otters on my tepee, he was frightened. He said it might cause his death; he had no right to use the otter design and asked that he be released from painting my tepee under any circumstances.

Then I went to White Grass, the medicine man, who was shrewd and more resourceful. He was not willing to paint the otter design, but found a way out of the difficulty. He proposed my using the Pine Tree, saying he could paint that design, because he had dreamed it himself while sleeping under a pine tree in the mountains.

So White Grass painted my lodge and made it into the Pine Tree Tepee. It had a black top for the night sky, the Morning Star in blue, also the constellations of the Great Bear and the Pleiades on both sides. At the bottom was a red band for the earth, on which were white discs for fallen stars, triangular projections for mountains and a yellow pine-cone at the back to symbolize the Pine Tree.

I also had a small traveling-lodge, which my friend Big Eyes gave me because I was kind to his children. It was decorated with pictures of both war and hunting — events which had happened in his own career. There were figures of men and animals and Indian camps in colors, red, yellow, and black, an attack by a band of hostile Sioux, a hand-to-hand conflict of Big Eyes with the chief of the Sioux, also battles with Cree Indians and with the Crows, and an attack they made on a settlement of white men.

On the north side of my traveling-lodge was the picture of a fight, which Big Eyes had with a band of five grizzly bears in the Rocky Mountains — a mother bear with two large cubs and two other grizzlies. In one of the scenes he was plunging his knife into the breast of the mother grizzly, and in another she was tearing him with her teeth and claws; and then she left him for dead to attack his horse.

Two of the most prominent tepees on the inner circle were the Yellow Buffalo and Black Buffalo — the oldest of all the Painted Tepees; and they were believed to have the greatest supernatural power; their bundles and the secrets of their ceremonies had been handed down through many years. Their founders were two warriors, who once looked down into a river and saw two lodges with decorations. Both had black tops, on which were white discs for stars, and a black band round the bottom with fallen stars; each had a pair of buffaloes painted about the center, using yellow for one tepee and black for the other, and the skins of buffalo calves for door-flaps. Their rituals were associated with power to call the buffalo in time of need or starvation. There were taboos against allowing dogs to come inside, the fire must not die out, the door must not be allowed to stand open, nor should any one strike the side of the tepee.

The founder of the Snow Tepee was caught on the open plains in a bad winter blizzard. He lay for days under a deep drift, and had a dream in which the Maker of Storms and Blizzards gave him the decorations and ceremony. The Snow Tepee was not often pitched in summer camps. It was a bad-weather-lodge and was believed to have power to bring storms and cold weather. It had a yellow top, like the color of the sky at sunrise, with a cluster of seven stars for the constellation of the Great Bear on the north side, the direction blizzards come from, and Pleiades on the other. At the back was a red disc for the sun, with a buffalo tail attached. Under the yellow top, and at the four sides where stood the four main lodge-poles, were four claws to represent the Thunder Bird. At the bottom was a yellow band for the earth, with green discs, the ice color. On both sides of the door were horse tails for good luck; and bunches of crow feathers, with small bells attached to tinkle in the wind, were fastened to the tops of the ear-poles. Inside no drumming was allowed, the fire must not go out, nor moccasins hung up; dogs were not allowed to enter, nor the tepee cover to be raised.

Medicine Owl was the owner of a large Snake Tepee, with black top for the night sky and the Morning Star and constellations of stars on both sides. Two large serpents were painted round the middle, with the male serpent on the south side and the female on the north. Above the snakes were four red bands for their trails and their den at the back of the tepee. No bones should be broken inside, lest the owner's horses go lame.

The Crow Tepee had a broad red band around its center, with a procession of crows holding pieces of meat in their bills. A buffalo head was painted over the door; at the back was a row of buffalo tails; and at the top a cross for the Moth, the Sleep Bringer — a symbol that the tepee had come to the owner in a dream. In the legend of its origin, the founder slept one night in the Rocky Mountains, where great flocks of crows came to roost. In his dream the crows gave their supernatural power which went with the tepee.

There was another Crow Tepee, which had a strip of fringed buckskin round the center part for a trail. A row of crows were walking in single file towards the front of the lodge, holding pieces of red flannel in their bills for meat. Under the top of this tepee were red and yellow bands, to represent the color of clouds at sunrise.

The Thunder Tepee was believed to bring fair weather. Its ceremony gave protection from storms and had power to clear the sky. Near the ground and at the back was painted a large yellow disc; the north half dotted with small blue spots for hail, the south half with yellow spots for rain. Near the top of this disc the Thunder Bird was represented with outstretched wings and flashes of lightning coming from its beak. At the time of the first thunder in the spring, a ceremony and feast were given.

The Rainbow Tepee had a red band at the bottom, surmounted by figures representing the heads of enemies. At the back was a figure for the founder of the tepee, with a pipe in one hand and a shield in the other, which he held as an offering to the Sun. The rainbow was represented by two curved lines in the form of an arch, and a red band for the color of clouds at sunrise.

The Beaver Tepee had a beaver painted at the top, with its chief organs in different colors — the kidneys, liver, brain, and life-line. Under the black top, with the groups of star constellations, were four bands to represent beaver trails. A ceremony was given at the end of the winter, the time beavers are accustomed to leave their winter dens.

The Big Stripe Tepee had a broad red band round the center. Its founder said it had been given to him by both the beaver and the otter. On the red band were figures of six otters going towards their home in the river bank. Their den was painted in red over the door. Inside this tepee was a string of buffalo hoofs, which rattled whenever any one entered.

The Water Monster Tepee came from the Sun. It had two serpent-like figures in red and blue round the center, with yellow and green plumes extending from their heads. Figures were painted on the back, to represent the crescent moon and the Morning Star; and on its altar were symbols for the

INNER CIRCLE OF THE TRIBAL CAMP
Crow Tepee in the Foreground

Moon, Morning Star, Mistake-Morning-Star, sun dogs and the rays of the sun.

There were two Eagle Tepees, one for the bald-headed eagle, with red top and yellow band for the color of the sky and clouds at sunrise; the other had a pair of eagles and a band round the center to represent a river. The Deer Tepee had figures of a buck deer and a doe, with two red bands for deer trails and hoof marks, with mountains at the bottom.

The Mountain Sheep Tepee had a procession of rams and ewes going from the rear of the lodge towards the door; at the bottom were triangular figures for mountains, and under the black top four red bands for mountain sheep trails. There was also an Elk Tepee, another covered with stars; and a Big Rock Tepee, representing a sacred rock on the prairies.

But the most interesting of all these decorated lodges was the War Tepee, covered with pictures of war and adventure. It belonged to an old chief named Running Rabbit; the men who had been associated with him on raids and hunts were also joint owners. The records represented the deeds of the owner and his nearest friends. Some of the songs they used in the ceremony were their individual war songs.

At the back of the War Tepee was the figure of a person holding a pipe, which was symbolic of the vision of the founder. On the left side of the door was a circle enclosing four figures surrounded by many others, to represent Running Rabbit as leader with three companions, standing in a pit and holding back a number of enemies. A series of crossed lines, representing picket stakes to which horses were tied, recorded the capture of a number of horses. There was one symbol for the number of times Running Rabbit was leader of war expeditions, and another for his being detailed as scout. The sign for scout was a curved line to represent the waiting warriors; and a zigzag line going off, to show his irregular course while scouting, in order to hide the position of his followers from the enemy.

Other brave deeds recorded were the cutting loose of a horse picketed close to the lodge of a Gros Ventre Indian and a dog barking; the enemy pursuing and their narrow escape; the seizing of a gun from the hand of an enemy; also the taking of a war bonnet, a lance, and a shield; there was the picture of a brave warrior who saved the lives of two wounded comrades, carrying one on his own horse and leading the horse with the other; their wounds were marked by dashes of red for blood; another picture showed Running Rabbit taking part in the making of a treaty with the white men.

In these pictures, the travois mark was used to indicate the direction taken by a war party; stops by day and traveling by night were marked by different colors — yellow for day and black for night. Mountains were marked, also lakes, streams, and rivers; a long crooked line ending in a fork represented a river; a red mark in the bend of this river showed where a fight took place with a war party of Crow Indians.

CHAPTER XXXVIII

A NATIVE DOCTOR AND HIS PATIENT

ONE evening I crossed the meadow and climbed the ridge on the north side of the plain to the big rock, which commanded a broad view of the circle camp, the billowy hills stretching away to the horizon, north, south, east, and in the west the snowy peaks of the Rocky Mountains. The sun was setting and the birds were calling. High over the mountains the sky was like a golden sea with many tints, broken into bays and inlets by cloud promontories, in purple and somber red.

The lodges of the big camp were a ghostly white in the fading twilight; and soon became illuminated by bright inside fires, until the camp looked like an enormous group of colored Japanese lanterns, the flickering lights of many outside fires resembling fireflies in a summer's dusk.

From my lofty seat on the hill, I heard the clear notes of a young brave singing a love song to his sweetheart, asking her

to come forth to meet him. He waited in a meadow just outside the camp, until she came with her water pails; and they went together to the stream — the common meeting place for Indian lovers.

Then, when the moon rose over the plains, the night-singers appeared. They rode around the camp circle, singing to an accompaniment of jingling bells, keeping time with the slow jog-trot of their horses and giving shrill war-whoops at the end of each song.

From different lodges came the sound of drumming, where dances and ceremonies were taking place. In one tepee the Brave Dog Society was giving a dance, shaking their rattles and singing; in another, a band of young men were singing and beating drums as a prayer for their Grass Dance on the morrow. And from Mad Wolf's lodge I heard the sound of solemn chanting by many voices in unison, both men and women, accompanied by rhythmical beating of rattles on the ground.

After dark I went down from the hill and entered the camp. But I soon lost my way; the plain was level with no paths to guide. The big Indian camp was over a mile in circumference and at night all the tepees looked alike. Then I met Rattler, the doctor, and his wife, First Strike, with drums and sacks of roots and herbs, on their way to visit a patient. I joined them and they took me to the lodge of Stuyimi, an old friend of mine who had been ill for many months.

We found the patient lying on a couch of robes and blankets. His wife and two daughters were seated on another couch across the lodge. Rattler and I took places at the back of the lodge, while his wife, First Strike, joined the women. I was no sooner seated than a small coyote puppy crawled from the blankets at my side. It had a long pointed nose and bright eyes, and his coat was soft and fluffy. I put forth my hand to stroke it. Like a flash it snapped viciously and narrowly missed; then snarled and showed his fangs, until one of the girls called him by name, "Apis" (Wolf), when he ran to her, hopping on three legs and dragging his hind quarters, after the manner of coyotes, and soon fell asleep in her arms.

They also had a pet dog named "Sa-sak-si" (Freckle Face). To show off his tricks, one of the girls said: "Ai im skotos" (laugh at him); the dog lifted his upper lip for a smile and wagged his tail. Then she called: "Iks katsit" (watch it), and the dog sat glaring at the door.

All this time the women were talking and gossiping and eating dried meat and service berries, while old Rattler waited in silence; he wanted to begin his doctoring. He was a large man, over six feet in height, with massive head and long gray hair, which fell in waves over his broad shoulders. He was genial and good-natured. Every one liked Rattler. He feigned an air of confidence in his own wisdom and power, which helped him with his patients and added greatly to his success as a doctor.

Finally, as a hint to the women, he took the cover from his medicine drum and began to warm it over the fire. It was painted yellow to represent a clear sky at sunset, with a red ball in the center for the sun. Then he signed for his wife to make ready; she left the other women and put four round stones to heat in the fire.

Never had I been allowed to see an Indian doctor at work; spectators were believed to weaken his power; even the members of a patient's family were expected to withdraw. I started to go with the others, when Rattler signed for me to remain. He asked me to join with him in the songs; it would give him greater power and would help him in his doctoring. I agreed to sing, on condition that he would allow me to bring my cameras next day, and make pictures of him doctoring his patient. Rattler hesitated; it was a strange request, and his wife, too, was afraid it might bring bad luck to their patient. But the sick man interceded in my behalf; he wanted me to take the pictures, that I might be able to show them to the white men in civilization. He persuaded Rattler; and thus it happened that I saw the doctoring of a patient and secured a set of pictures.

Now an Indian has the same confidence in the native doctor that a child of civilization has in the family physician. Susceptible to mental impressions, the Indian has faith in the methods of his doctor. The doctor inspires in his patient a feeling of confidence and hope of recovery, which acts favorably upon the body. The weird songs, incantations and drumming of the medicine man, are often more effective for the Indian than the skilled white doctor whom he does not trust.

With the medicine men, suggestion had a great power for healing. Some of them practiced in good faith; others were frauds and quacks, in about the same proportion as in civilized communities. Many of them were inspired and had faith in their art. They relieved suffering and held positions of influence in their tribe. Thus modern science had its origin in the blind gropings of primitive doctors and medicine men.

Rattler and his wife stripped the patient to his waist. He lay on a couch, with his head against the back-rest. The woman doctored first, while Rattler and I sat together at the back of the lodge to help by our singing.

She took some roots and herbs from an old sack and brewed them over the fire for a hot drink. She burned sweet pine as incense, holding both hands in the rising smoke and praying to her helper, the Buffalo Spirit, that he would give her power to heal. She kneeled by the patient's side, holding her hands in the sweet smoke and laying them on his body and feeling him gently with her fingers; she said the trouble was in his chest, and was bad on the left side. Then she took a hot stone from the fire, and placing it in a kettle of water, prayed:

"Sun, pity and help me.
Listen, Sun, to what I say.
Help this sick man, that he may live to old age.
Take heed and pity him, for the sake of wife and children.
May they live long.
May they all be happy and see many snows."

Then Rattler signed that it was time for us to sing. He raised his medicine drum and beat slowly and rhythmically. Holding his head back and with eyes closed, he began to sing, while I joined with him. In the meantime, his wife was going through dancing motions on her knees, moving her body in time with the beating of the drum and joining with us in a chant.

Her power to heal came through the medium of a dream. A buffalo bull appeared and said: "You will profit from my body. Behold! I give these herbs whereby you can heal the sick."

In her doctoring, First Strike imitated the actions of her dream-buffalo, the way she saw it doctoring another buffalo. She covered herself with a buffalo robe and knelt beside the patient. She pawed the ground, hooked with her head, and imitated the sounds of a buffalo. Then she breathed on a piece of buffalo-skin to give it power; she held it towards the patient, swaying her body in time with the beating of the drum. She laid the buffalo-skin on a hot stone and then placed it quickly on the left side of the sick man, the place where the trouble lay. She put her hands into the root medicine; she touched a hot stone with the wet tips of her fingers and, with a quick movement, placed them on the body of her patient. In this way she made hot applications on both sides of his body, using three hot stones, one after the other.

When First Strike had finished her doctoring, Rattler made ready. With his massive figure and benign countenance, his long gray hair in waves over his shoulders, he was an imposing doctor, one to inspire confidence in a sick person. Rattler did not make use of herbs or roots. In his dream an eagle had bestowed upon him power to heal, directing him how to proceed and showing him the motions to use.

First, Rattler beat loudly on his medicine drum. He signed to me to join him in a song and swayed his body in time with the drumming. Then he used an eagle wing, imitating the flying of an eagle; he beat the wing against the body of his patient — the way he saw the eagle do in his dream. He sprayed yellow paint through the hollow wing-bones of eagles, first over his arms and breast, then over his entire body, and prayed:

"Listen! I beseech you, the power in my dream.
Help me cure this sick man.
Do not deceive me.
You said this was the way to doctor.
Here is the wing; I use it right.
Sun, help me, pity me.
Help me cure this sick person."

But Stuyimi did not recover. One night he called to his wife that the ghost of his dead father was outside the lodge, and said:

"Listen! He says he has been waiting for me and it is time for me to go with him to the Sand Hills."

After that the sick man kept seeing the ghost all the time. He said it did not go away; and he died that same night.

For burial they dressed him in his best clothes — a suit of soft-tanned deerskin, with leggings and moccasins to match. They wrapped the body in a robe and placed it on the summit of a high ridge — his favorite place to sit and dream.

The Blackfoot believed that the spirit went eastward to the Sand Hills, a barren country on the plains. It was inhabited by the ghosts of people and animals, which exist together as in this life.

They placed their dead upon scaffolds in trees, on the summit of a hill, or in a death lodge hidden away among the trees. The dead were clothed according to their station in life, believing they went to the Sand Hills in their burial clothes. Often the things a person valued most were left beside the grave. Sometimes the best horses of a chief were killed, that they might go with him to the Spirit Land.

Beating the Medicine Drum and singing

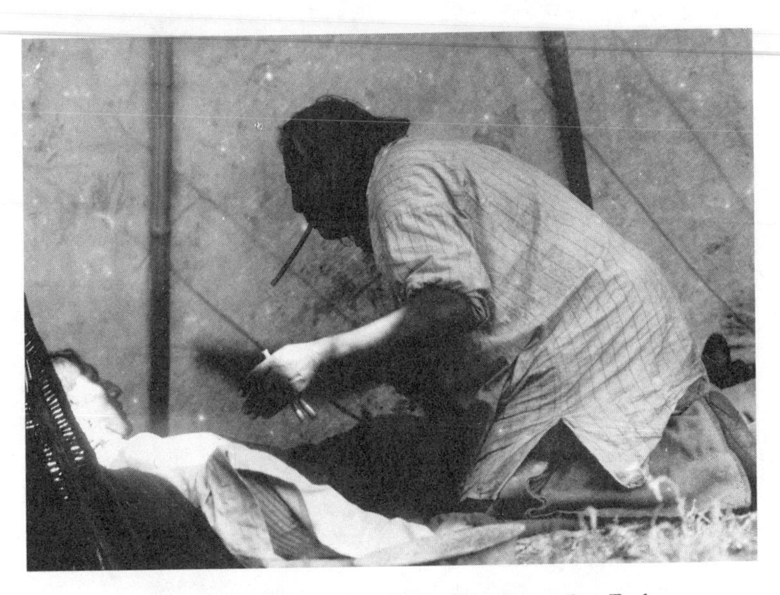

Spraying Yellow Paint through the Wing-Bone of an Eagle

RATTLER DOCTORING STUYIMI

In mourning they denied and tortured themselves to excite the pity of the Great Spirit, to show their indifference to pain and to manifest their high regard for the dead. During the time of mourning, which lasted several months, they went daily at sunset and sunrise to a lonely hill, to weep and cut themselves with arrow-points and knives. As a sign of deep mourning, they cut off a finger, generally the first joint of the small finger. Sometimes they made the tepee smaller to bring discomfort to all the family. When a prominent chief died, his family would place their lodge at a distance from the others. Parents who lost a son led his saddle horse through the camp and made public lamentations. People in mourning wore old clothes; they gave up painting themselves and all ornaments. They kept away from public gatherings, dances, and religious ceremonies. Sometimes they wore neither moccasins nor leggings; they cut off the manes of their saddle horses, but they had a superstition against the cutting of their horses' tails.

No Chief, a prominent man, mourned so deeply at the death of his brother that he journeyed several hundred miles to the place where he was killed and brought the body home. After that he carried the skeleton in a rawhide case wherever he went, and had it buried beside him when he died.

It was customary for a man and his wife to give their sacred bundles into the care of another couple who were expected to make new clothes and give ceremonies for the couple in mourning. Finally friends of the mourners came and tried to make them forget their sorrow, and to persuade them to return to their ordinary life.

CHAPTER XXXIX

DANCE OF THE HAIR-PARTERS (GRASS DANCE)

ONE morning Elk Horn, the herald, galloped through the camp, holding aloft a standard with eagle feathers along its staff. He called in a loud voice that the Grass Dancers would hold their ceremony, and invited every one to come. He wore a deerskin suit, a beaded breast ornament of many strands, and a blanket draped about his waist. His horse was painted, and decorated with clusters of feathers and sleigh bells; and there were coyote tails hanging from his stirrups.

The Grass Dancers, or Hair-Parters, was an association of young men. They held their meetings through the winter months, and a public ceremony at the time of the Sun Dance. Any one who had a suitable dance outfit could take part. They had four unmarried women as members, who rode around the camp with them at night and helped them in their singing.

Their drummers opened the ceremony by seating themselves where the dance would take place. They beat the drums steadily and in perfect rhythm — the signal for the people to come together.

Soon the dancers began to assemble. Some were naked, except for loin-cloths and beaded dance moccasins, and had their faces and bodies variously painted. Others wore fine costumes, with war shirts of soft-tanned buckskin, which were decorated with colored beads and trimmed over the shoulders and legs with black-tipped ermine tails. They had breast ornaments and necklaces of beads, of elk teeth and grizzly bear claws. They carried tomahawks, bows and arrows, and rattles made of bunches of deer and elk hoofs;

and wore war bonnets of eagle feathers and headdresses made of colored horsehair and porcupine-skins, caps of otter and mink skins, which were wound about their heads and had the tails hanging down behind. They had skin ankle-bands with small bells attached, and strings of sleigh bells strapped about their legs and hanging from their waists.

The dancers sat in a circle, with the drummers in the center, having large cowhide drums of different colors. They used single drumsticks with which they beat with spirit; they sang rhythmically and in perfect unison. In the dance the drumming was a continued booming that did not break, growing faster and faster, until it ended suddenly with a crash and in a chorus of shrill war-whoops. Such was the music the Hair-Parters had for their ceremony.

Some of the dancers had distinguishing marks; and their movements had meanings, which an outsider would not understand. One warrior wore leggings with eight parallel black lines, to show the number of men he had killed in battle. Another had a war shirt covered with marks, representing picket stakes with short ropes attached, to show the number of horses he had captured from enemies, cutting them loose at the risk of his life. Another, who was a noted taker of horses, carried a painted horse carved from wood. Others had long whips, feathered wands and fringed bags decorated with colored beads and porcupine quills.

They had one dance figure, in which only warriors took part; those who had escaped after being surrounded in battle. Another dance was for men who had never turned away from a fight; and another in which only generous men took part — those who were known to give freely of their possessions.

When an eagle feather fell in the dance from the war bonnet of Night Gun, he did not try to recover it himself; this might bring him bad luck. He chose Bear Chief, a famous warrior, to pick it up. Then, led by Bear Chief, the dancers circled three times round the feather; the fourth time, Bear Chief took the feather; and, after recounting four of his brave deeds in battle, he gave it back to the owner.

There was a special dance for those who had been wounded in battle. Wolf Eagle, a warrior with only one arm, danced with spirit and abandon, carrying in his single hand the decorated bone of his missing arm. Another dancer, "Behind-the-Ears" by name, held his rifle ready to shoot. In battle he had once made a good shot and hit an enemy behind the ear; in this dance, he went through similar motions to recall that deed.

The leader of the Hair-Parters was Black Weasel. His seat in the dance circle was marked by a wand decorated with eagle feathers and driven into the ground. He wore a war bonnet of selected eagle feathers and a soft-tanned suit of deerskin trimmed with ermine tails. Across his shoulders and along arms and legs were broad strips of quill work.

Black Weasel opened the dance by moving about the circle, striking the seated warriors with his feathered wand to make them join in and whipping any who lagged behind. It was also his duty to look out for strangers, and to see that women and children had seats.

Among the spectators was Nokoa, a small boy with his mother. He wore a fringed buckskin suit and a beaded necklace of many strands. During one of the figures his father, Wolverine, took him into the dance. At first he was abashed before so many people, but soon forgot himself and danced fearlessly, his moccasined feet keeping time with the rhythmic beating of drums, swaying his small body like the warriors and aiming a stick for a gun.

The Grass Dance lasted throughout the day and ended after sunset with a feast. During intermissions, they had speeches and stories of brave deeds in war. Mountain Chief stood up and told how he used to dance in former days. He urged the Hair-Parters to be generous and to give many horses to visitors, especially those who came from a distance. In his hand he held a stick which represented a horse. He crossed the circle and handed the stick to a visiting Sioux Indian. Then from the spectators came shouts of approval; and an aged chief sang: "Good man, to give away your horse so generously."

During the feast, the venerable chief, Running Crane, stood up and spoke, saying:

"My children, I am glad in my heart to see you gathered here, the young men all dressed in fine clothes. Only at the Sun Dance, which comes once a year, can we have a good time together. Our Great Grandfather (President of the United States) should not put an end to our Sun Dance; it makes our people happy and we do no harm to white men. Let the old people restrain our young men, that we may return to our homes without trouble. That is all. My name is Running Crane."

On this same day, and in a different part of the camp, were sham battles of former fights with hostile Indian tribes — dances by warriors on foot and mounted on horses. Their functions were to excite the people, both old and young, and to stir up enthusiasm for war and make young men eager to fight.

One of these sham battles on foot enacted a fight between Crows and Blackfoot. The warriors, representing the Crow Indians, were led by Flat Tail; and the Blackfoot by Little Dog, their war chief. They advanced in line with rifles, beating drums and singing war songs. When the waiting warriors fired their guns, some of the enemy fell and the rest retreated. Then the visitors scalped the dead amid cheers and war-whoops from the spectators.

The horseback dances were spectacular sham battles by

mounted men. In former days, warriors took part before starting on the warpath, to stimulate their courage. The mounted men were dressed in war clothes and had their horses painted with war signs — pictures of weapons, guns, bows and arrows; a red hand stood for blood lust and red marks for men wounded or killed in battle. They wore head-dresses of eagle feathers and horned bonnets, and carried war bundles — the sacred War Bridle, the Lance, and the Shield. They used decorated saddles and bridles and tied up the tails of their horses; and had strings of bells strapped to their legs and around the necks of their horses.

I saw a group of men and women gathered in a circle, drumming and singing, waiting for the horsemen to come. Soon the riders appeared on the summit of a hill, where they stood for a while in sight of the people; then rode down at a gallop in single file, with Little Plume their war chief in the lead. First they rode round the inner circle with shrill war-whoops, and came to the place where the people were gathered. They circled round and round, shouting and firing their rifles. Then they gave horseback dances, reënacting scenes of former battles. One band rode at full speed against another, maneuvering with war cries and shooting. Then they formed in line, and with Little Plume in the lead, marched slowly through the camp, with rifles in position, singing a song of victory and holding aloft their sacred Lance.

Just outside the circle camp was the race track, a level stretch along a low range of hills. The head of the course lay towards the snow-capped Rockies and extended eastward toward the open plains. On one side were grass-covered prairies, decked with lovely wild flowers; and on the other the outskirts of the big camp with its smoke-colored tepees.

For the most exciting race of that day, a large crowd of Indians gathered at the finish; they wagered horses, robes, and blankets. The young riders were naked, wearing only loin-cloths and moccasins. They rode wild broncos without saddles, using rawhide ropes for bridles. At the start I heard shouts, and saw a cloud of dust moving swiftly. The riders came, lying low along the backs of their broncos and beating them with rawhide whips. A famous race horse named "Bull Shoe" won, amid shouts from the throng of spectators.

Then Elk Horn, the herald, rode through the camp and announced that White Grass, the medicine man, would take out his Dancing Pipe; he invited every one to come to the ceremony.

Now the Dancing Pipe was the oldest and most powerful of the medicine pipes. Many came to follow it, both men and women, dressed in their best, each carrying some sacred object to which they prayed. A throng soon filled the lodge of White Grass and crowded about the outside. They watched him remove the wrappings from the pipe, one by one, each with a different song, until at last he held up the long stem. It was wrapped with fur and decorated with eagle feathers and bright-colored plumes.

White Grass lifted the Pipe reverently, holding it to the north, south, east, and west; and prayed to the Sun for all the people. Two chiefs arose and recounted their brave deeds in war; and, after that, four men sounded their drums.

Then White Grass stood up and held the Pipe in front of him. He danced slowly from the lodge, men and women and even children following in single file, until there was a long line of dancing Indians moving in and out among the tepees. White Grass and the four drummers led the dancers, beating their drums and singing the songs of the Dancing Pipe. They moved once around the big camp circle and then back to the lodge of White Grass.

Another crowd gathered at the tepee of Night Gun, to see some women choose their men in the Kissing Dance. The men stood in line on one side of the lodge, the women on

the other. When the lines came close together, the man who was chosen put a blanket over his head and the woman's, and they kissed each other while dancing between the lines. For this favor, the man had to make the woman a present, generally a blanket, though sometimes other gifts were added.

But a tragedy put an end to the Kissing Dance. There was a married woman who liked the dance so much she neglected home and children. When her husband found out that she kept choosing a former lover, he came to the dance lodge and killed her.

I saw a band of visiting Sioux warriors parade on horse-

ELK HORN, HERALD OF THE BRAVE DOG SOCIETY
He announced their orders and warnings through the camp

back, singing a Celebration Song. Lone Dog was their leader;

also Red Boy, Bear Paw, and White Eagle. They wore feathered shields fastened to their backs and carried rifles and feathered wands. Their horses were painted and had bunches of feathers attached to manes and tails. They also had head ornaments and beaded flaps of rawhide, which were fastened to their stirrups. While parading the camp circle, they sang:

> "Oh, Blackfoot! In the past we heard you boast,
> You would never live like white men.
> But we see you now,
> With few of your fine Indian clothes left."

According to an old custom, these visiting Sioux warriors stopped to sing at the lodges of prominent men who gave them presents and food. After going once around the camp circle, they stopped at the lodge of Áhkiona, who gave a Pipe Ceremony for them. A few years before, while visiting the Sioux in North Dakota, they gave him a Medicine Pipe; and now they were going to take it home.

In the evening a party of warriors came to the lodge of the head-chief to sing a Wolf Song, according to an ancient war

custom. They stood in a circle holding a large rawhide between them, upon which they beat with sticks. They sang no words, but gave the wolf howl at intervals. Their wives and sweethearts who stood near did not sing, but joined in the wolf howls. In former days, the Blackfoot sang the Wolf Song before starting to war or on a hunt, in the belief that the spirit of the wolf, the craftiest of all wild animals, would lead and inspire them with his cunning. To express the desire of the singer, the song always ended with the wolf call, because a wolf always howls when it hunts.

That same night, I was wakened by a dog fight close to our lodge. Quickly other dogs came and joined in a mass fight, with barking, yelps and snarls. Then hundreds of dogs in all parts of the circle camp, roused by the noise of the fight, united in a deep-throated and mournful howl — a weird sound, like the wailing of a great wolf-pack.

When their dismal chorus died away, I went outside the lodge. It was a glorious night; the sky was clear and a full moon rising over the prairie. All about me were white tepees with their picturesque clusters of tapering poles. In the west a brilliant planet was sinking behind the dim outlines of the Rocky Mountains. The camp was throbbing with life. On all sides I heard singing and drumming. The Sioux warriors were again making their rounds, singing a Traveling Song. Then Red Fox and his sweetheart passed, singing in unison a Riding Song. The girl sat in front of her lover, wearing his

war bonnet. His robe of soft-tanned elkskin flowed gracefully back as they rode. Some of the night-singers were riding, mounted two on a horse, singing and marking time with clusters of sleigh bells, in perfect time with the slow jog-trot of their horses.

It was an old custom for young people to ride all night and sing, while guarding camp and protecting the horse herds. Then it became a social custom with special songs, sung in unison by different groups riding two on a horse.

CHAPTER XL

SOCIETY OF BRAVE DOGS

My tepee was near the three dance lodges of the Brave Dog Society, which were somewhat apart from the others, near the center of the circle camp. There they kept their costumes and weapons and dressed for parades and dances. Day after day I watched them in their interesting customs.

As a society they had power, because of their reputation for bravery. Every one feared to oppose them. They did not maltreat people, but sometimes punished severely offenders against the public welfare. Their function in the tribal camp was primarily to preserve order.

The first evening of the camp, they rode round the circle shouting their orders to the people, saying:

"Let every one be quiet to-night. Young people must not act thoughtlessly or play pranks. The sacred woman has important ceremonies and should not be disturbed."

For parades and dances out of doors, the Brave Dogs went forth in their best costumes. They marched by twos. Short Robe, their leader, wore a beaded suit of deerskin trimmed over shoulders and arms with black-tipped weasel-skins; also a large coyote-skin, with his head thrust through a slit in the middle of the skin and the tail hanging down his back. According to their society custom, he carried a rattle in his right hand and a blanket over his left arm. Sometimes in their parades, Short Robe's youngest son, a boy of twelve, walked by his father's side, wearing a miniature costume like the chief.

Next in rank to Short Robe were two mounted men, Big Moon and Elk Horn. They were the assistant leaders, and

SOCIETY OF BRAVE DOGS MARCHING THROUGH THE CAMP
In front is Short Robe, the head man, with his small son

CHARACTERISTIC COSTUMES OF BRAVE DOGS
In the center is Lone Chief as a grizzly bear. The four others — Blood, Flat Tail, Mountain Chief, and Drags-his-Robe — were known as Old Men Comrades

wore war bonnets of selected eagle feathers. Their horses were painted with war pictures, representing the brave deeds of their riders.

Two members, Lone Chief and Cream Antelope, represented grizzly bears. They alone of the society carried bows and arrows. Their faces were painted with the "bear face" pattern — red all over, with black marks downward from the eyes and corners of the mouth. They wore headdresses of bearskin, with bear's ears and two bear claws on top for horns; and on their arms were bands made of bearskin with bear claws attached. The lower part of their bodies was naked and painted with bright colors. They wore loin-cloths and beaded belts with daggers and short-sleeved shirts of soft-tanned skins covered with fringe.

Four other members were known as "Old Men Comrades." They were Flat Tail, Mountain Chief, Drags-His-Robe, and Blood. They carried rattles and wore eagle feathers in their hair. Flat Tail had a beaver-skin cap, Mountain Chief a red band round his head and carried a skin shield decorated with clusters of eagle feathers. It was the duty of the Old Men Comrades to call the society together, to act as advisers in the ceremonies, also as heralds and to make announcements to the people.

The lay members wore whatever they pleased. They were mostly from prominent families, who were chosen because of their fine costumes; also because their relatives had property and could make liberal presents to the society. They were — Lazy Husband, Raven Eyes, Drags Behind, Makes-Cold-Weather, Bad Married, Big Spring, Bird Rattler, Bear Shoe, Three Bears, Two Spears, and Black Bear. In parades it was their custom to carry blankets over their left arms and rattles in their right hands. They painted their faces to correspond with the designs on their rattles. These rattles were looked upon as ceremonial objects and were all different. If a member wanted to withdraw from the society, he sold his rattle. Thus the transfer consisted in the purchase of a rattle.

In parades the four drummers walked behind, wearing blankets tied about their waists, beating on drums and singing. Some of the members carried sacred objects; Drags-His-Robe had a Medicine Pipe, Mountain Chief a Shield, and Big Moon, one of the mounted men, the War Bridle.

They all marched in time with the beating of drums and sang. A throng of women and children, the families of members, followed in the rear. Every now and then they stopped in their march, and, turning about, faced the drummers and danced backwards and forwards; then reversed and moved on. Sometimes they stopped to give a formal dance in front of the lodge of a prominent man. They seated themselves in a circle in their regular positions on both sides of the door. Short Robe, as chief of the society, was at the head with his son; and then the four Old Men Comrades. The two grizzly bears were at the other end of the circle, with the lay members between. The families of members stood near and helped in the singing.

In the dance they rose in their places. The two mounted men rode round and round the circle in opposite directions, forcing the dancers toward the center, and at last pretended to ride them down. This figure was used, because the founder of the society had a way of killing enemies by riding them down with his horse. Finally, all members who had performed the brave feat of unhorsing an enemy, took hold of the two mounted men and dragged them from their horses. Then they all danced together. When they were ready to stop, they held their rattles high in the air and the drummers their drums; they shouted and returned to their seats.

Whenever the Brave Dogs stopped at a lodge and gave their dance, the owner was expected to give them a feast,

BRAVE DOGS GIVING THEIR SOCIETY DANCE

They kept on dancing until food appeared. Any man of prominence dared not refuse, lest people think him stingy.

After their feasts, the head men of the society were accustomed to make speeches; and they all sang together accompanied by the beating of drums. One of their songs was: "It is bad to live to be old; it is better to die young, fighting bravely in battle."

One evening, I saw the Brave Dogs marching through camp in the golden light of sunset. They went to the beating of drums, singing in unison and shaking their rattles, dressed in gorgeous costumes of wild animal skins and war bonnets, carrying weapons and their standards of black-tipped eagle feathers. Elk Horn, as herald, rode in advance, shouting their orders and warnings; and announced their society dance.

That night I saw the lodges of the Brave Dogs, glowing with light from inside fires. Their drums beat steadily and became louder and louder. Then people began to assemble, coming from all parts of the camp, until the dance lodge was thronged.

I stood outside, listening to the war-whoops and singing. The rhythmical beating of the drums increased until it reached a climax; then, with loud beating and shouts, would suddenly cease.

For a while I waited; then crawled under the canvas and found myself inside, among a crowd of women and children — the families of the Brave Dogs. But, they were so interested in the dance, they took no notice of my sudden appearance in their midst.

The dance was at its height and the Brave Dogs had laid aside their costumes and blankets. They looked savage and wild, with the red glow of the fire on painted faces and bodies. They wore only loin-cloths and moccasins. Some had bone whistles in their mouths on which they blew shrilly, others sang and gave war-whoops at intervals.

Short Robe as leader wore his large coyote-skin, with head thrust through a slit in the middle, the tail hanging down his back and almost touching the ground. Four of the dancers were covered with white clay and represented gray wolves. They carried long sticks decorated with eagle feathers. They imitated wolves driving buffalo, circling round the dancers. Their step was an alternate lifting of the feet, slow or fast, according to the beat of the drums.

The two grizzly bear dancers sat in a hole for a den. They wore the bear headdress, with bear's ears and bear claws on top for double horns. Their faces were painted red with black streaks across the eyes and corners of the mouth, representing the "bear face."

Whenever the spectators wanted to see them dance, they threw at them; but, like bears, they were lazy and stayed in their den until a point in the dance when the wolf dancers had herded the buffalo and were closing in; then the two bears rose slowly and entered the dance, driving back the wolves from the buffalo, after which they returned to their den and all the dancers sat down. This figure was repeated many times.

Before they separated, the Brave Dogs had a feast; and then marched through the camp, singing their society song and shouting:

"Let every one be quiet to-night. Do not disturb the sacred woman. All the young men should rest and be ready to help. To-morrow we will build the Sun Lodge and will make it a great day."

CHAPTER XLI

A MEDICINE-PIPE CEREMONY

It was twilight in the camp. Bright fires lighted up the inner circle of Painted Tepees and revealed in soft colors their fanciful bird and animal pictures. A fresh breeze blew from the mountains, whistling through the ropes of the lodges, tinkling the small bells on top of the ear-poles and rattling the bunches of deer hoofs over the doors.

While wandering among the tepees, I saw a group of young men on their way to a dance, singing to an accompaniment of jingling bells, then two night-singers making their rounds on a horse. Suddenly a crowd rushed from a lodge and laid hold of the two riders; their horse bucked and plunged, but the singers held fast and galloped away amid shouts of laughter.

Then I came to a small lodge of a poor family, where the fire burned low, and heard a medicine man doctoring a patient, snuffing and grunting and stamping his feet.

In another lodge I heard a man shout angrily, so his neighbors could hear: "What has become of the woman who went for water?"

Soon he shouted again, louder and more angrily: "What has become of the woman who went for water? She has been gone a long time."

And then I heard a strange method of public rebuke. Indians in near-by lodges took up his cry; they mocked his impatient and angry tone, shouting one after the other: "What has become of the woman who went for water?" It spread quickly from one band to another; and ended in laughter and a general disturbance throughout the camp.

While I stood in the shadow listening to the many interesting sounds of camp life, I saw two figures muffled in blankets move stealthily from lodge to lodge. Finally they stopped at the tepee of Big Spring, a well-known chief. It glowed with light from an inside fire and they peered cautiously through a crack in the door. They were medicine-pipe scouts on the lookout for a victim. That night Lone Chief was giving up his sacred Pipe. He told some of his friends secretly; he wanted to catch Big Spring and make him his successor; he was prominent and could afford to pay well for the Pipe.

The owner of a Medicine Pipe could force any one to purchase it, regardless of the wishes of his victim, provided he could catch him. If he found him asleep and touched him with the Pipe, he dared not resist; death and ill luck were the penalties for refusing a Medicine Pipe.

But Big Spring had warning that Lone Chief was after him. He did not want the care and expense of owning a Pipe. So he stayed away from his tepee that night. The scouts could not find him and Lone Chief had to make another choice.

Some medicine-pipe men were assembled in the lodge of Lone Chief. They had opened his Pipe Bundle and were singing and drinking. They kept on with the ceremony, waiting for their scouts to report favorably. Then they would go forth together. In their actions they imitated the grizzly bear, stealing quietly upon their victim, to take him by surprise in the night, the way a bear does; because the power of the Pipe came from the grizzly bear. They sang bear songs and imitated the sound the grizzly makes when he charges, also owl songs to cast a spell over their victim, so he could not escape; the owl is a bird of night and its power also belongs to the Pipe. So Lone Chief and his friends kept on with their ceremony throughout the night, awaiting their scouts.

In the meantime, I returned to my lodge and lay down on my couch. That night the noise and confusion of the camp kept every one in our tepee awake. Even the baby, Tears-in-Her-Eyes, was restless in her little hammock-bed. Strikes-on-Both-Sides sang to her, rocking the hammock, singing over and over the old Indian cradle song: "Come, wolf, eat this baby if she don't sleep."

It was clear moonlight. The dogs were restless, barking and fighting and on foraging expeditions. Near midnight, a dog came silently into our lodge and tried to steal a side of bacon, but Strikes-on-Both-Sides followed him so closely he dropped his prize and fled yelping through the door.

Then a party of young men came close to the lodge and gave a begging dance, expecting me as the owner to make presents; it added to the prestige of every lodge owner in the camp to have a reputation for generosity. After we gave them food, they went to dance at another tepee. In this way it was customary for a party to visit four places, and then disband for the night.

Morning Plume's lodge was so close I could hear every sound. His small son was restless and bothered his aged grandmother. When the fire burned low he was cold and began to cry. He wanted her to cover him warmly. She was no sooner back in her own bed than he cried again for water. This wakened his baby brother. So the mother sang a cradle song and rocked him to sleep.

Near by was the lodge of a young man named Two Eagles. That night his only child was ill. I heard a medicine man enter and begin his monotonous drumming. The beating was soft and regular, unlike the lively drumming for a ceremony or dance; this was slow and steady and sounded muffled, like the steady throbbing of a human heart. After midnight the beating suddenly ceased, and I knew the child had died. For a moment there was silence; I heard the mother sobbing as she took up the lifeless body; then realizing it was dead, she broke into a mournful wail.

Just before dawn a rider galloped through the camp, calling for every one to get up and go to work. But it was only a joke; no one took it seriously; every one knew it was a man who was humorously inclined.

Then came the morning breeze from the mountains, making a humming sound against the ropes; and the ears of our lodge began to flap. I heard the beating of a horse's hoofs on the soft turf, going towards the meadow where the tribal herds were feeding; and knew it was the day man going to relieve the night herder.

Suddenly the sound of drums, with shouts and singing, came from the band of Fat Melters. At last Lone Chief had caught some one with his Pipe.

Then Elk Horn, the herald, rode forth beating a drum. He shouted as he galloped through the camp:

"You Fat Melters! Get up and cook breakfast. Wolf Plume has been caught with the Pipe. Let every one help. He must pay many horses, robes and blankets. Do not delay; the sun will soon rise. The dance will take place in the lodge of Wolf Plume. Let every one come."

Quickly I dressed and made ready my cameras. When I went out from the lodge, a bright morning star was rising over the prairie. In the dim light, I saw a crowd gathered about one of the tepees. Then the drums began again — the signal for Lone Chief and his friends to come forth with the sacred Pipe. I saw them march through the camp and made picture records of these interesting events, though the sun had not risen.

Lone Chief and Wolf Plume were at the head of the procession with the Medicine Pipe. Then came their wives carrying the sacred bundles. The drummers were behind; also prominent men with their wives, who were to help Lone Chief in the ceremony.

MOUNTAIN CHIEF

WOLF PLUME

When they came to Wolf Plume's tepee, they halted; but the singing and drumming continued. In the doorway of the lodge stood the aged mother of Wolf Plume. She had snow-white hair and leaned heavily on a staff. When she saw Wolf Plume with the Pipe, and heard the singing and drumming, she was so overcome with emotion that she joined in the song. She waved her stick in the air and shouted: "Good boy! Wolf Plume! Good boy! My son! You are now a great chief."

Then the drumming ceased and the procession entered the lodge. The women laid their sacred bundles at the back, and all took seats. Lone Chief, as the officiating pipe man, sat in the center. Wolf Plume, the new pipe man, was on his right; and the seven men who would help in the singing and drumming, on his left.

Next to Wolf Plume sat his wife and the wife of Lone Chief. Beyond them were the head wives of the seven drummers, also the aged and people of prominence. Indians came from all parts of camp and crowded into the tepee.

Members of Wolf Plume's band (blood relatives) and his friends brought presents to help him in the payment. Lone Chief was paid forty horses for the Pipe, and besides a large pile of clothing, blankets, and provisions. Tearing Lodge, father-in-law of Wolf Plume, received them, calling in a loud voice the names of each giver. My present, a blanket of bright colors, was announced with the rest.

Then Lone Chief dressed Wolf Plume in the ceremonial clothes — a headband of white goatskin with an eagle feather, beaded buckskin shirt trimmed with ermine tails, and leggings and moccasins to match. He also gave him a horse, which could only be ridden by the pipe owner, and a saddle, bridle, whip and lariat, to go with the horse.

The ceremony of transfer began while the sun was still low over the prairie. Its first golden rays streamed into the open front of the lodge and fell upon the seven singers with their painted medicine drums. Sweet pine burned as incense. Lone Chief and his wife placed their hands in the rising smoke and sang the first song of a series of seven. During these songs the women removed the outer coverings from the bundle. Then they all sang the Buffalo Song, making the buffalo sign with forefingers curved, while Wolf Plume and his wife untied the outer thongs of buffalo-skin. During the Antelope Song the singers imitated with their hands the graceful motions of antelope. While loosing the wrapper of elkskin they sang the Elk Song, making the elk sign by holding their hands to their heads with fingers extended to represent antlers; and the women shook their heads at the bundle, as if they were elk about to charge and tear loose the wrapper with their horns. Thus the sacred bundle of the Medicine Pipe was opened, exposing many skins of birds and animals and other relics.

Now came the time for dancing with the Pipe. Only pipe owners could dance with a Medicine Pipe; but, if a man had made a vow, he could fulfill that vow by dancing with one of the sacred skins, which was taken from the bundle. Whenever a prominent man arose to dance, he was applauded and received with special attention by the spectators. Because Wolf Plume was receiving the Pipe, he did not rise to dance; he sat beside the bundle and received the skins and relics from those who took part in the ceremony.

For the grizzly bear dance, the drummers sang the words:

"In the spring I grow restless."

In this dance, Lone Chief imitated the actions of a bear coming from its winter den; and sang while he danced:

"I wander in the summer."

Then he took the Pipe, and holding it in both hands, sang:

"Sacred Chief, every one shall see you."

He slowly raised the Pipe, that all might see it, and sang:

"The Chief is powerful."

After that, they beat on the drums and sang bear songs, while Lone Chief arose and danced like a bear, holding his hands as a bear does its paws; and imitated a bear by putting his feet together, moving backwards and forwards with short jumps and breathing hard; he also imitated the awkward motions of a bear running, digging in the ground and turning over stones for insects.

For the Thunder Dance, Lone Chief blew shrilly on his whistle, made from the wing bone of an eagle, to represent the sound the Thunder Bird makes with its wings when it first comes in the spring; also the time the bear leaves its winter den. Then he danced, holding the Pipe in his right hand and spreading out the fingers of his left, to represent the wings of the Thunder Bird.

During the singing of the Swan Song, Bear Child danced alone. He represented the chief swan, the leader of the flock. He made the swan sign, by holding both hands extended with fingers spread out in imitation of a swan flying.

In the Antelope Dance, Red Fox made motions with his hands to imitate an antelope running; and moved his head like an antelope on the alert for danger.

When the drummers sang the Crane Song, several dancers arose. They all gave the crane call and imitated the motions of flying cranes. Several songs were sung for different water birds and for ducks and geese. And, after a short rest, while both men and women smoked, seven owl songs were sung; and buffalo songs for the white-skin band worn about the head of the pipe owner. The ceremony came to an end with the singing of the Good Luck Song for Wolf Plume, the new pipe owner; thereafter, he must always sing it if he wanted anything very badly.

At sunset, Lone Chief and his wife led the new pipe owners outside the lodge. They faced the four directions in turn and sang:

(Towards the west)

> "Over there, towards the sunset, are the mountains.
> May you see them as long as you live.
> From them you will get your sweet pine as incense.

(North)

> "Over there, is the star-that-never-moves (Pole Star).
> May you live to see that star for many years.

(East)

> "Over there, you will get old age.
> From the east comes the light of the Sun.

(South)

> "Over there, are warriors coming with scalps.
> May the warm wind of the south bring plenty of food."

It took Lone Chief four days to confer upon Wolf Plume the rights of the Pipe — to instruct him in its care and impart the secrets of the ceremony. As owner of a Medicine Pipe, there were taboos that Wolf Plume and his wife must avoid; it would inconvenience them both and interfere with their daily life.

They must never point at a person with fingers, only with the thumb. They must never move anything burning with a knife, lest it cause their teeth to ache. They must not pick up a lost article without first singing a certain song. They must never allow a dog to leap upon them; it would cause the body to ache. If Wolf Plume let any one ride or use his medicine horse, some of his herd would sicken and die. The word "bear" must never be used near the Pipe; it would cause bad dreams and bring sickness. But the evil power might be averted by burning sweet pine for incense. Sweet pine must be burned every morning before lighting the fire,

A BLACKFOOT CAMP ON THE PRAIRIE

also before taking out the Pipe and before carrying it back in the evening.

It was customary for a pipe owner to take a seat at the back of a lodge, never by the door. No one should walk in front of him, lest it cause blindness or sore eyes. He must not light his pipe with a willow stick, but must use either cottonwood or service berry. The firewood inside his tepee must always lie in the same direction with the Pipe; and none of the firewood could be taken from the lodge. Near the place where the Pipe Bundle was kept, no one should talk loud, aim a gun, or throw anything. The owner must never touch a dead person, or say anything against the character of any one.

A Medicine Pipe was not allowed to hang outside in bad weather. It must be taken out after sunrise on a clear day and hung from a tripod behind the lodge. It was carried out by the south side and returned by the north, using the same direction the sun moves through the sky.

As soon as the first thunder was heard in the spring, the pipe owner gave a ceremony. He invited the people to come, both old and young. And they came gladly, in order to be prayed for and given tobacco from the Pipe Bundle; it brought one under the good will of the Thunder. During the pipe ceremony in the spring an owner took his pipe out of doors and held it towards the sky, praying for every one present, that none of them might be killed during that year by the Thunder.

A Medicine Pipe was a great burden to both husband and wife, but especially to the woman. On the other hand, its possession gave them both a prominent position in the tribe; they gained social and religious recognition. It was said of Lone Chief, that he profited by his Pipe. His property increased. He followed carefully its rules and had good luck throughout his ownership.

CHAPTER XLII

A SACRED CEREMONY IN MAD WOLF'S TEPEE

MAD WOLF called upon the Society of Brave Dogs to build the framework of the sweat-lodge. It held a prominent place in the Sun Dance.

Then the Brave Dogs rode to the river valley for willow branches to be used in constructing the framework of the lodge; and on their return, they entered the camp on the east side, parading around the circle and the tepee of Mad Wolf, where the sacred woman was fasting and praying, singing in unison and holding aloft their green branches, which they finally deposited on the side of camp toward the setting sun. There they built the sweat-lodge by sticking the willow branches into the ground and bending them into the form of an oval; they interlocked them on top and made the entrance toward the rising sun, digging a hole inside for the heated stones and covering the entire structure with robes and blankets.

When the Brave Dogs had everything ready, the medicine men and women came from Mad Wolf's tepee. White Calf, as the "father," was in the lead; then came Mad Wolf, and Spotted Eagle, the head medicine man; and then the wife of White Calf with Gives-to-the-Sun, the fasting woman.

They walked in single file, slowly and by stages, with eyes fixed upon the ground, passing around the south side of the sweat-lodge from east to west, following the direction of the sun through the heavens. They stopped on the west side, where Gives-to-the-Sun took her seat beside the structure with the wife of White Calf; the men stood on the south side, while the two women bowed their heads in prayer.

Then Mad Wolf, White Calf, and Spotted Eagle removed their clothing and entered the sweat-lodge. The fasting woman prayed over the skull of a buffalo bull, which the Brave Dogs handed to Mad Wolf inside the lodge. He laid the skull on a bunch of meadow grass, because it was the favorite food of the buffalo.

Then Spotted Eagle painted black marks on the skull to represent stars, and red for the Sun; and they chanted together, while Spotted Eagle put meadow grass into the nose and eyes of the skull, to symbolize the feeding of the buffalo. The Brave Dogs took the skull outside, fastening it on top of the sweat-lodge with the nose pointing towards the rising sun.

Then the Brave Dogs passed hot stones to Mad Wolf inside the lodge. He laid sweet grass upon them and held his hands in the rising smoke, rubbing them over his body for purification, and sang this prayer to the Sun:

"May our lives be as strong as these stones."

He sprayed water on the hot stones; as the steam rose, he sang:

"May our lives be straight.
May we live to be old and always have water to drink."

Throughout the ceremony, Mad Wolf and his associates prayed to the Sun, Moon, and Morning Star. Then the procession returned to Mad Wolf's tepee, walking slowly and in single file, with heads bowed and eyes fixed on the ground, carefully avoiding the trail by which they came out.

On this same day the tribe had a parade, in which men, women, and children took part. They dressed in their best and painted their faces. The two war chiefs, Little Plume and Little Dog, were in the lead, wearing fine costumes of deerskin decorated with colored beads and black-tipped tails of weasels. Little Plume had a foxskin wound around his head for a cap, with the tail hanging down behind and two eagle feathers in his hair.

Some of the women riders wore dresses decorated with quill work and elk teeth; their saddles had pommels of deer antlers, beaded pendants, and buckskin cruppers; clusters of eagle feathers hung from the necks of their horses and bright-colored feathers from their tails.

Red Fox was dressed as a clown or jester. He rode a black horse and had his face and hands painted black; his robe too was black and extended from his shoulders, back over the tail of his horse, waving gracefully in the wind when he rode at a gallop.

Before the parade, Two Spears rode through the camp, leading the white horse of Morning Eagle, the aged warrior. It was covered with painted pictures, to remind the people of Morning Eagle's brave deeds in war, both as leader and as a scout.

The pictures told how he cut loose a horse close to the lodge of an enemy — a hand with a knife, a picket pin and a horse; also the time he took many horses in an open fight; how he killed some Gros Ventres and took their weapons — a lance, a shield, and bows and arrows. He even seized a gun from the hand of an enemy and escaped without hurting him; and killed a Crow Indian who entered his camp at night and tried to steal his horses. While Two Spears rode through the camp, leading this horse of victory, he proclaimed in a loud voice the brave deeds of old Morning Eagle and then joined in the parade.

When the tribe had assembled, they marched slowly around the inner circle, with their two war chiefs in the lead, and singing in unison. Some held aloft human scalps tied to long branches; others held standards of eagle feathers, guns and lances and feathered shields fastened to poles.

That evening, Mad Wolf invited to his lodge prominent

men and women who had taken part in former Sun Dances, to pray and sing throughout the night. And the Brave Dogs sang in their lodge the dancing songs of the weather makers, to keep the weather clear. Then they rode through camp and commanded the people to be quiet and not disturb the medicine men and women in their ceremony in Mad Wolf's tepee; next day would take place the building of the sun lodge and the ceremony of raising the center pole.

Round the outside of Mad Wolf's lodge green branches were placed — the sign of an important ceremony and only those invited should enter. For a while I watched from my tepee the chiefs and their wives coming to the ceremony. I went nearer and listened to a solemn chant led by Mad Wolf and White Calf. At intervals the low monotone of the men was joined by the higher voices of the women. Then I stood close to the door and heard the song die away. In the silence that followed I decided to enter. So I raised the door-flap and looked inside. Mad Wolf and White Calf were seated at the back, behind a sort of altar, made by cutting away the grass and forming sod-walls on three sides, with an open space toward the rising sun. An Indian seated by the door motioned me to withdraw, but my Indian father signed for me to stay, so I took my place among the singers and priests. At one side sweet grass was burning on a hot coal as incense. The base of the altar was covered with light-colored earth and had painted symbols to represent sun dogs, the Moon, Morning Star, and Mistake-Morning-Star.

Mad Wolf and his wife sat quietly in their places, with heads bowed in prayer and eyes cast down. As the fasting woman, she was the central figure; all the serious and solemn aspects of the Sun Dance centered about her. She wore a tanned buffalo robe, which covered her from head to foot; her hair was unbraided and concealed her face. She and Mad Wolf did nothing for themselves; others took care of their lodge and looked after the fire. No one spoke aloud; every one whispered. All who came to the ceremony entered quietly and reverently. That night throughout the big camp no noise was allowed, because of the fasting woman and her ceremony.

It was Morning Plume's duty to attend to the fire. He kept the blaze down, so that the light was subdued. Every one sat quietly in their places without talking, and left the moving about to Morning Plume. If Mad Wolf or his wife had anything to say, they whispered it to White Calf or his wife; and they repeated it in a low voice to the others.

Morning Plume also attended to cutting the tobacco and filling the pipes for all the company. Beside him was a tobacco outfit — a large beaded bag, extra pipe stems and a cutting-board. Two redstone pipes were passed around the circle, one for men and the other for women. Whenever they burned out, they were handed back to Morning Plume, who emptied the ashes into a hole in the ground and refilled them with tobacco. After food had been distributed, they were ready to begin the ceremony.

White Calf brought forth some buffalo rawhides, which were spread on the ground in front of the men singers, and pairs of rattles distributed. My Indian father asked that two of the rattles be given to me, so that I could join them in the singing.

White Calf opened the ceremony with a prayer. Then Bear Child took a hot ember from the fire with the prongs and laid it before White Calf; he placed sweet grass upon it to burn as incense and sang to the Morning Star. Then we all joined in singing seven songs to Morning Star and seven each to the Sun and Moon. There were seven songs for a sacred eagle feather; in the Sun Dance legend, the Sun God used an eagle feather to brush the scar from the face of Scarface. We also sang songs to the raven and songs to the sacred

CEREMONY OF THE SUN DANCE INSIDE THE SACRED TEPEE

The man and his wife giving the ceremony are seated behind an altar; men and women helpers on both sides

headdress, which was worn by the fasting woman. There was a song for everything that made up this bonnet — the white weasel-skin, the feathers and plumes, flint arrow-point, snipe, buffalo tail, and a small bundle filled with seeds of the tobacco.

Then White Calf, the head-chief, prayed, saying:

"Father, the Sun, I am praying for my people.
May they be happy in the summer and live through the cold of winter.
Many are sick and hungry,
Pity them and let them live.
May we go through this ceremony right,
The way you taught our people to do in the days of long ago.
If we make mistakes, pity us.
Mother Earth, pity us, help us; may the grass and berries grow.
Morning Star, shine into our lodge and give us long life.
Father, the Sun, bless our children, relatives and visitors.
May our trails lie straight through a happy life; may we live to be old.
We are all your children and ask these things with good hearts."

During this prayer, the Indians sat silently and with heads bowed reverently; and at the close, they united in a long-drawn "ah-h-h-h-h-h" to express their approval, while some added a few words of prayer.

This ceremony lasted until long after midnight; day was beginning to dawn when the company went away. But before they separated, White Calf as the "father" gave instructions for the important events of next day — the big day of the camp. Then the Sun Dance Bundle would be transferred to Mad Wolf and his wife; they would have the tribal feast, when the sacred tongues would be distributed; women would make their vows before all the people; and at sunset they would raise the center pole and finish the sun lodge.

CHAPTER XLIII

THE TRIBAL DANCING-LODGE

EARLY the following morning, Elk Horn, the herald, rode around the camp circle beating a drum, and announced:

"This is the great day; now we raise the sun pole; it is time to get ready; every band should send men to help; bring trees and branches from the river valley; all must do their share and take part in building the dancing-lodge."

Then the different bands sent young men to help in the work. Young women dressed themselves in their best costumes and rode forth on horseback to help drag in the trees, using lariats fastened to the pommels of their saddles. They returned from the river valley and entered camp amid shouting and firing of guns. They dragged the trees and branches to the place for the sun lodge in the center of the camp circle. In the construction of the big lodge, nine forked tree trunks were used for posts; also long branches for stringers and rafters, and a lot of green boughs to cover the sides.

The men who were chosen to get the center pole went forth as a war party and cut down the tree with a ceremony. They selected a large cottonwood with forked branches. Double Runner was the warrior chosen for the honor of felling it, because of his brave deeds in war. He came forward with an axe, the blade painted red. First, he told a war story — how he had killed an enemy in battle, then struck the tree with his axe. In this manner, after recounting four brave deeds, Double Runner cut down the tree. When it began to fall, the waiting warriors shouted and gave war-whoops and fired their guns into its crown; as it struck the ground, they made a rush and broke off the branches, counting "coups" as trophies of war. Then they trimmed the trees and rested the forked end on a travois. Indians on horses helped with lariats; and in this way they bore the center pole to camp, placing it beside the open hole in the medicine lodge, with its forks pointing toward the setting sun.

Prominent men were chosen for the honor of digging the post-holes. They also put the stringers into place and long poles for rafters. Thus they made everything ready for raising the center pole at sunset, when all the bands of the tribe would assemble and do their share.

In the meantime, the ceremony of transferring the Sun Dance Bundle was taking place in the lodge of Mad Wolf. Then the people had their first chance to see the fasting woman, and a large crowd assembled. The men who sang and beat with rattles sat together on the north side of the lodge; across from them were the women, who had made vows at former sun dances. Directly behind the altar and in the center were Mad Wolf and his wife, as the givers of the Sun Dance, together with White Calf and his wife who were giving up the bundle.

First, a small cottonwood tree was planted in the ground close to the altar by Middle Calf, who recounted four of his brave deeds in war. Gives-to-the-Sun and the "mother" kneeled together and sang. They made dancing movements in unison, as they took up the sacred headdress and hung it upon the tree.

Then the "mother," still kneeling beside the headdress and swaying her body in time with the beating of rattles on the ground, made hooking motions at the tree and imitated an elk; she rubbed her head against the branches and made a whistling sound like an elk. Finally she took the headdress and, with many symbolical movements, placed it upon Gives-to-the-Sun. While clothing her in the ceremonial dress of deer and antelope-skins, the women attendants sang in unison. They placed the elkskin robe about her and sang the Elk Song, making the elk sign and imitating the movements of elk, swaying their bodies like trotting elk and giving the elk call.

In the meantime the entire tribe had assembled about the unfinished sun lodge, seating themselves in long rows on the prairie, waiting for the feast. When they heard the women singing the Elk Song in Mad Wolf's tepee — the last song in clothing the fasting woman, they knew it was time for the medicine woman to come out.

When she finally appeared, the throng was so great prominent men stood on both sides of the doorway to hold the people back. First in the line came White Calf, the head-chief, followed by Mad Wolf; then the wife of White Calf as the "mother," and Gives-to-the-Sun, the fasting woman, with her attendants bearing the parfleches of sacred tongues. They moved by slow stages, all with heads reverently bowed and eyes fixed on the ground. The face of Gives-to-the-Sun was hidden by her headdress. Weakened by her fast, she walked slowly and feebly, leaning on a staff. Mad Wolf also used a staff and kept his head bowed, holding aloft a stalk of wild parsnip, with eagle feathers on the branches.

This solemn procession moved slowly around the unfinished sun lodge, going from the east towards the south, following the sun's daily course through the sky; and finally entered a temporary shelter, to remain there during the tribal feast.

Then many Indians came before them, bearing offerings, which they presented to White Calf; and, with each offering, White Calf prayed to the Sun in behalf of the giver and painted his face. Women who brought offerings, handed them to the wife of White Calf who also prayed and painted their faces.

A fresh hide was stretched on the ground in front of the shelter, to be cut into strips for binding the rafters of the sun lodge. For this honor, Bear Chief, a warrior of renown, was chosen by Eagle Head, who had cut these thongs at the former Sun Dance. Then Eagle Head transferred to Bear Chief the right to cut; and the relatives of Bear Chief came forward with gifts to help him pay for the honor.

In the ceremony of transfer, Bear Chief was painted over the face and body by Eagle Head, who prayed to the Sun that Bear Chief might have power to cut the hide without mistake.

Then Bear Chief stood before the people with a knife painted half red for the Sun and half black for the Moon. Holding it aloft, he prayed for power. Then he recounted four of his brave deeds in war, making a stroke after each tale, as though he were cutting the hide, saying:

"Hear! Men and women, for what I tell you is true. I went to war in the south against our enemies the Crows. I took a band of horses and killed two warriors."

After making a stroke towards the hide, Bear Chief counted another "coup":

"Behold! I went again to war in the north and fought with a chief of the Crees; I killed him and took his scalp."

In this manner, Bear Chief told four tales; and then cut the hide into strips, while his relatives stood near and shouted words of praise.

Women, who had made vows, came forward and took pieces of the sacred tongues, standing beside the persons in behalf of whom they had vowed and facing the setting sun. They prayed aloud so that every one could hear and confessed their temptations. Some made known the names of men who wanted them to commit adultery. They told the Sun how they had power to resist. But none of the men who were implicated came forward to defend themselves.

These groups of praying women, standing in the evening sunlight, before the venerable medicine men and women, and the long rows of Indians, men, women and children seated on the prairie, was a solemn and impressive scene.

The aged wife of Tearing Lodge came forward and prayed in behalf of her daughter who was ill; and the wife of Heavy Breast prayed for her husband who stood beside her. But one of the most interesting of all the groups was old Awasáki, wife of Painted Wing, with four small grandchildren. She stood them in line before the throng of people; after eating one of the tongues, she faced the setting sun and prayed:

"Sun! Behold! Pity us, help us!
You know I have lived straight; I give you my life to-day.
Now I eat this tongue that my grandchild may live,
The boy who is ill.
I pray also for these children who stand before you.
May they grow and be strong.
May they never suffer from hunger.
May all of them have long life.
Sun, hear us and pity us."

After this prayer, the old woman planted a piece of the tongue in the ground as a sacrifice to the Underground Spirits and divided the remainder among her relatives, that they might be able to lead better lives.

By this time the sun was nearing the summits of the Rocky Mountains. White Calf, the head-chief, arose and called upon the people to make ready for raising the sun pole. The men returned to their lodges and dressed in their best costumes. They gathered into lines at the four quarters of the camp, bearing long lodge-poles, which were tied in pairs near their tops, each pair carried by two men, for lifting into place the heavy rafters of the dancing-lodge.

The band that was first in line started to sing the tribal hymn, "Raising the Sun Pole"; it was quickly taken up by

RAISING THE CENTER POLE FOR THE SUN LODGE
Warriors advancing, singing the tribal hymn

THE SUN LODGE FINISHED AND READY FOR THE TRIBE
Three society lodges of the Brave Dogs stand on the left

other bands as they formed into line. The Indians believed this song was given by the Sun through Scarface, the founder of the Sun Dance. It was sung as a prayer by all the people for the safe raising of the center pole.

In the meantine, White Calf and Mad Wolf walked slowly to the prostrate pole and stood upon its trunk, while their wives took positions by its forks. Then the four lines of warriors, holding aloft their poles, advanced by four stages. During the pauses, they waited to sing the hymn to the pole, each band singing in unison regardless of the other bands, in different intervals of time and pitch; and, as the notes of the melody all belonged to one chord, the different groups combined harmoniously in a sort of grand fugal effect, the deep and resonant voices of the warriors booming and sliding up to the last notes of the song. Finally, the four lines met in a large circle round the sun lodge, and stood while all the people, men, women and children joined in singing the tribal hymn.

Then the head-chief called in a loud voice to raise the pole. Mad Wolf blew his medicine whistle; he threw off his black-colored robe and jumped from the pole. With shouts and war-whoops, the circle of warriors ran towards the unfinished lodge, followed by the throng of Indians. The pole was quickly raised with ropes; and the warriors with lodge-poles lifted the rafters into place, tying them to the frame with rawhide thongs, and placed green cottonwood branches against the sides.

Thus the dancing-lodge was finished and made ready for the tribe. There the people assembled during the remaining days of the circle camp, to hear tales of war by prominent chiefs, to witness the rites of the Weather Dancers and the dances and ceremonies of the men's societies.

CHAPTER XLIV

END OF THE SUN DANCE AND FAREWELL OF MY INDIAN FATHER

NEXT day Elk Horn rode through the camp and summoned every one to the dancing-lodge. The first to go were the three Weather Dancers, the medicine men, Spotted Eagle, Bull Child, and Medicine Bull. When the sun was high they appeared, coming from their tepees in different parts of the camp, wearing their medicine charms and with faces and bodies painted.

The Indians looked to the Weather Dancers to drive away all storms; during the time of the dancing-lodge, they were expected to keep the weather clear. Through their medicine charms, incantations, and dances, they were believed to have power over nature.

Bull Child wore a ceremonial robe,[1] which came from Brings-Down-the-Sun, the famous medicine man of the north. It was yellow in color and had blue corners; many skins and feathers of birds were attached. Clusters of stars were painted over its surface, to represent the constellations of the Great Bear and the Pleiades. Near the center was a circle with a blue border for the Sun; below, a blue crescent for the Moon and a small cross for the Morning Star. Wound around his head was an otter-skin, with a plume in front and long eagle feathers behind. The plume came from the Thunder and gave him power over the weather. In one hand he held an eagle wing and a wand of raven feathers in the other. The painted designs on his body had been revealed to him by the Sun in a dream. On his forehead was a red disc to represent

[1] This robe is now in the Indian collection of the American Museum of Natural History, New York City.

the Sun; across his temples, yellow streaks for sun dogs; clusters of stars were on both cheeks, and on his arms marks to represent the rainbow.

The three Weather Makers were followed by drummers, who beat time for their songs. On their way to the sun lodge, they stopped four times to dance and sing. In their dances they moved up and down in time with the drumming, holding bone whistles in their mouths, on which they blew steadily while gazing fixedly at the sun, facing in turn the rising and setting sun and making motions with both arms extended.

Thus Spotted Eagle, Bull Child, and Medicine Bull, came before the people as weather makers, and entered the booth inside the dancing-lodge. The floor of this booth was made of earth from the foot of the sun pole, with a surface of white clay. On three of its sides were low walls of sod, which were covered with creeping juniper. The back and sides of the booth were interwoven with branches of ground pine, to shield the medicine men from the curious gaze of the spectators.

Then many Indians came before the three Weather Makers, to have their faces painted and to be blessed with sun power — men, women and children. They took young children in their arms, gazing steadily into the Sun, and prayed for long life and good fortune.

In the dancing-lodge a place was reserved for Mad Wolf and his wife near the center pole and close to the booth of the Weather Dancers. Gives-to-the-Sun had now finished her fast and was happy. Her work and troubles were over; family and relatives were proud of her position in the tribe; she was the most honored and revered of all the women.

Then a fire-pit was dug in front of the sun pole, and a famous warrior was called upon to start the fire. After his war story came other warriors. Each of them took a piece of firewood and, holding it up, related one of his brave deeds in battle; after which he put the stick upon the fire, amid the beating of drums and "cheering-songs" by the musicians. The bravest warriors were those who narrated so many brave deeds they made the fire blaze high.

Mountain Chief, a warrior of renown, stood before the people with his weapons — a shield and bow and arrows. He gave his war cry; and, drawing his bow, aimed it in different directions, telling how he killed an enemy and took his scalp. After his story, Mountain Chief sat down, amid the beating of drums and shrill war cries from the spectators.

Then Bear Chief, a famous war leader, his horse painted with war pictures, rode into the dancing-lodge with a band of warriors and acted out a sham battle. He was chief of a band that went against the Sioux Indians. In the sham battle, Bear Chief kept firing his rifle into the air, over the heads of the crowd; and after every shot an acting warrior fell dead. An old woman, a relative of Bear Chief, stood up and sang a song of gladness, proclaiming his bravery; and one of the head men made a speech, in which he urged all the young men to emulate the brave deeds of Bear Chief.

In the meantime a storm was gathering over the Rocky Mountains and extended toward the plains. The Indians in the dancing-lodge eagerly watched the black clouds, to see if the Weather Makers would drive them back.

Now it happened there were two rivals among the medicine men. Medicine Bull was clearing the weather and Spotted Eagle praying for rain. Medicine Bull came first from the booth and faced the clouds. He blew shrilly on his bone whistle and called in a loud voice:

"Behold! A storm comes from the mountains. But I have power over the weather. I shall dance and drive it back."

Short and sinewy, he danced gracefully in a circle, holding his otter-skin toward the storm; and with a final sweep waved it over his head, as if driving back the clouds. Suddenly the wind changed; the clouds divided and the sun shone.

Then Spotted Eagle, jealous of his rival's success, came from the booth. He wore medicine charms, which had been handed down from Four Bears, a famous medicine man and weather maker of former days — a belt of great power and an otter-skin cap. In one hand he held a minkskin and in the other an eagle feather. With these powerful charms, he stood confidently before the people and announced that he would bring back the storm, saying:

"My power over the weather comes from the Sun; it is very strong. Behold! The clouds will come together again and it will rain."

Spotted Eagle danced and prayed and made motions toward the storm clouds, which continued to spread, until they passed over the camp with a heavy rain.

The Blackfoot were hero worshipers. They believed that men who were brave and were successful in war attained a certain power to help relatives who were ill. For this reason Wolf Plume, a famous warrior, stood before the people and prayed:

> "Sun, have pity and hear me.
> My mother is ill. May she become strong and well."

After this prayer, Wolf Plume enacted a sham battle — a night attack he had made on a hostile camp. He built a miniature lodge of branches; he showed how he entered the tepee of an enemy and took two scalps.

Then Big Beaver came forward with his sister and said:

"Hear, men and women, for what I speak is true. In the winter-moon I went with Two Eagles on a visit to the Crow Indians. We crossed the Yellowstone River on the ice and my partner was drowned. I thought my time to die had also come. But I made a vow to the Sun — if I ever came out of that danger alive, my sister would come forward with me and take one of the sacred tongues at the next Sun Dance."

Then his sister held up a tongue and prayed to the Sun; while Big Beaver announced that he gave his saddle horse and its equipment to Spotted Eagle, the medicine man, and asked him to pray for him.

Then a woman aroused the interest of all by singing a mourning song to her dead lover, saying:

> "The dancing-lodge is the place where I was last with my lover.
> Now I am lonely.
> He left me and went to the Spirit World.
> Where I want to join him soon."

Shortly after this, the woman committed suicide by jumping from a cliff in view of the people of her camp.

In former days, when the Indians were free, there was self-torture at the Sun Dance, by warriors who had made vows to the Sun in time of peril. Slits were cut on both sides of the breast and sticks were inserted under the muscles. By means of rawhide ropes hanging from the center pole and fastened to these sticks, the warriors danced before the people, amid the beating of drums and applause of the spectators, until the sticks were torn loose from the flesh. Many of these warriors did not live long after the torture. It was believed they gave themselves to the Sun and the Sun took them.

Throughout the ceremonies, Mad Wolf and Gives-to-the-Sun came regularly to the dancing-lodge. He took his pipe and plenty of tobacco and gave to those who sat near. She wore her best clothes — deerskin trimmed with elk teeth and with leggings and moccasins to match.

Then the men's societies, the All-Brave-Dogs, Pigeons, and Mosquitoes, gave their rituals and dances; and their members told of brave deeds in war. They also gave war dances and counted "coups," accompanied by the beating of drums and of rattles on a rawhide; they had a feast and

TWILIGHT IN THE CIRCLE CAMP

Tepees illuminated by inside fires

passed around a Medicine Pipe for every one to smoke and pray.

On the last day of the Sun Dance, when the time had come for the tribe to break camp and separate, Mad Wolf stood before the people. He spoke to them in a strong voice so that all could hear, saying:

"Hear, my children, for I speak to you with a good heart. It does us all good to come together once every year for the Sun Dance. We have smoked the Medicine Pipe and the rising smoke has carried away all of our bad feelings. Some have fulfilled their vows and others made presents to the Sun. The old people have fasted and prayed and now feel better in their hearts. The young men have heard the wise counsels of our chiefs, and young girls have seen the medicine women who fast and pray, because their lives are pure and they are good to every one.

"The Sun is our father. He is kind. He covers the trees with leaves and makes the grass green in the spring. He also gave the Indians good hearts, that they might be kind and help each other.

"The grass is now long and the sun is warm over the prairie; but the cold and frost of winter, with its deep snows and biting winds will soon come; and I know not where our women and children will get their food.

"We are not moving; we are just standing still. The buffalo are all gone, the antelope and the rest of the game also. The white men continue to drive us towards the setting sun; but now the Rocky Mountains face us like a wall, and we can go no farther. I do not care for myself; I shall soon go to the Great Spirit. But I am anxious for our little children; I know not what will become of them.

"You have all heard of our Great Father (President of the United States), who calls us his red children. He is the only one upon whom we can depend. Now, you must look to him, as in the past we looked to the Sun God. My children, you must obey his laws and give heed to his advice. He lives far away toward the rising sun. I shake hands with him now, for our hearts feel warm toward him.

"Prepare to return to your homes and to care for your horses and cattle. Look after them well and send your children to school. If they learn the language of the white men, they will be a great help to us; for the way of the white man is now on top.

"My children, I shake hands with all of you. I want you to feel the sunshine of joy in your hearts and to have no trouble. What I speak with my mouth, I feel in my heart. Farewell!"

Early on the following morning, Running Crane and his bands of Indians took down their lodges and started south. Then Mad Wolf with his followers departed for the north. The great tribal camp melted quickly away; and I was left alone on the prairie.

The golden rays of the rising sun shone over the rounded uplands with their long grass-covered slopes and wide valleys; upon the giant peaks of the Rockies with towering precipices, dark forests and everlasting snow. Many birds were singing, meadow-larks, white-crowns, and thrushes. The west wind bore the scent of pine and cedar from the mountains, the fragrance of prairie wild flowers and sweet grass. I took a last look at the broad plain with its great circle of deserted lodge-fires; and turned my face toward the rising sun. That was the last I ever saw of Mad Wolf, my Indian father. He soon went over the Wolf Trail to the ghostly Sand Hills. And now all that old generation of Indians have followed him.

THE END

APPENDIX

APPENDIX

MEDICINAL AND USEFUL PLANTS OF THE BLACKFOOT INDIANS[1]

BY WALTER McCLINTOCK

THE following collection of herbs and plants with their Indian names, uses, and methods of preparation by the Blackfoot, is deposited in the Carnegie Museum of Pittsburgh. The specimens were identified by Mr. O. E. Jennings, Curator of Botany in the Museum and Professor of Botany in the University of Pittsburgh.

1. Materia Medica of the Blackfoot

KATOYA. Sweet Pine. Balsam Fir. *Abies lasiocarpa.* Burned for incense in ceremonials. It was used in poultices for fevers and colds in the chest, also for hair oil by mixing with grease and for perfume. It is more fragrant than ordinary balsam. When it grows in dry places it has a more concentrated and sweet odor.

SE-PAT-SEMO. Sweet Grass. Vanilla Grass. *Savastana odorata.* After drying, Sweet Grass was generally kept by plaiting several strands. It was burned for incense and used also for making hair tonic by soaking in water. In northern Europe and Sweden it is called Holy Grass, because with other sweet-scented grasses, it is strewn before the churches. It is found throughout the world in the cold north-temperate zone, northern Europe and Asia, Newfoundland to Alaska, south to New Jersey and Wisconsin to Colorado.

EK-SISO-KE. Sharp Vine. Bear Grass. *Yucca glauca.* The roots were boiled in water and used as a tonic for falling hair. The Blackfoot thought there was no better remedy than the Ek-siso-ke for breaks and sprains. The roots were grated and placed in boiling water. The inflammation was reduced by holding the injured member in the rising steam. The roots were also placed upon cuts to stop bleeding and to allay inflammation.

NITS-IK-OPA. Double-Root. Squaw-Root. *Carum Gairdneri.* Used for sore throat and placed on swellings to draw out inflammation. It was also eaten raw or boiled as a vegetable and used for flavoring stews.

[1] Published in *Zeitschrift für Ethnologie,* Berlin Heft 2. 1909.

OKS-PI-POKU. Sticky-Root, also called AP-AKS-IBOKU. Wide Leaves. Tufted Primrose or Alkali Lily. *Pachylobus caespitosus.* The root was pounded up and applied wet to sores and swellings to allay inflammation. It grows in alkali soil and is generally found in gravel beds.

APOS-IPOCO. Tastes Dry. Alumn-Root. *Heuchera parvifolia.* It was pounded up and used wet as an application for sores and swellings. It grows on gravel bottoms and alkali flats.

MATOA-KOA-KSI. Yellow-Root, or Swamp-Root. Willow-leaved Dock. *Rumex salicifolius.* It was boiled and used for many complaints but generally for swellings. It grows in swamps.

MAIS-TO-NATA. Crow-Root. Dotted Blazing-Star. *Lacinaria punctata.* Named because of the scarlet brilliancy of its flowers. It was called Crow-Root by the Blackfoot because it was eaten by crows and ravens in the autumn. The root was boiled and applied to swellings. A tea was also made with it for stomach-ache. It was sometimes eaten raw.

O-MUCK-KAS. Big Turnip. Parsnip. *Leptotaenia multifida.* Belonging to the carrot family, the Big Turnip is found on the sides of hills, growing in sandy loamy soil. It was gathered in the fall, the root being used to make a hot drink as a tonic for people in a weakened condition and to make them fat. The root was also pounded up and burned for incense. When horses had the distemper they were made to inhale smoke from this root. It was also mixed with brains and used in soft tanning.

PA-KITO-KI. Gray Leaves. Double Bladder-Pod. *Physaria didymocarpa.* It is to be found growing on gravel bottoms. The Blackfoot chewed the plant for sore throats, also for cramps and stomach trouble. It was also placed in water with hot rocks and used to allay swelling.

A-SAT-CHIOT-AKE. Rattle-Weed. Purple Loco-Weed, Crazy-Weed. *Aragallus lagopus.* Some of the flowers are purple, others blue, yellow, and white. It grows on gravel bottoms. The Blackfoot chewed it for sore throat, also to allay swelling.

A-SA-PO-PINATS. Looks-like-a-plume. Wind-Flower or Round-fruited Anemone. *Anemone globosa.* It is adapted for a windy place and is found growing on hillsides where the wind strikes it, either on the plains, or in the mountains. In midsummer the flower turns into cotton, which the Blackfoot burn on a hot coal for headache.

ET-A-WA-ASI. Makes-you-sneeze (Snuff). American White Hellebore. *Veratrum speciosum.* The plant grows to be about six feet high and is found in the mountain forests. The root is poisonous to eat. It was gathered by the Blackfoot both in the fall and in the spring and was used for headache. They broke off a small piece of the root, which was very dry, and snuffed it up the nose.

SIXA-WA-KASIM. Black-Root. Red Bane-Berry. *Actaea arguta.* The berries are both red and white. It is found near the mountains in the underbrush along rivers. The roots were boiled and used for coughs and colds.

SIXIMAS. Black-Root. White Bane-Berry. *Actaea eburnea.* The root was boiled and used for coughs and colds.

SIX-OCASIM. Indian Horehound. It is not found on the prairies but in the mountains along streams. It was generally used, after mixing with other plants, for baby colds.

KAKSAMIS. She Sage. Sweet Sage, Old Man, Pasturage Sage-Brush. *Artemisia frigida.* The roots or tops were boiled and used as a drink for mountain fever. It was also chewed for heart-burn. Sage was generally tied to articles that were sacrificed to the Sun.

OTSQUE-EINA. Blue Berry. Oregon Grape. *Berberis aquifolium.* The roots were boiled and used for stomach trouble, also for hemorrhages. It grew in the forest on the mountains.

A-POKS-IKIM. Smell-Foot. Northern Valerian. *Valeriana septentrionalis.* A hot drink was made from the roots for stomach trouble.

A-MUCH-KO-IYATSIS. Red-Mouth Bush. Paper-Leaf Alder. *Alnus tenuifolia.* A hot drink was made of the bark and taken for scrofula. The bark split readily and was also used for making stirrups, which were covered with raw-hide. The Indian name originated because it was observed that when people chewed the bark it colored their mouths red.

MA-NE-KA-PE. Young Man. Horse-Mint. *Monarda scabra.* An eye-wash was made by placing the blossoms in warm water and was used to allay inflammation.

SO-YA-ITS. Lies-on-his-belly. Long-plumed Avens. *Sieversia ciliata.* It grows on the plains and in the mountains. The Blackfoot boiled it in water and used for sore and inflamed eyes.

KINE. Rose Berries or APIS-IS-KITSA-WA. Tomato-Flower. Say's Rose. *Rosa Sayi.* A drink was made of the root and given to children for diarrhea. The berries were sometimes eaten raw.

OMAKA-KA-TANE-WAN. Gopher-Berries. Wild Potato, Ground Cherry, Cut-leaved Nightshade. *Solanum triflorum.* The berries were boiled and given to children for diarrhea. The plants grow on prairie-dog hills.

KITA-KOP-SIM. Garter-Root, or Pachsi, Dry-Root. Silver-Weed. *Argentina anserina*. The root was used for diarrhea.

NUXAPIST. Little Blanket. Indian Hemp, Dogbane. *Apocynum cannabinum*. A drink was made by boiling the root in water and taken for a laxative. It was also used as a wash to prevent hair falling out. It grows on high cliffs and was gathered at all times of year.

A-PO-PIK-A-TISS. Makes-your-hair-gray. Pore Fungus. *Polyporus*. A small quantity was used as a purgative. It was said to make the hair gray if too large a dose was taken. It was also used for cleaning buckskin.

AT-SI-PO-KOA. Fire-Taste. Sharp-leaved Beard-Tongue. *Pentstemon acuminatus*. The Blackfoot named it At-si-po-koa because of its biting flavor. It was boiled in water and taken internally for cramps and pains in the stomach. It was also used to stop vomiting.

SIX-IN-OKO. Juniper. Red Cedar. *Juniperus scopulorum*. The berries were made into a tea to stop vomiting. The Juniper was used on the altar of the sacred woman at the Sun Dance.

AKS-PEIS. Sticky-Weed. Gum-Plant. *Grindelia squarrosa*. The root was boiled and taken internally for liver trouble. It grows on the prairies.

OPET-AT-SAPIA. *Gutierrezia diversifolia*. Grows on the prairies in the foothills to the mountains. The roots were used by medicine men in doctoring. Red-hot stones were placed in water with the roots. Fumes arose with the steam.

E-SIMATCH-SIS. Dye. *Evernia vulpina*. A lichen that grows on pine trees. It was used as a yellow dye for porcupine quills. The quills were placed with the dye in boiling water. It was also used for headache.

E-SIMATCH-SIS. Dye. The Yellow Orthocarpus. *Orthocarpus luteus*. Used for dyeing gopher skins red. The plant was first pounded up and then pressed firmly upon the skin. It grows on the prairies.

ANA-WAWA-TOKS-TIMA. Buffalo-Food. Yellow Cancer-Root. *Thalesia fasciculata*. Used by Buffalo medicine men in doctoring wounds. They chewed and blew it upon the wound.

SA-PO-TUN-A-KIO-TOI-YIS. Joint Grass. Scouring Rush. *Equisetum hiemale*. The grass was boiled in water and used as a drink, for horse medicine.

PACH-CO-I-AU-SAUKAS. Smell-Mouth. Western Sweet Cicely. *Washingtonia divaricata*. It was given to mares in winter. The

Blackfoot say that it put them in good condition for foaling. They placed it in the mares' mouths and made them chew it. A pleasant drink was made with a small piece of the Western Sweet Cicely root, a little more of the Sixocasim (Indian Horehound) to three cups of water. It was taken hot for colds or tickling in the throat.

Tobacco

KA-KA-SIN. Larb, or Kinnikinick. Bearberry. Arctostaphylus uva-ursi. The leaves, which are thick and evergreen, were dried and used for tobacco. The berries were eaten raw and also used mashed in fat and fried. It grows in Northern North America, also Northern Europe and Asia.

O-MAKSE-KA-KA-SIN. Big Larb. Pipsissewa, Prince's Pine. *Chimaphila umbellata.* It flourishes among decaying leaves in a sandy soil in the mountain forests of Northern North America. The dried leaves were used for tobacco by all the Mountain Indians. The Blackfoot had a special preference for the Big Larb in smoking.

2. Plants for Ceremonials

PONO-KAU-SINNI. Turnip. Elk-Food. Narrow-leaved Puccoon. *Lithospermum linearifolium.* The tops were dried and used for burning as incense in ceremonials.

SO-YO-TOI-YIS. Spring Grass or I-TA-PAT-ANIS, Cut-your-finger. Slough Grass Sedge. *Carex nebrascensis praevia.* The Blackfoot said it was the favorite grass of the buffalo and for this reason the medicine men tied it around the horns of the sacred Buffalo head used in the Sun Dance ceremonials. It grows in marshy places on the prairies.

A-PONO-KAUKI. Paper-Leaves or O-TO-KAP-ATSIS. Yellow Flower. Arrow-leaved Balsam-Root. *Balsamorrhiza sagittata.* The large leaves were used in roasting Camas roots.

3. Berries and wild vegetables used for eating

OK-KUN-OKIN. Berry. Sarvis-Berry, June-Berry, Service-Berry, Shadbush, May Cherry. *Amelanchier oblongifolia.* A tall shrub or small tree growing on the prairies along side-hills and in river bottoms. The berries ripen in midsummer generally about the middle of July. The Blackfoot used them in great quantities with stews, soups, and meat. They also dried them for winter use. Violent pains often followed the eating of raw Sarvis-Berries.

PUKKEEP. Chokecherry. Western Wild Cherry. *Prunus demissa.* The Blackfoot say it does not ripen till later than the Sarvis-Berry, generally September or even October. They were used for soups, eaten raw and pounded up and mixed with meat. The bark was boiled and used internally in combination with roots of the Western Sweet Cicely, Northern Valerian, and Sixocasim (Indian Horehound).

MISS-IS-A-MISOI. Stink-Wood. Buffalo-Berry, Silver-Berry. *Elaeagnus argentea.* The Blackfoot gave it the name of Stink-Wood because of the bad smell of the smoke. In gathering firewood a person was ridiculed if he brought in Stink-Wood. The berries were used for soup. The bark was very tough and made strong rope for tying skins and parfleches when rawhide was not at hand.

IM-A-TOCH-KOT. Dog-Feet. *Disporum trachycarpum.* It bears yellow berries, which are eaten raw.

PO-KINT-SOMO. Wild Rhubarb. Cow Parsnip. *Heracleum lanatum.* In the spring the stalks were eaten after roasting over hot coals. The Blackfoot say the stalks are of two kinds, which they designate by Napim (He) and Skim (She). They peeled and split the stalk of the Skim before roasting but only peeled the Napim. A stalk of the PO-KINT-SOMO was placed on the altar of the Sun Dance ceremonial.

PACH-OP-IT-SKINNI. Lumpy-Head. Wild Potato, Spring-Beauty. *Claytonia lanceolata.* The Wild Potato grew on the prairies and in the foothills of the mountains. The Blackfoot dug them in spring for eating, preparing them for eating by boiling.

EK-SIK-A-PATO-API. Looks Back. Smartweed. *Polygonum bistortoides.* The root was used in soups and stews.

PESAT-SE-NEKIM. Funny Vine. Wild Onion. *Allium recurvatum.* Eaten raw and also used for flavoring.

KACH-A-TAN. Tender-Root. Carolina Milk Vetch. *Astragalus carolinianus.* The root was gathered in the spring or fall and eaten raw or cooked by boiling in water. It grows on the gravel bottoms or side-hills of the prairies.

EXIXIX. White-Root. Bitter-Root, State Flower of Montana, Red-Head Louisa. *Lewisia rediviva.* The Blackfoot believed it was healthy food. They prepared it by boiling in water. It grows plentifully in the mountains.

SAX-IKA-KITSIM. Quick Smell. American Wild Mint. *Mentha canadensis.* The leaves were placed in parfleches to flavor dried meat. It was also used to make tea.

MASS. Wild Turnip. Elk Food. *Lithospermum linearifolium.*

The roots were prepared for eating by boiling or roasting. It grows on the prairies.

O-MUCK-AI-IX-IXI. Big White-Root. Evening Primrose, Alkali Lily. *Musenium divaricatum.* The Blackfoot say the root has no flavor until dried. It was gathered in the fall and eaten raw. It grows on the prairies.

MISS-ISSA. Camas. *Camassia esculenta.* The roots were generally dug in the fall after the blossoms had fallen. They were baked by placing in a deep hole with heated rocks, leaves, and grass. A fire was also kept burning on top of the ground. It was said to require two days and two nights to cook them thoroughly in this way.

4. Perfumes

AT-SINA-MO. Gros Ventre Scent. Meadow-Rue. *Thalictrum occidentale.* The berries were dried and placed in small buckskin bags for perfumery.

KATOYA. Sweet Pine. Balsam Fir. *Abies lasiocarpa.* The leaves had a delightful odor when confined in a buckskin bag. Sweet Pine was also mixed with grease in making hair oil to add fragrance.

MAT-O-AT-SIM. Perfumed Plant. Rayless Camomile, Oregon Dog-Root, Dog Fennel. *Matricaria matricarioides.* The blossoms were dried and used for perfumery.

SE-PAT-SEMO. Sweet Grass. Vanilla Grass. *Sevastana odorata.* Sweet Grass was the most popular perfumery among the Blackfoot. It was made into braids and placed with their clothes or carried around in small bags. It was also used for a hair-wash and as incense.

Pieces of punk from the Cottonwood tree, leaves of the Balsam Poplar and the ring-bone from a horse's leg were used for perfumes.

Blackfoot names for flowers

SIK-A-PIS-CHIS. White Flower. *Aster commutatus.*

OTA-KAP-IS-CHIS-KIT-SIMA. Yellow Flower. Clasping-leaved Arnica. *Arnica amplexifolia.*

A-PIS-IS-KIT-SA-WA. Tomato-Flower. Red Rose. *Rosa Sayi.*

OT-SKA-A-PIS-IS-KIT-SA. Blue Flower. Oblong-leaved Gentian. *Gentiana affinis.*

A-SA-PO-PIN-ATS. Looks-like-a-plume. Round-Fruited Anemone. *Anemone globosa.* Its name was derived from the appearance of the flower when it turns into cotton and resembles a soft, downy feather.

A-PO-NO-KAU-KI. Paper-Leaves. Arrow-leaved Balsam-Root. *Balsamorrhiza sagittata.* In the hot weather its large leaves become very dry and resemble paper.

STO-O-KAT-SIS. Ghost's Lariat. Columbian Virgin's-Bower. *Atragene columbiana.* A vine, with a beautiful light blue flower, that trails along the ground and also climbs trees. The Blackfoot have named it Ghost's Lariat because it catches people and trips them up unexpectedly.

INDEX

INDEX